S0-BOL-092

23

Print and Cover Design: Nora Pauwels

Cultural Critique

Cultural Critique is published three times a year by Oxford University Press in association with the Society for Cultural Critique, a nonprofit, educational organization.

Manuscript submissions. Contributors should submit three copies of their manuscripts to Donna Przybylowicz, *Cultural Critique,* Department of English, University of Minnesota, Minneapolis, MN 55455. Manuscripts should conform to the recommendations of *The MLA Style Manual;* authors should use parenthetical documentation with a list of works cited. Contact the editorial office at the address above for further instructions on style. Manuscripts will be returned if accompanied by a stamped, self-addressed envelope. Please allow a minimum of four months for editorial consideration.

Subscriptions. Annual subscription rates are $26 for individuals and $49 for institutions. Outside the United States please add $11 for normal delivery and an additional $8 for air-expedited delivery. Subscription requests and checks (payable in U.S. funds) should be sent to Journals Customer Service, Oxford University Press, 2001 Evans Road, Cary, NC 27513.

Back issues. Single copies of back issues are $9.95 for individuals and $20 for institutions. Outside the United States please add $4. Copies may be obtained from the Journals Fulfillment Department, Oxford University Press, 2001 Evans Road, Cary, NC 27513.

Advertising and permissions. Advertising inquiries and requests to reprint material from the journal should be directed to the Journals Department, Oxford University Press, 200 Madison Avenue, New York, NY 10016.

Abstracts. *Cultural Critique* is indexed/abstracted in *The Left Index, Alternative Press Index, Sociological Abstracts* (*SA*), *Social Welfare, Social Planning/Policy and Social Development* (*SOPODA*), *International Political Science Abstracts, MLA Directory of Periodicals,* and *MLA International Bibliography.*

Postal information. *Cultural Critique* (ISSN 0882-4371) is published by Oxford University Press, 2001 Evans Road, Cary, NC 27513. Postage paid at Cary, NC, and additional post offices. *Postmaster:* Send address changes to Journals Customer Service, Oxford University Press, 2001 Evans Road, Cary, NC 27513.

Photocopies. The journal is registered with the Copyright Clearance Center, 27 Congress Street, Salem, MA 01970. Permission to photocopy items for internal or personal use, or the internal or personal use of specific clients, is granted by Oxford University Press provided that the per page rate of $.05 is paid directly to the CCC for copying beyond that permitted by the U.S. Copyright Law. Requests for permission to photocopy for other purposes, such as general distribution, resale, advertising and promotional purposes, or creating new collective works, should be directed to the Journals Department, Oxford University Press, 200 Madison Avenue, New York, NY 10016.

Printed on acid-free paper effective with Number 1.

the way things are

Carnival Culture

THE TRASHING OF TASTE IN AMERICA

JAMES B. TWITCHELL

Twitchell takes an entertaining look at the changes in television, publishing, and movies since the 1960's and assesses the damage: vulgarity has become the national norm.

"It's the best combination of profundity and pizzazz this year."

—The Philadelphia Inquirer

306 pp., 51 illustrations., $24.95

The Terms of Cultural Criticism

THE FRANKFURT SCHOOL, EXISTENTIALISM, POSTSTRUCTURALISM

RICHARD WOLIN

Diving into the rifts among three currents of thought, Wolin sees the blurring of "science" and "reason" as one of the most fatal intellectual mistakes of our age.

256 pp., $35.00

Black Sun

DEPRESSION AND MELANCHOLIA

JULIA KRISTEVA

Translated by Leon S. Roudiez

"An absorbing meditation on depression and melancholia... A persuasive theory... that is both moving and provocative."

—The New York Times

300 pp., $14.95, Now a paperback!

Radical Parody

AMERICAN CULTURE AND CRITICAL AGENCY AFTER FOUCAULT

DANIEL T. O'HARA

Most critics agree that no positive social or ethical consequences result from the practice of theory, but not O'Hara. By analyzing the later works of Foucault, Derrida, Kristeva, Said, Bloom, and others, he shows that theory does have social and ethical consequences.

264 pp., $37.50

Left Letters

THE CULTURE WARS OF MIKE GOLD AND JOSEPH FREEMAN

JAMES D. BLOOM

In the 1930's Mike Gold won acclaim for *Jews Without Money* and Joseph Freeman for *An American Testament*. Despite these and other contributions, both authors, ironically, have largely been forgotten. Bloom examines their works and rescues them from obscurity.

156 pp., $37.50

COLUMBIA UNIVERSITY PRESS

TO ORDER, CALL OR WRITE. CREDIT CARDS ACCEPTED. DEPT. S19, 136 SOUTH BROADWAY, IRVINGTON, NY 10533 • TEL: (800) 944-UNIV • FAX: (800) 944-1844

Ludic Feminism, the Body, Performance, and Labor: Bringing *Materialism* Back into Feminist Cultural Studies

Teresa L. Ebert

Contemporary feminism has, for the most part, retreated from "materialist" politics into a form of "discursive" or what I call "ludic" politics.[1] Broadly, materialist feminism is a political practice aimed at social transformation of dominant institutions that, as a totality, distribute economic resources and cultural power asymmetrically according to gender. But this project has been put in question by postmodern theories that announce the end of transformative politics (indeed, the end of history itself) and substitute a ludic cultural politics in its place. In this essay, I will argue for the possibility of a postmodern feminist cultural studies devoted to materialist politics—transformative social change—and indicate why I find ludic or discursive politics ineffective for feminism. I will thus use a materialist frame to engage both levels of politics: cultural politics (intervening in and changing cultural representations, specifically those concerning gender, sexuality, and race) as well as transformative politics (radical social inter-

© 1993 by *Cultural Critique*. 0882-4371 (Winter 1992–93). All rights reserved.

ventions in the historical economic, political, and labor relations underlying cultural representations). My discussion, however, will focus on a critique of and engagement with cultural politics, first, because cultural politics, in its ludic mode, has become the primary form of dominant feminism and, second, because a materialist critique of cultural representations is an effective inaugural move in opening up a space for transformative politics.

Whether postmodernism is seen as what Fredric Jameson calls "the cultural logic of late capitalism" or is associated with the writings of Jean-François Lyotard and Jean Baudrillard, with Derridean poststructuralists or Lacanian psychoanalysts, it has intimated the end of transformative politics. In short, the dominant postmodern theories—what I have called "ludic" postmodernism[2]—have problematized the notion of politics and rearticulated it as solely a cultural politics: that is, as a language-effect, a mode of rhetoric aimed at changing cultural representations, rather than as a collective practice through which existing social institutions are changed so that (economic) resources and cultural power can be distributed without regard to gender, race, class, sexuality. This prevailing ludic postmodernism has so displaced and discredited politics as emancipation as to make it nearly impossible. After Lyotard, Jacques Derrida, Michel Foucault, and such ludic feminists as Luce Irigaray, Alice Jardine, Susan Suleiman, and Donna Haraway, emancipation—the collective social struggle to end exploitation—becomes simply a metaphysical project: a metanarrative. The appropriate critical and political stance is thus, in Lyotard's words, an "incredulity toward metanarratives" (*The Postmodern Condition* xxiv): an incredulity, in short, toward emancipation as the necessary social struggle against "real" systems of exploitation, like patriarchy or capitalism.[3] Such social systems (totalities) are, for ludic postmodernists, merely discredited metanarratives rather than social "realities" to be contested. As a leading ludic social critic, Ernesto Laclau, claims, even "'society,' as a founding totality . . . is an impossible object" ("Transformations" 40).

Moreover, power, as Foucault argues, is now seen as a "multiplicity of force relations" engendering "local and unstable" states of power that are "everywhere" (92–93). Power, then, is diffuse, asystematic, and "aleatory" (that is, marked by chance and arbitrariness) rather than historically determined. It produces its own immanent "plurality of resistances": for as Foucault says, "where there is power, there is resistance" (95), rather like the natural resistance to a physical force. The ludic notion of power, in short, substitutes a logic of contingency for the logic of social necessity. In doing so, it preempts any need for collective, organized social transformation—any need, in other words, for emancipation, and more important, it dispenses with the necessity for organized social and political revolution to overthrow dominant power relations. All we need to do, according to ludic postmodernists, is recognize and validate the multiplicity of local points of resistance power itself already generates. As a result, it is increasingly common to call our age "postpolitical."

The new postmodern culture studies taking hold in the United States, Britain, and a number of Commonwealth countries, notably Canada and Australia, subscribes, in large part, to these ludic assumptions and in the name of the political it becomes, in effect, "postpolitical." Increasingly it substitutes validation for critique and affirmation for opposition. John Fiske, for instance, argues for a "cultural theory that can both account for and validate popular social difference."[4] In other words, the affirmation of already existing differences (rather than *explaining* why and how these have become differences) is largely seen as in itself an effective mode of social resistance to the hegemonic. Obviously this position has widespread appeal for many feminist critics—especially for those who regard the affirmation of women's experience, in and of itself, as the political basis for feminism—but we need to ask difficult and by now quite unpopular questions: What is the effect of such validation? Does it affirm "what is" rather than critique how these differences have been produced out of regimes of exploitation—and perhaps support these regimes and even be "necessary" to their continued existence and domination? Can we afford to dispense with critique if we are to transform these regimes and the differences they produce? Is critique necessary to social struggle and to a transformative cultural studies?

Instead of an interventionist critique, (ludic) postmodern cultural studies tends to focus on pleasure—pleasure in/of textuality, the local, the popular, and, above all, the body (*jouissance*)—as in and of itself—a form of resistance. This is a "new generation" of intellectuals, according to Andrew Ross, who "appeal to the liberatory body, and the creativity of consumption" (11). Thus, postmodern feminist cultural critics like Constance Penley increasingly engage not in critique but in affirmative descriptions of local sites of pleasure. For instance, in Penley's popular studies of a genre of *Star Trek* fan magazines (called "slash zines" because they eroticize and sexualize the relationship between Kirk and Spock and are designated by a code with a slash, "K/S") her "aim" is to "show" the "range and diversity of identifications and object relations" in these texts because "once shown, it will then be possible to give a fuller and more complex account of what women *do* with popular culture, how it gives them pleasure, and how it can be consciously and unconsciously reworked to give them *more* pleasure" ("Feminism" 488). Ludic feminist cultural studies, in other words, seeks to "show" or "give . . . account," that is, to *describe* but not to *explain* through conceptualization, for any attempt to "conceptualize" experience or pleasure is seen by ludic critics as a violent erasure of the unique, local, specific, and concrete individual: to conceptualize is to totalize and to totalize is seen, at all levels, as totalitarian.

But such a validating, affirmative, and pleasure-ful culture studies—concerned primarily with the liberation of (individual) desire and the body as zone of sensuousness—is to my mind a very class-specific inquiry. Pleasure and desire can be the overriding concern only for the classes of people (middle and upper) who are already "free" from economic want and have the means to pursue or, more specifically in commodity cultures, to consume the means for pleasure. It is also these classes who have the relative luxury of displacing the body as means of labor onto the body as pleasure zone. This fetishization of pleasure validates the priorities and privileges of the middle class—in spite of its attention to the "pleasures" of others—for it produces a cultural studies that largely erases the needs, conditions, and exploitation of the working poor and the impoverished underclass in this country and globally: an underclass that is denied basic economic and human rights, an underclass that is overwhelmingly not "white."[5]

This ludic valorization of "pleasure" as liberation, the affirmation of existing social differences, and the fetishization of the "local" and specific raise serious problems for feminist and oppositional culture critique. It will not take us far in understanding or explaining the socioeconomic conditions and desperation underlying the uprising in Los Angeles or causing women in India to sell their kidneys and women in the United States to rent out their uteruses in order to feed their children; nor will it help us much to intervene in and change these conditions. The verdict in the Rodney King trial—for many of us—was not a local, contingent, arbitrary, and aleatory play of power; rather, it was part of the systematic exercise of inequality, injustice, and oppression against African Americans in this country. It urgently impresses on us the need not simply to "account for and validate social differences" but to *critique* them in order to explain the underlying social relations of exploitation and to transform them.

Perhaps I need to clarify here what I mean by critique. First, I do not regard "critique" as an end in itself. Critique is a practice through which the subject develops historical knowledge of the social totality: she or he acquires, in other words, an understanding of how the existing social institutions ("motherhood," "child care," "love," "paternity," "taxation," "family," etc.) have in fact come about and how they can be changed. Critique, in other words, is that knowledge-practice that historically situates the conditions of possibility of what empirically exists under patriarchal-capitalist labor relations and, more importantly, points to what is suppressed by the empirically existing: what *could be* (instead of what actually *is*). Critique indicates, in other words, that what "is" is not necessarily the real/true but rather only the existing actuality which is transformable. The role of critique in resistance postmodern feminism is exactly this: the production of historical knowledges that mark the transformability of existing social arrangements and the possibility of a different social organization—an organization free from exploitation. Quite simply then, critique is a mode of knowing that inquires into what is not said, into the silences and the suppressed or missing, in order to uncover the concealed operations of power and underlying socioeconomic relations connecting the myriad details and seemingly disparate events and representations of our lives. It shows how seemingly disconnected zones of culture are in fact linked through the highly differentiated and dispersed operation of a systematic logic of exploitation informing all practices of society. In sum, critique disrupts that which represents itself as what is, as natural, as inevitable, as the way things are and exposes the way "what is" is historically and socially produced out of social contradictions and how it supports inequality. Critique enables us to *explain* how gender, race, sexual, and class oppression operate so we can change it.

A number of contemporary feminists, from Haraway and Penley to Jane Gallop and Judith Butler, have embraced the ludic mode of postmodern cultural studies and argued for its liberatory potential. But I believe if feminists are to engage in postmodern cultural studies without jeopardizing feminism's political effectiveness, we need to rigorously critique postmodernism's fundamental presuppositions and, above all, to write a materialist politics back into postmodernism. My essay is a contribution to this effort. Thus it *insists* on a transformative emancipatory politics in postmodernism and on the necessity of critique for an oppositional culture studies. In other words, I contend that the *ludic postmodern* erasure of the political in the name of discursive difference is only one way of constructing postmodern difference. In contrast, I want to argue for feminism to radically retheorize postmodern difference itself and to articulate what I call a *resistance postmodernism* that will be the basis for *postmodern materialist feminist culture critique.*

I

But first I need to address the question of theory. It has become customary, among ludic postmodernists, to dissociate oneself from "theory": theory is seen as an act of "totalizing" that, as I have already indicated, has become synonymous in ludic circles with "totalitarianism." For instance, Judith Butler—who is, in spite of her disclaimers, one of the elite theorists—distances herself from theory by assuming the familiar pose of "ignorance" (which, of course, in ludic discourses is the genuine mark of "knowing"). She states, in a recent essay, that she "do[es] not understand the notion of 'theory,' and [is] hardly interested in being cast as its defender . . ." ("Imitation and Gender Insubordination" 14). J. Hillis Miller, another elite theorist, regards himself basically as a "local" reader—a producer of pleasure or what he calls the "joys of reading"—and claims that he is a "theorist" almost by accident; he practices theory, as the title of his most recent book indicates, only "now and then" (*Theory Now and Then*). Similar acts of distancing have almost become part of a ludic ritual among those elite theorists who command considerable power and prestige in the academy precisely because they are theorists. Jane Gallop, for example, prefaces her well-known book on Lacan by not only proclaiming her "inadequacy" and her "attempt to read (Lacan) from that position" but also granting it a special status as "both Lacanian and feminist" (*Reading Lacan* 20). However, we should not take literally their distancing of themselves from theory: this gesture is itself theoretical in that it puts in question one notion of theory (theory as explanatory critique) and favors another (theory as play, as affirmation and not explanation). Since I oppose the notion of theory as play—affirmation of that which already exists—and argue for theory as explanatory critique, I need to say more about the role of this "different" kind of theory that I am producing here.

It is not enough to write a "different" theory if such difference does not fundamentally challenge the way theory often participates in power relations. A new and different theory must contribute to the struggle to build a more multicultural and equal socioeconomic order. But the "new" and "different" are easily commodified in patriarchal capitalism as mere variety in a supposedly "free marketplace" of choice, thus promoting the illusion of diversity and free will and concealing the oppressive restrictions on people's possibilities. In other words, the idea of theory as play and the notion of theory as explanatory critique are treated in the contemporary academy as simply two different choices. In such a view choices are understood as merely a matter of personal taste or preference, as if such tastes and preferences are not themselves historically produced. However, the two understandings of theory are not only related to each other but they also contest each other in their assumptions and presuppositions and in the socioeconomic orders they legitimate. They are, in other words, not simply two different choices, but two contesting modes of understanding existing social institutions and political arrangements as well as the role of gender, sexuality, race, and class in such arrangements. In short, there are material and historical conflicts between them. Theory as play or performance and theory as materialist explanatory critique should not just be pluralistically accepted as two (free) choices but rather rigorously examined so that their historicity and their (political) role in contemporary feminism are clearly articulated.

Feminist theory, I believe, must be a politically transformative practice: one that not only disrupts the specific conditions and features of a racist, patriarchal, and capitalist oppression but also transforms the systematic relations of exploitation and moves toward producing nonexploitative social arrangements. At the same time, feminist theory needs to be especially self-reflexive and adept at critiquing its own historical situation and limits; at resisting the patriarchal appropriation and usurpation of its oppositional logic; and at insuring that its alternative practices and modes of knowing circulate and are used on behalf of an emancipatory agenda. While many may agree with this principle, its realization is the most difficult and hotly contested issue in feminist theory today.

In addressing these issues, I thus speak as a feminist engaged in a self-reflexive dialog with other feminists over a critique of the limits, aporias, and presuppositions, in short, the problematic of feminist theory as it struggles to end exploitation. As I have already made clear, I am also speaking from an oppositional space within the postmodern that is a *resistance postmodernism.*

Theory, for many feminists, is seen as masculinist, abstract, elitist, and phallogocentric, and as a form of instrumental reason. Above all theory is considered antithetical to women's experience and thus betrays feminism. At the core of this controversy over theory is the issue of the relation of theory and *experience*—whether the humanist notion of the experience of the moral self (as in cultural feminism) or the postmodern celebration of the experience of the ethical subject of pleasure, the *jouissance* of the body (as in ludic feminism).[6] Much postmodern theory is, in fact, an "antitheoretical theory." We need only look at Derrida's *Post Card,* Lyotard's *Just Gaming,* de Man's *The Resistance to Theory,* Gallop's *Thinking through the Body,* or Fish's *Doing What Comes Naturally* to see this opposition to theory as a phallogocentric rationalism and the use of such "ludic" strategies as the play of tropes, parody, punning, autobiography (what Ulmer calls "mystory"), and anecdote to deconstruct theory, its concepts and principles. This antitheoretical stance also informs ludic postmodern cultural studies as the anthology *Cultural Studies* demonstrates. In writing the afterword to the volume, in which she both sums up its major themes and comments on the current state of cultural studies, Angela McRobbie celebrates "the absence of the tyranny of theory," which has been displaced by a "speculative 'writerly' approach" (Grossberg et al. 724). But this view of theory, whether adopted by humanists, postmodernists, or feminists, is, to my mind, politically very disenabling.

Instead of conventionally (and conveniently) dismissing theory as a masculinist and rationalist instrumentalism that acts as an abstract metalanguage or a violent closure of meaning, we need to reunderstand theory as a historical critique of the politics of intelligibility. By this I mean theory is most effectively understood in resistance postmodernism not in an "idealist" way (theory as metalanguage) but as an explanatory critique of the ways in which meanings are materially formed and social reality is constructed in relation to various strategies of power. This reunderstanding of theory enables us to acquire a historical knowledge of social totalities and the relations of power, profit, and labor rendering certain forms of daily practices legitimate ("meaningful") and marking others as "meaningless." Theory, in this sense, is a double operation: it is both the frame of intelligibility through which we organize and make sense of reality, and the critical inquiry into and contestation over these modes of meaning making. Practice is inscribed in theory as I am articulating it here. Thus theory is not simply a cognitivism but a historical site of social struggle over how we represent reality, that is, over how we construct reality and the ways to change it.[7] Theory, in other words, is a political practice and not simply a metaphysical abstraction or discursive play. This means that even such a seemingly natural and nontheoretical practice as common sense (as Gramsci argues in *Prison Notebooks*) is a frame of intelligibility, a theory, but one that conceals its mode of knowing, representing it as the "way things are." Theory, then, is not opposed to experience but is the necessary *supplement* of experience (to use Derrida's term in order to deconstruct his deconstruction of theory): theory historicizes experience and displays the social relations that have enabled it to be experienced as "experience." Such a knowledge prevents us from essentializing experience and makes it possible to produce new experiences by transforming the dominant social relations.

The pressing issue for social change then is not to reject theory (knowledge) but first to *critique* how specific theories are produced and used, in the interests of what power relations, and second to engage in the struggle to produce new opposing theories (contesting knowledges)—in short, to participate in the struggle over opposing ways of constructing and changing the world. To theorize postmodernism and difference in the terms I am proposing here is an instance of such a contestation over theory: an effort to produce opposing knowledge for social change.

Thus the question of postmodernism is itself the question of contesting theories—contesting modes of intelligibility and their different political consequences. By postmodern, then, I do not mean a monolithic discourse but the ensemble of conflicting discourses produced in late patriarchy in which capital and the sexual division of labor are deployed in new ways. Among these discourses, as I have already indicated, I distinguish two key formations: "ludic postmodernism" and "resistance postmodernism." At the core of this conflict is the opposition over how to theorize difference.

Ludic postmodernists address reality as a theater of "simulation," marked by the free-floating *play* (hence the term ludic) of disembodied signifiers and the heterogeneity of differences as in the works of Derrida, Jardine, Lyotard, Baudrillard, Suleiman, and Butler. For instance, for Butler gender is a simulation—what she calls "performance": it is, in other words, the effect of performative acts of the subject and not the outcome of some pregiven interior essence. This sexual indeterminism is what also marks the writings of Marjorie Garber, *Vested Interests;* Teresa de Lauretis, "Film and the Visible" (*How Do I Look? Queer Film and Video*); and Diana Fuss, *Essentially Speaking*. Gender and sexuality in the writings of all these theorists are effects of the circulation of discourses and not part of the operation of socioeconomic arrangements. In fact the very term "gender"—which has been an important enabling concept for politically radical feminism—

is displaced by the new emphasis on "sexuality," which is seen as a ludic excess of gender. "Gender," in other words, is considered a regulatory mechanism that can best be overthrown not by collective social practices but by excessive individual performances that fracture its rules and set the subject free in its libidinal quest.

Ludic postmodernism is best conceptualized as a crisis of representation, a crisis in which texts constituted by difference can no longer provide reliable knowledge of the real because meaning itself is self-divided and undecidable: the access of the signifier to the signified is delayed and deferred, divided by a *difference within*. This movement of differ*a*nce deprives politics of its groundedness in such categories of seeming presence and identity as gender, race, class, nationality: for as one of the contributors to *Cultural Studies* argues, following Laclau and Mouffe, "[I]ndeterminacy and ambivalence . . . inhabit the construction of every social identity" (Mercer 426). Differ*a*nce dismantles the notion of politics itself as "outside" representation, as a "referent" for action. Politics, for ludic postmodernists, is instead a textual practice (such as parody, pastiche, fragmentation, and so on) that has no reliable reference "outside" itself: like texts, as Paul de Man argues (*Allegories of Reading*), its only meaning is that it has no meaning outside its processes of signification. Politics, in this sense then, is a *process* without a *product;* it is a mode of semiotic activism. Politics as semiotic activism obscures prevailing meanings: it disrupts the oppressive totality of what Lyotard calls "cultural policy" (*Postmodern Condition* 76) through play, gaming, experimentation in writing, and transgressive readings (Barthes's "writerly" text) that subvert the "rules" of grand narratives and prevent the easy circulation of meaning in culture. Thus, radical politics for ludic postmodernists problematizes signifying practices and established meanings, demonstrating that in every entity there is a surplus of meaning, an excess, a difference preventing that category from being a reliable ground for reality in general and politics in particular. Such a subversive politics of signification is seen as a liberating gesture, deconstructing the totalities—that is, the grand narratives—organizing reality. Ludic postmodernism substitutes a politics of *differences within* signification for the politics of *differences between* identities such as race, class, and gender. "Identity," for ludic postmodernism, is nothing but a metanarrative inherited from the Enlightenment.

I want to stress that the postmodern problematization of signifying practices is a necessary move in that it denaturalizes dominant meanings and opens up a space for the disarticulation of established signifiers constituting identities. The problem is that ludic critics do so in a way that isolates signifying practices from the historically specific social relations producing them. Ludic postmodernism is, in effect, a cognitivism and an immanent critique that reduces politics to rhetoric and history to textuality. It removes the ground from under both the *revolutionary* and the *reactionary* and in the name of a multiplicity of differences effectively conceals radical difference. Ludic politics is, in the last instance, a Socratic, dialogic, discursive apparatus that does not so much transform practices as merely problematize their continuation.

In feminism this postmodern rewriting of difference has meant a shift away from differences *between* genders to a concern with the differences *within* the category of women along the various trajectories of race, class, and sexuality, as in the work, for instance, of de Lauretis, Joan Scott, and Elizabeth Meese. For others, such as Jardine and Shoshana Felman, it has meant the erasure of woman as historical subject and her construction as a subject of desire: a signifying excess. As a result, feminism risks losing sight of women as collective subjects systematically exploited in patriarchy according to their gender and is in danger of textualizing and thus losing its transformative politics.

Feminism, I argue, needs to rewrite the postmodern *difference within*—differ*a*nce—not as a ludic difference but as a historical, *political difference,* a materialized, resisting differ*a*nce. But this is not a call to return to the essentializing difference between identities as in a logocentric humanism. Rather it proposes that we need to realize the historicity of identities, particularly of gender sexuality and race, and their relations to labor processes.

I would thus like to propose *resistance postmodernism* as the activation of this political difference. Resistance postmodernism contests the ludic notion of difference as simply discursive—as textuality, as a formal, rhetorical space—and instead insists that difference is social and historical. Difference, I suggest, is rewritten in resistance postmodernism as always *difference in relation,* that is, as *difference within a system of exploitation and the social struggle it engenders.* Resistance postmodernism, then, does not simply reject textuality or rhetoric, nor does it return to a predetermined reference; rather, it contends that textuality and difference—the relation of signifier and signified—are themselves the site of social conflict and struggle. They are not panhistorical spaces of eternal ahistorical slippage and excess. In short, significations acquire meaning not from their formal system as Saussure proposes but from their place in the social struggle over "meanings," as in the conflicts over "negro," "black," and "African-American," or over "Ms" or the pronoun "he." The "sign" itself is an arena of social conflict, to paraphrase Volosinov-Bakhtin in his *Marxism and the Philosophy of Language,* because it is always situated in the socio-economic and power relations of a specific social formation. In other words, the relation of signifier to signified is not a free-floating play of signification but an ideological process in which the signifier is related to a matrix of historically possible signifieds. The signifier becomes temporarily connected to a specific signified—that is, it acquires its "meaning"—through social struggle in which the prevailing ideology and social contradictions (arising from labor relations) insist on a particular signified or set of signifieds and suppress others. Such a signifying relation is insecure, continually contested, and changeable—that is, opposing ideologies can disarticulate a specific relation and propose an opposing set of signifieds or meanings, as in the struggles to displace the derogatory signifieds of "black" with more affirmative and emancipatory signifieds as in "black power" and "black is beautiful."[8]

In theorizing difference as always *difference in relation within a system of exploitation* feminism can open up new spaces for radical political action and cultural critique. Instead of merely subverting signification, resistance postmodernism seeks to *critique* and *intervene* in the systematic relations and uses of signification for exploitation.

II

I would like to elaborate more specifically here on the two radically different notions of politics in postmodernism I have been discussing. Ludic politics seeks *open access* to the free play of signification (through parody, irony, and experimentation) in order to dissemble the dominant cultural policy (the totality) that tries to restrict and stabilize meaning. Resistance or materialist postmodern politics insists on *politics as the practice aimed at "equal" access for all to social, cultural, and economic resources* and also as an end to the exploitative exercise of power. The first is a politics aimed at the liberation of the individual, particularly the individual libido—the celebration of pleasure, excess *jouissance*. It advocates cultural equality through semiotic activism. The second seeks the emancipation of the collectivity of subjects from exploitation—specifically from a capitalist, racist patriarchy: its aim is primarily economic equality through social struggle.

In short, the rewriting of difference as difference in relation raises anew the issue of totality. To transform people's access to socioeconomic resources and to end exploitation will require a notion of totality in order to critique the systematicity and global relations of oppression. But the first mode of politics—"ludic politics"—does not merely disrupt specific totalities, it rejects any inquiry into the concept of totality as itself an instance of totalitarianism and occludes any critique of power as a *system* of unequal relations involving the powerful and powerless.[9] As I have already indicated, ludic politics relies on an immanent notion of power and instead of systems of power such as capitalism or patriarchy, it proposes localities (like prisons or clinics) in which power is not merely repressive but positively enabling since it produces its own "resistance." Power in ludic politics is aleatory and *a*systematic; it is never "necessary" or "determinate" but always subject to the unpredictable slippage of the sign. Thus for many postmodernists, especially cultural critics, the main agenda of ludic politics follows Lyotard's battle cry to "wage war on totality."

This ludic war on totality with its local, micropolitics and aleatory notion of power has become the primary site for feminist engagement with the postmodern largely because ludic discourses and practices are seen as synonymous with postmodernism. In short, feminists, by and large, have failed to see that postmodernism is itself divided by a radical difference. As a result, feminists as diverse as Butler, de Lauretis, Donna Haraway, Nancy Fraser, and Linda Nicholson are articulating a politically very counterproductive form of postmodern feminist cultural studies in their celebration of a local pluralism and their "war" on other feminists as totalizing. An exemplar of this ludic postmodern feminism is, of course, Haraway's "A Manifesto for Cyborgs," in which she attempts to rewrite a socialist, materialist feminism as an "argument for pleasure in the confusion of boundaries," as a local network of differences among women and a rejection of any notion of system and totality as an "erasure of polyvocal, unassimilable . . . difference" (150–59). Haraway's notion of socialism is influenced more by the post-Marxist idea of politics as discourse and the ludic notion of libidinal liberation than by the concept of politics as social struggle over economic equality. In fact, in Haraway's "socialism"—as indeed in the work of many contemporary feminists who regard(ed) themselves as socialist—concepts of "labor," "class", "history" (notions that underwrite socialism and differentiate it from radical democracy or liberal politics) are conspicuously missing. This is a socialism which is, by and large, utopian, idealist, and metaphoric: it is grounded on metaphors of labor, class, struggle, economics (if it uses them at all) rather than on actual historical, materialist practices.[10]

At the core of Haraway's essay is her attack on Catherine MacKinnon's radical feminism as "a caricature of the appropriating, incorporating, totalizing tendencies of Western theories of identity grounding action" (200). In fact, MacKinnon has become the straw woman for attacks on feminist theories of totality: one critic has even called her both Lenin and Hitler (Mullarkey 720). Such attacks on committed feminists like MacKinnon, who have long been on the front lines of critique and intervention in the systematic exploitation of women's sexuality and labor, should be a serious warning to us to rethink the political consequences of feminist involvement in ludic postmodernism.[11] Much recent feminist theory under pressure of ludic postmodernism is not only denying the insights of radical feminism but is also abandoning the sustained critique of patriarchy as an ongoing system of exploitation based on gender—so much so, that patriarchy, which the socialist-feminist Maria Mies has called the necessary "struggle concept" of feminism (*Patriarchy and Accumulation* 36), has now become the taboo word of recent feminist theory: it cannot be said without the speaker taking the risk of being labeled a reductive totalizer, Lenin or even Stalin.

"Patriarchy" has become a taboo concept because, from a ludic perspective, it is not only totalizing but it also essentializes "men," "women," and "oppression." From an orthodox Marxist perspective, patriarchy cannot be deployed because it is seen as reifying gender issues while erasing class and economics. However, the concept of patriarchy is vital to the struggle against women's oppression.[12] Thus, I want to put forth a materialist concept of patriarchy as a regime of exploitation that produces gender difference in order to construct asymmetrical, unequal divisions of labor, accumulation, and access to social, economic, and cultural resources, guaranteeing not only the privilege of one gender (male) over the other (female) but, more important, the subjugation and exploitation of the "other" gender as the very grounds of wealth and accumulation. In other words, patriarchy is a historically diverse, ongoing, and unequal system of gender differences and exploitation: one that is "necessary" to the very existence and prosperity of the majority of socioeconomic systems in the world and is fundamental to the global expansion and colonization of capitalism.

I am quite aware that most ludic feminists will dismiss this position as itself reductive and repressive. But the local pluralism they advocate, which also informs (ludic) postmodern cultural studies, is far from being a new, nonrepressive inclusivity. Instead, it involves a very insidious exclusion of any politics of change: it excludes and occludes global or structural relations of power, as I have already indicated, by simply dismissing them as "ideological" and "totalizing" effects of discourse itself. It excludes, in effect, the systematicity of regimes of exploitation on the basis of what Jameson has called "that silliest of all puns, the confusion of 'totality' with 'totalitarianism'" (60).

In contrast, resistance postmodernism, as I am articulating it here, enables feminists to retheorize totality and to insist on system and patriarchy as necessary struggle concepts for cultural critique and social transformation. Instead of considering totality to be an organic, homogeneous, unified whole (a Hegelian expressive unity) we can reconceptualize totality as both a system of relations and an *overdetermined structure of difference,* a system which is historical and thus articulates social contradictions: it is thus materialistically (not discursively) always self-divided, different from itself and multiple. It is traversed by *differences within,* by differ*a*nce, and, at the same time, produces a logic of connection that operates through this self-division.

We can thus reunderstand patriarchy as a "system of differences," but not one that is either a homogenous undifferentiated "totality" or fragmented, dispersed, free-floating, and unconnected sites of power. Instead, the ongoing exploitative organization and production of gender differences, especially in relation to the division of labor, and the ideological effort to represent them as natural and inevitable, provide a logic of connection through all the diverse historical formations of patriarchy. Yet the specific articulations of these differences are not fixed and stable but historically traversed by contradictions and continually contested and struggled over by the other, that is, by differences excluded, suppressed, and exploited. *Patriarchy is thus a totality in process,* a self-divided, multiple arena of social struggle. But it is able to represent itself as a seeming unity that is coherent, inviolable, and always the same, in other words, continuous, but this is an ideological effect. Patriarchy thus *seems* transhistorical and synonymous with human nature and society. But this seeming historical "continuity" is not so much the continuity of the same but rather *different* reconfigurations of an ongoing socioeconomic structure of gendered oppression. Patriarchy, then, is continuous on the level of the structure or organization of oppression and discontinuous, that is, heterogeneous, in its historically specific and conjunctural practices.

In short, patriarchy is a differentiated, contradictory structure that historically produces *identical effects* differently. For instance, the specific configuration of the political economy of differences in postmodern or late capitalist patriarchy in the United States is quite distinct from the configuration of differences in contemporary fundamentalist Iran, and both of these vary from those found in feudal Europe. Yet for all their *differences in relation* to each other, they share the same dominant organization of differences according to the gender opposition of male/female.[13] All these various patriarchal arrangements, in short, produce the same *effects:* the oppression and exclusion of woman as other, the division of labor according to gender—specifically, the exploitation of women's labor (whether in the public or private sphere)—and the denial of women's full access to social resources. Women thus occupy the "same" position within patriarchy *differently,* divided by the conjunctions of race, class, nationality, (post)colonialism, and so on. Their "identity" is not identical; they are not the "same" as each other, yet they are all subjects of the same structures of oppression. By understanding women's subjectivities as the effects of difference-in-relation, I believe, we can rearticulate a collective subject for feminism.

A move toward an emancipatory politics for feminism needs to be based on a materialist cultural critique. But in order to be effective, cultural critique must intervene in the system of patriarchal oppression at *both* the macropolitical level of the structural organization of domination (a transformative politics of labor relations) and the micropolitical level of different and contradictory manifestations of oppression (cultural politics). Ludic postmodern cultural studies and much recent feminist theory all tend to confine their analysis to the micropolitics of oppression and the local level of differences. In doing so, they inhibit any effective intervention in the structures of totalities like patriarchy. I believe resistance postmodern cultural studies and postmodern materialist feminism, with their dialectical critiques of both the structures of difference-in-relation and the specific enunciations of these differences, will develop a transformative theory and practice that can contribute to the end of patriarchal exploitation. For it is through the unrelenting critique of the socioeconomic relations of differences, particularly the division of labor, and the way they construct and restrict the meanings and subjectivities they require that feminist cultural studies can help bring about the nonexploitative future.

III

How does this resistance postmodern critique enable feminism to reunderstand some of the specific concepts, practices, and issues it engages in cultural studies? I want to demonstrate some of these consequences by taking up the politics of the "body" in feminist cultural studies. The body, increasingly, is the primary site for new articulations of cultural understanding for a wide range of feminist and ludic postmodern critics. Not only is Ross calling for a "new generation" of critics and intellectuals to "appeal to the liberatory body," but many feminist and postmodern critics are more and more following Foucault, for whom, as Fiske argues, the "body replaces the subject" (161). In fact, much of the valorization of the body in feminism and cultural studies participates in the ludic postmodern (re)turn to the body, evident in the writings of not only Foucault but also Barthes, Deleuze, Guattari, Bourdieu, and others. Thus, Fiske argues for a cultural studies of "everyday life" that deals not with subjects but with "the body [as it] enters into immediate, performed relationship with the different settings or spaces it inhabits" (162), and one of the most innovative of recent feminist cultural theories, Butler's *Gender Trouble,* similarly displaces the subject and builds a theory of gender and sexuality on this postmodern performativity of the body. Perhaps more than any other issue, this concern with the body bridges the considerable differences dividing feminism today, and we find humanist feminists like Adrienne Rich, socialist feminists such as Nancy Hartsock, and poststructuralist feminists like Gallop all attempting to "think through the body" as a new basis for a feminist social dynamic. Elizabeth Grosz, in fact, calls for a new "corporeal feminism" since "the body can be seen as *the* primary object of social production and inscription" (qtd. in Barrett xxviii).[14]

One of the main questions for feminist culture critique, then, is what is the political effect of these rewritings of knowledge and everyday culture through the body? Do they disrupt and transform patriarchal knowledge and practices, or do they end up reproducing the division of subjectivities and significations necessary to patriarchal oppression—in spite of their feminist agenda?

The body in feminist theory is the site of the concrete, the specific, the particular in opposition to abstraction—which is considered masculinist and phallogocentric. As Rich puts it, women's

> need to begin with the female body—our own—[is] understood . . . as locating the grounds from which to speak with authority *as* women. Not to transcend this body, but to reclaim it. To reconnect our thinking and speaking with the body of this particular living human individual, a woman. Begin . . . with the material, with matter, mma, madre, mutter, moeder, modder. . . . Pick up again the long struggle against lofty and privileged abstraction. (213)

We are all well aware, since it has become a commonplace of both feminist and postmodern discourses, that abstraction marks the hierarchical dualism dominating Western rationalism in which the abstract, the ideal, the concept, and mind are privileged over the concrete, the material, experience, and the body. And as Hartsock writes in *Money, Sex and Power,* "[I]t is not accidental that women are associated with quasi-human and nonhuman nature, that woman is associated with the body and material life, that the lives of women are systematically used as examples to characterize the lives of those ruled by their bodies rather than their minds" (241). Diverse feminists thus share a commitment to overturning this hierarchical dualism dominating the binary other, whether nature, woman, or men and women of color. Thus we find Gallop beginning her book *Thinking through the Body* by decrying the "systematic mind-body split that is killing our children" and quoting Rich: "Culture: pure spirit, mind . . . has . . . split itself off from life, becoming the death-culture of quantification, abstraction, and the will to power which has reached its most refined destructiveness in this century" (2). Abstraction, in short, represents the alienation and destructiveness of dominant modes of knowing—especially the primacy of concepts—in Western thought.

In opposition to this alienating abstraction, feminists increasingly posit the body as a concrete, anticonceptual, material knowledge that is both disalienating and creative. For many humanist feminists, such as Rich, Susan Griffin, and Andrea Dworkin, the *experience* of the female body—what Sandra Harding has described as "female embodiment . . . [m]enstruation, vaginal penetration, lesbian sexual practices, birthing, nursing and menopause . . . bodily experiences men cannot have" (661–62)—is seen as locating women in a specific, particular, material knowledge of daily life and involving them in creative, nondominating relations of nurturing and connection with others. Female embodiment is considered to overcome masculinist, rationalist dualism, for as Hartsock argues, a "unity of mental and manual labor . . . grows from the fact that women's bodies, unlike men's, can be themselves instruments of production" (*Money, Sex and Power* 243). Thus, Hartsock seeks to base an unalienated production with its "erotic possibilities" and a "reunderstanding of power and community" on women's "bodily, sensual, creative" experiences (257). In fact, Hartsock argues that "the body—its desires and needs, its mortality . . . would be given a place of honor at the center of the theory" (259) as both a feminist standpoint of epistemology and a specifically feminist historical materialism. The body, in short, has become such a privileged site of nonalienating, concrete, unifying experience that even a complex theorist like Hartsock bases her feminist historical materialism—with its theory of power, women's labor, and epistemology—in the end all on the female body, in other words, on a form of biological essentialism. Hartsock's feminist materialism reverses the very relations of historical materialism: instead of critiquing how the body—that is, our experiences and understanding of the body, how we make the body intelligible—is produced through the political economy of social relations, she instead grounds her theory of social relations, in the last instance, on a biology and erotics of reproduction: on the menstruation, pregnancy, lactation of the female body as if these were self-evident, invariable, essential processes.

And that is the question isn't it? Are these bodily processes natural, material grounds for social relations or are they always already mediated and thus constructed, made intelligible and experienced through the structuring of the symbolic order and the operation of the political economy of social relations and the division of labor? In other words, is the "meaning" of menstruation in the "experience" of menstruation (its physical bodiliness) or is the meaning in the way that experience gets read in a given social formation on the basis of the frames of intelligibility and labor practices that society produces. To answer this question we need to look more closely at how the body functions in feminist discourses.

First, as I have already mentioned, the body is posited as the opposite of abstraction, of conceptuality, but the body as it circulates in feminist theory is a *concept:* a specific historically produced articulation or way of making sense of experience. Rich makes this dilemma especially clear when she says, "Perhaps we need a moratorium on saying 'the body.' For it's also possible to abstract '*the*' body. When I write '*the* body,' I see nothing in particular. To write 'my body' plunges me into lived experience, particularity: I see scars, disfigurements, discolorations, damages, losses . . ." (215). Rich, in other words, recognizes that the body is itself a concept, an abstraction, but she is, I think, wrong in believing we can overcome this abstraction if only we can make the body more particular, more specific—"my body," my scar, my color. We are back again to the bourgeois isolate, the monad so necessary to capitalist patriarchy: the specific, local me cut off from any understanding of the operation of the social relations of exploitation.

This concept of the body as anti-abstract continues to be trapped in the hierarchical dualism it is used to contest. The body is not so much a unifying experience as it is merely a reversal of the binary hierarchy. Instead of privileging mind, we privilege body; instead of reifying abstractions, we reify the concrete. The mind-body split still operates, and women are still located in the body. Only now it is women who confirm our place there in the name of change. Certainly such a move alters the relations of privilege—it valorizes what the dominant order denigrates—but it does not overthrow the system underlying oppressive dichotomy. It merely reverses its privileged terms without touching the structure that produces the binarism. The dualistic system thus remains intact, only now it is partially concealed behind a false monism of the body.

The second question for us is whether those feminists engaged in ludic postmodern—specifically poststructuralist and Lacanian—discourses have conceptualized the body in a more productive way for a transformative feminist politics, or do they reproduce the same aporias and limits in new terms? Gallop's

Thinking through the Body is a lesson text for us to use in addressing this question not only because it is considered by many to be a primary discussion of the subject, but also, and perhaps more important, because its contradictions and confusions so vividly enact the contradictions over the body in postmodern feminist theory at this historical moment.

In *Thinking through the Body,* Gallop contests what she calls the "mind-body split" that is "exemplified in an opposition between philosophers and mothers" (8). She begins by drawing on Roland Barthes to posit the body as a "bedrock given, a priori to any subjectivity." As she says:

> Not just the physical envelope, but other puzzling and irreducible *givens,* arising from the 'body' if that word means all that in the organism which exceeds and antedates consciousness or reason or interpretation. By 'body,' [she goes on to say] I mean here: perceivable givens that the human being knows as 'hers' without knowing their significance to her. In such a way a taste for a certain food or a certain color, a distaste for another, are pieces of the bodily enigma. (13)

Taste or "predilection" for Gallop "indicates a bodily enigma; it points to an outside—beyond/before language" (16). It is through this unrepresentable, uninterpretable bodily enigma, this taste or predilection, in excess of language, of textuality—that we know (in other words, experience) the givenness of the body. This positing of the body as the experience of a given outside, in excess of language and social relations and in opposition to abstract systematicity, is quite close to the humanist conception of the body discussed above.

Gallop's text is fraught with contradictions: on the one hand, she asserts the poststructuralist position on textuality and the crisis of referentiality; on the other, she ends up affirming the body as referent and valorizing the experience of the body. For example, she claims at one point in the text that "everything is real *and* everything is textual, mediated, interpretable" (90). And at another point in discussing the work of Irigaray she says that

> belief in simple referentiality is . . . politically conservative, because it cannot recognize that the reality to which it appeals

> is a traditional ideological construction, whether one terms it phallomorphic, or metaphysical, or bourgeois, or something else. The politics of experience is inevitably a conservative politics, for it cannot help but conserve traditional ideological constructs which are not recognized as such but are taken for the "real." (98–99)

This is an eloquent statement of the politics of referentiality and experience, but the question is, does it end up being a description of Gallop's own politics? For in her critique of the phallus in Lacan, for example, she repeatedly argues that the penis is the referent for the phallus and condemns Lacanians for attempting to dispense with the penis as the referent grounding the power of the phallus. To erase the penis as referent, she contends, turns the phallus into a self-referential transcendental signified. Her argument thus defends an essential reference that she has herself already rejected. This, obviously, is one way to understand and critique Lacan. However, we can also read Lacan more politically—read him, that is, as saying that the "phallus" is a social entity and, as such, its meaning does not reside in any secure ground such as the physicality of the penis. The meaning of the phallus, in short, is not secured in the penis, but is basically a matter of power. As Volosinov argues, the sign (phallus) is the site of contestation: the meaning of the phallus is "determined" through social struggles and labor relations and *then* attributed to the penis/clitoris as a way of naturalizing what is essentially a social phenomenon. Gallop's critique of Lacan is itself a very conservative critique: it takes us back to the essentialism of humanism. A postmodern materialist critique, on the other hand, is aimed at moving beyond Lacan (not regressing to a "before") by teasing out the political possibilities in problematizing the referent of the phallus.

Gallop's reading of Lacan, in short, is a serious misreading that ends up restoring the experience of the body as she quite clearly states: "By insisting on the penis, I was looking for some masculine body, some other body, some bodily object of female heterosexual desire, trying to find not just the institution of heterosexism but also the experience of heterosexuality" (131). This move is not just confined to the phallus/penis; rather much of Gallop's reading of the body puts forth a conservative politics of experience that, to use her own words, "conserves the traditional ideological constructs" of patriarchy and does not offer us a possibility for an emancipatory politics.

The more poststructuralist aspects of her text, on the other hand, participate in the limits of a ludic postmodern politics, specifically the textualization of resistance and the reification of the local and the particular. Gallop's discourse, like ludic postmodernism as a whole, is an antitheory theory—think of Derrida's *Glas,* Richard Rorty's *Objectivity, Relativism, and Truth,* de Man's *Resistance to Theory,* or Gregory Ulmer's *Teletheory,* a text which also reifies experience as "mystory." Theory in these discourses is essentialized as a phallogocentric, abstract, instrumental, dominating system whose main apparatus is the concept (which is equated with an identity of language and reality) with its rigid, reductive fixity. Ludic opposition to this mastering theory involves displacing its concepts and subverting its categories through such deconstructive strategies as punning, parody, and cultivating the tropic play of signifiers—the dissemination of differ*a*nce—that exceed the controlling argument of the system. Thus we have Ulmer's "puncept" (147) and Naomi Schor's "patriody": a form of tropic play and difference that "hovers between parody and parricide" (xii). This ludic notion of theory, to which Gallop and other poststructuralist feminists subscribe, is obviously similar to the dominant feminist essentialization of theory as a masculinist abstraction and provides a site for many for the convergence of some forms of feminism and ludic postmodernism.

But the limits of the feminist ludic resistance to theory are quite evident in Gallop's claims for the disruptive potential of the body. As she points out in her discussion of the Marquis de Sade, the conflict is "between rational order, that is, 'philosophy' and irrational bodily materiality. . . . [T]here is always some disorderly specific which exceeds the systematizing discourse" (*Thinking through the Body* 47) and disrupts the mastering impulse of knowledge. Thus, in her discussion of *Justine* and *The New Justine* Gallop claims that

> [t]he pedagogical examination which attempts to regulate the student on the basis of external rules, of the teacher's rules, is messed up by the *regles,* the rules, flowing from within. The

> bodily, fluid, material, feminine sense of *regles* [as "woman's bloody (menstrual) 'rules'" or period] undermines the Sadian pederastic pedagogue's attempt at exact examination, at subjugation of the pupil to his rational, masterful rules. (52)

This is a fairly subtle and sophisticated reading of Sade, exposing both rationalism's violence toward the body and the body's uncontainable excess. But what is its political effectivity? It exposes and disrupts dominant rational categories, but does it move beyond a local, subversive annotation? Does it transform them? Gallop asserts that "the really disturbing violence is not physical violence but the physical as it violates the rational categories that would contain and dominate it" (18). In other words, in a very ludic move, she proposes that what is disturbing is not the violent exploitation and abuse of the body but the body's violation of rational categories. And by this she does not mean a revolutionary act of resistance by the body as agency of conscious social change but rather the excessive, disorderly, irrational details and predilections of the body—its differences—that passively escape rational logic. This, in effect, is a textualizing of violence, of the physical, a dehistoricizing of the social, and an erasure of the economic, all in the name of the body. It is a subversion of linguistic categories on behalf of a concept—that conceals its own conceptuality—a concept of the body as fragmented, nomadic details that escape knowing: its difference from itself.

We need to keep in mind that the texts Gallop is attempting to disrupt through the tropic excess and violence of a textual body are ones in which teachers and fathers sexually assault, physically abuse, cut up, and murder mothers and daughters. This is not merely some pornographic fantasy, some libertarian rationalism gone amuck—this is the reality, the historical situation of exploitation of innumerable women in racist, patriarchal capitalism today. According to MacKinnon, only "7.8% of women in the United States have *not* been sexually assaulted or harassed in their lifetime" (*Feminism Unmodified* 6). Moreover, only 17% of all incidents of rapes and attempted rapes are committed by strangers; the majority are committed by men the women know—acquaintances, friends, lovers, relatives, authority figures (247)—and "women of color (. . . specifically . . . Black women) are raped four times as often as white women" (82). The ludic textualization of violence that Gallop is articulating ends up erasing the political economy of the body in the social relations of exploitation and turning resistance into a tropic game.[15]

In what way does Gallop's textualized body in excess transform the mind-body split? It merely reinscribes woman in the same place she has also been in the patriarchal hierarchy: in the unknowable, unrepresentable, bloody body that exists in opposition to concepts. This anxiety over concepts in ludic postmodernism and humanist feminism is, to my mind, especially counterproductive for an emancipatory politics. Concepts are not only unavoidable, they are also a necessary means for social change. Thinking/experience without concepts is impossible: concepts are the "mediating" frames of intelligibility through which we know the world. Experience—which is put forth as liberation from concepts/thinking by ludic feminists (such as Gallop) and cultural feminists (as different as Susan Griffin and Camille Paglia)—is itself intelligible only through the mediation of concepts. The issue here is not to romantically dismiss concepts but to question how we theorize and use them.

Gallop, however, does not so much contest concepts as abandon them. When she is forced to recognize that *jouissance* is a "principle," that is, a concept, it loses its unsettling, disruptive features for her, and she essentializes it as "a 'general rule,' a 'fixed form' . . . 'strong, muscular, and phallic.'" In its place, she substitutes the weaker, "mediocre and unworthy word, pleasure" (*Thinking through the Body* 123–24), whose conceptuality is still veiled for her. Like Adrienne Rich, who abandons the concept of "the body" for the details of "my body," Gallop and other ludic feminists flee in the face of concepts, taking refuge in the autobiographical (or mystorical) and the local, anecdotal, minute details of differences: as if the local were not "local" precisely because of its relation to the political economy of the total.

I believe a politically effective feminism and cultural critique needs to refuse to essentialize theory and concepts as phallogocentric, masculinist, and dominating or to seek refuge in a seemingly anticonceptual biological, biographical, textual, or performative body. Nor can it acquiesce to the pervasive and "universal" (in spite of all its seeming particularity) ludic displacement of concepts—and the theories they help construct—into an indeterminate chain of differences. For theory is not in and of itself controlling and oppressive; rather, it is the question of the specific historical constructions, appropriations, and uses of theory and concepts in relation to the struggles over exploitative socioeconomic relations. Indeed, historically theory has been largely the province and property of the privileged, hegemonic gender, class, and race: concepts have been used—in the name of a transhistorical "reason"—to establish and maintain an oppressive patriarchal and racist hierarchy of knowledge. But we need to critique theory and show its historical limits, and then reunderstand it as a site of social struggle. It is especially important that we engage in the materialist retheorization of theory as the historical frames of intelligibility and conceptual strategies through which we know the operation of power and socioeconomic oppression in the world in which we live. For it is through the struggle over theory, the critique of the limits and uses of existing modes of knowing and the effort to construct new frames of intelligibility, that we can produce emancipatory knowledges (rather than merely subversive pleasures) and thus generate the new subjectivities necessary to transform the world as it is.

It is, therefore, politically more productive to move beyond the upper-middle-class antirationalism of ludic critics in order to focus on a materialist feminist reunderstanding of concepts. I believe it is necessary for feminism not to fetishize an identitarian Hegelian notion of concept as a moment of rational plenitude, in which the signifier and the signified correspond without "difference." Instead, we need to reunderstand concepts as "struggle concepts": as historical, material practices through which the subject engages the social contradictions, the exploitative effects of patriarchy. Concepts, in other words, are historical matrices of intelligibility that display the relations among apparently disconnected entities and thus enable us to grasp the logic of domination that underlies the seemingly disparate and isolated experiences of individuals in culture. Concepts allow us to perceive the way experience is produced and thus empower us to change the social relations and produce new nonexploitative experiences and collective subjectivities. The aim of such conceptual knowledge, then, is not cognitive delight—the joys of knowing—but explanatory critique: a critique that explains the conditions of the possibility of patriarchal practices and thus points to ways that they can be transformed. Concepts, contrary to the bodyism of Gallop, are not philosophical, epistemological, and cognitive but, in fact, the very materiality through which social struggles in the realm of cultural politics take place.

These struggles have meant that women, people of color, and oppressed classes historically have been restricted in their ability to produce theories and concepts as well as "silenced" by the dominant regime that excludes and discredits the knowledges they do construct. In large part they have been denied access to those cultural and institutional subject positions and practices—such as education (including literacy), "philosophy," and "theory" itself—through which individuals are enabled to produce new concepts and to legitimate those concepts they do generate (in short, to be "heard"). Patriarchy has used the practices of theory and institutions of knowledge to try to keep women and others from entering into the struggle over theory and producing new modes of intelligibility that would radically reconceptualize and organize reality in nonexploitative ways. One of the most recent (and pernicious) forms of this de-educating of women has been antitheoretical theory itself. In a politically damaging move, theory is used to argue against theory, to delegitimate concepts productive for social struggle and to dissuade women from "theorizing," from offering explanatory critiques. As Hartsock has quite rightly pointed out:

> Somehow it seems highly suspicious that it is at the precise moment when so many groups have been engaged in "nationalisms" which involve redefinitions of the marginalized Others that suspicions emerge about the nature of the "subject," about the possibilities for a general theory which can describe the world, about historical "progress." Why is it that just at the moment when so many of us who have been silenced begin to demand the right to name ourselves, to act as subjects rather than objects of history, that just then the concept of subjecthood becomes problematic? Just when we are forming our own theories about the world, uncertainty emerges about whether the world can be theorized. ("Foucault on Power" 163–64)

Feminists thus must ask, what are the consequences of grounding feminist politics in a biological, textual, or performative body that is posited as anticonceptual? Does this not reproduce the dominant regime of patriarchal control over theory and the historical marginalization of women from the struggle over concepts, relegating them to their traditional position as passive objects rather than the makers of concepts?

What was consciousness raising if not a grassroots struggle by women to contest the hegemonic concepts that concealed the relations of domination underlying their disparate experiences as individual women and their effort to produce new concepts that revealed the systematic operation of patriarchal social relations, concepts that constructed new subjectivities for women?[16] Feminism, in fact, has long had a history of producing and rearticulating struggle concepts—such as "sexual harassment," "child abuse," "date rape," or gender—that have radically altered our understanding of reality and thus our ability to change it. These struggle concepts have made it possible to make intelligible as historical and social effects those practices that have been thought of as "natural" and inevitable aspects of the "normal" order, thus opening up those practices to the possibility of intervention and social change. The concept of "date rape," for instance, allows women to make distinctions (that is, to intervene in the order of the seemingly "natural") and thus to transform those practices that—according to a perverse patriarchal semiotics—equate a woman's "no" with another signifier, "yes," and block it from signifying anything at all. "No" needs to be recognized not as the playful slippages of a signifier without a signified—a self-divided signifier which actually means its other ("yes")—but instead as a signifier related through the social struggles of women to a "decided" signified: stop the violence!

We have reached the stage in the postdeconstructive moment of patriarchy in which we need to recognize the political consequences of the ludic Laws of the Postmodern Fathers—Nietzsche, Derrida, Barthes, de Man, Fish, Rorty—which subvert the (supposedly) totalitarian "reason" and thereby render impossible an explanatory critique of capitalist patriarchy. The Romantic antirationalism informing the ludic textualism of the body is itself a masculinist pseudorebellion against rationalism. A feminist transformative politics needs to see what is at stake in this resurgence of antirationalism that represents itself as a liberatory cultural politics but in actuality functions hand in hand with the dominant power structures of postmodern patriarchal capitalism.[17]

An especially telling site for pursuing this issue more specifically is the work of Butler in which the ludic trope of the "body" as resistance against rationality receives a philosophically much more sophisticated turn than in the writings of Gallop. In a series of texts, most notably *Gender Trouble* (which will be the focus of my analysis here), Butler deploys the notion of language/textuality as "performative" (language *doing* something) as distinguished from language/textuality as "constative" (language merely *saying* something) to argue that sexual difference is indeterminate. Sexual difference, according to Butler, is not "determined" by some inner "essence" but is a sliding, slipping play of differences "performed" by the subject of/as body. At the outset, I would like to say that Butler's ludic "feminism" takes its founding concepts ("performative" and its other, "constative") from the Fathers of deconstructive performance theory—Austin (who "authored" the founding text of performance theory, *How to Do Things With Words*), Husserl, Derrida, Lyotard, Fish, and Rorty.

The body, for Butler, is "a variable boundary, a surface whose permeability is politically regulated, a signifying practice within a cultural field of gender hierarchy and compulsory heterosexuality" (*Gender Trouble* 139). What does such a concept of the body mean for how we can understand and effect the daily realities of women and men? Does it overcome the limits I have been critiquing? First, Butler frames her entire theorization of gender, sexuality, and the body within the prevailing poststructuralist dichotomy of epistemology and signification, continually attempting to "shift from an *epistemological* account of identity [the "constative" in Austin's terms] to one which locates the problematic within practices of *signification* [the "performative" in Austin's words]" (144). While such a move could be a useful one, the problem is that its understanding of epistemology (reason) is ahistorical and its account of sexuality only partial: the scope of Butler's analysis never moves beyond the boundaries of a discursive or rhetorical arena (whether understood as epistemology or signifying practices) to relate these to material socioeconomic conditions. In fact, the notion of "performance" is deployed to provide an independent, free subject who acquires freedom outside the collectivity of the social. This elision is all the more significant since Butler attempts to engage a materialist social analytics, but she identifies it entirely with Monique Wittig, whom she considers a "classic idealist" for whom "'Nature' and the domain of materiality are ideas, ideological constructs . . . mental representation" (125). In short, materialism is itself reduced to epistemology and thus (in the absence of a historical series) subjected to the indeterminate play of differ*a*nce and subversive repetitions of signifying practices. In its place, Butler—like Rich, Hartsock, and Gallop—substitutes a bodily "matterism" (an ahistorical "objectism") of "flesh" and the sensuousness of both body and sign (gesture). Ironically, even though Butler privileges concrete gesturality, her analysis is itself a mode of cognitivism that fails to link the embodied performances of ideas and significations to historically specific socioeconomic relations.

Following Foucault, Butler absorbs the social into a set of discursive practices, the most fundamental being "compulsory heterosexuality and phallogocentrism . . . understood as regimes of power/discourse" (xi) regulating the production of gender and sexuality. In other words, Butler takes the discursive practice of "compulsory heterosexuality" as the basis for explaining the generation and production of gender and sexuality, but in doing so she occludes the socioeconomic relations of gender and sexual exploitation. She is unable to account for *why* heterosexuality is compulsory and instead takes it as a given. She thus diverts attention from the political economy to rhetoric and ends up replacing explanation with description. A materialist social analytic, on the other hand, *explains* the compulsory nature of heterosexuality by situating it within the historical relations of (gender) differences within a system of exploitation—patriarchy—as a necessary means of the system. In other words, compulsory heterosexuality is a necessary means by which patriarchy naturalizes gender divisions of social relations, particularly labor, but to replace patriarchy with compulsory heterosexuality, as Butler, Wittig, and a number of other feminists do, is a reductive move, isolating heterosexuality as a closed system cut off from socioeconomic relations and erasing patriarchy as a regime of exploitation: in short, it cuts off gender and sexuality from labor. By confining her critique to the discursive regime of compulsory heterosexuality, Butler is never able to move beyond an immanent critique—constrained by its rhetorical boundaries—to relate it to the underlying social forces. She thus substitutes ludic agency—a form of semiotic activism that in fact reifies the dominant power structure—for transformative critique and intervention in the social system itself. Part of the reason is, of course, Butler's participation in the ludic rejection of "totalizing gestures" and her concern to prevent the reduction or "colonizing" of "differences that might otherwise call [the] totalizing concept into question." For "feminist critique," according to Butler, "ought to explore the totalizing claims of a masculinist signifying economy" and even feminism itself (13). In the name of a seemingly inclusive complexity of local, specific differences, Butler, in a common ludic move, excludes the connections of local signifying practices/performances, and their discursive regulatory frames, to global socioeconomic relations.

Butler thus puts forth not only an anticonceptual notion of the body—"bodies are so many 'styles of the flesh'" (139)—but of gender as well: she asks us to "consider gender, for instance, as *a corporeal style,* an 'act'" (139), in short, a signifying or discursive performance inscribed on the surface of the body. This notion of gender, as a corporeal or textual "style," marks ludic feminism, which, in effect, abandons the category of gender (as a materialist and historical construct, emphasizing the way the socioeconomic totality produces gender subjects) in favor of sexuality, as the effects of the a-regular excess of performance and desire. The history of feminism is, in a sense, the history of conceptual contestations over fundamental struggle concepts, like gender, and the way such contests articulate, in the realm of theory, the socioeconomic contestations over the distribution of economic resources and cultural power in society. But this history is radically different from the prevailing "ludic" history of feminism, Gallop's *Around 1981,* which constructs this history in terms of a closed system of textualities as manifested in different anthologies of feminist writings in literary theory and criticism. Gallop acknowledges quite specifically that in writing this history her "project is a struggle . . . over whose version of history is going to be told to the next generation. . . . I am clearly trying to write that history . . .

to undo . . . the effect of books like *Sexual/Textual Politics*. . . ." (Gallop, Hirsch, and Miller 362).

Butler herself argues that "the very different ways in which the category of sex is understood depend[s] on how the field of power is articulated" (*Gender Trouble* 18). However, she articulates power in terms of a generalized, ahistorical, a-causal Foucauldian notion that "encompasses," as she says, "both the juridical (prohibitive and regulatory) and the productive (inadvertently generative) functions of differential relations" (29). In short, power is understood in largely rhetorical terms as regulatory or rule governing, and as such it is not simply restrictive, but, like a grammar, also generative: its "productions," according to Butler, "inadvertently mobilize possibilities of 'subjects' that do not merely exceed the bounds of cultural intelligibility, but effectively expand the boundaries of what is, in fact, culturally intelligible" (29). In short, power, for Butler, is a regulatory system that produces excesses that subvert its own rules. Thus a discursive-power regime like compulsory heterosexuality generates "rules governing signification [that] not only restrict, but enable the assertion of alternative domains of cultural intelligibility, i.e., new possibilities for gender that contest the rigid codes of hierarchical binarisms. . . . The injunction *to be* a given gender produces necessary failures, a variety of incoherent configurations that in their multiplicity exceed and defy the injunction by which they are generated" (145). Gender, for Butler, is thus a ludic play of differ*a*nce; it is unstable, continually deferring and differing from itself: "gender," Butler writes, "is a complexity whose totality is permanently deferred" (16). It simultaneously constructs and undoes itself through an indeterminate series of repetitive acts or performances that exceed and subvert the regulatory power of compulsory heterosexuality.

Such an understanding of the political construction of gender is, I think, seriously misleading and disenabling for a socially transformative feminism. Indeed, gender is not naturally fixed or secure, as psychoanalysis has shown, but neither is it simply discursive or performative. Nor can it be so easily disrupted or exceeded as Butler argues. Gender is a historical and ideological effect of a socioeconomic regime of exploitation, namely patriarchy, and in particular the sexual division of labor. Thus, it cannot be effectively transformed through an indefinite series of individual acts ("performances") of parodic repetition. To disrupt, undo, or exceed the gender binary requires a collective social struggle not only on the level of ideological constructions but, more importantly, against the systematic socioeconomic relations requiring and maintaining the specific forms of gender and sexual difference. This also means that rewriting—reducing—the notion of power to a rhetorical practice that is little more than a grammar does not take us very far in our struggles.[18] Such a ludic notion of power—developed in the name of the concrete, local, specific—turns out to be an abstract, generalized, isolated concept of power cut off from the economic realities of daily life, especially the labor of women. Contrary to Foucault and Butler, power is not some kind of a-causal, contingent, and free-floating series of rules and injunctions generating its own demise. Rather, power, from a materialist or resistance postmodern frame, is always situated in relation to social conflicts over regimes of exploitation. While power can be harnessed for opposition and revolution, it is not automatically generated but must be struggled for since power by and large operates on behalf of the dominant interests. One of the primary functions, then, of a transformative feminist cultural critique is to expose the hidden operation of power, the underlying global connections that relate the disparate, diffuse instances of power to systematic practices of exploitation according to socially and economically produced differences of gender, sexuality, race, and class.

The overriding purpose of feminist cultural critique, I believe, is to help construct the historical knowledges and explanations necessary for the social struggle against oppression—including our own social and historical limits (see, for example, Ebert, "Detecting the Phallus"). From the site of a materialist feminist critique, the most serious and damaging blind spot in ludic feminist theories of gender, sexuality, and the body is the occlusion of labor, especially the erasure of body/sexuality/gender as all *effects of labor*. It is largely a class blindness. The ludic notions of discursive subversion, semiotic activism, disruptive pleasures, and flexible notions of gender have a strong appeal to (upper) middle-class women. They play to the (upper) middle-class desire for individual freedom from economic constraints and the obsession to escape the demands of labor, through gestures of self-expression, pleasure, excess. Ludic postmodern theories of gender and sexuality, including the new (ludic) "queer theory" (in which bodily axes of desire-as-performance provide the conditions of possibility of "queerity"), all tend to construct the differences, pleasures, and excesses of gender/sexuality as sites of escape and denial of the demands and effects of labor: as recreational breaks erase the very parameters of our identities, pleasures, desires, and needs become functions of our participation in the production process, a process that is not only (self)alienating but also produces us as specific kinds of consuming/desiring subjects in patriarchal capitalism.

IV

Gender and sexuality are not simply the result of discursive or signifying practices performed on the body but also, and more importantly, they are the effect of labor performed by, on, and through bodies as historically determined by the division of labor and the unequal access to economic and social resources. The way we live in/through our bodies as men and women, the way our bodies take shape, the way we make sense of and signify our bodies, and even the way we desire and are pleasured in and through our bodies are all affected by our participation in gender-divided labor relations—especially those of racist patriarchal capitalism, whose scope now reaches around the globe.

By labor I do not mean only work for paid wages or work for the production of surplus value and commodities—although it is particularly important to stress the ever-increasing involvement of women in all classes, races, and even nations in the production of surplus value and feminization of more and more sectors of commodity production as in "light-assembly work, whether . . . Barbie dolls or computer components," textiles, and, especially important in the "underdeveloped countries," such as Thailand, "sex-tourism."[19] But also, more broadly, I mean labor as the human activity of transforming nature involved in the reproduction of human life itself as well as the basic means to sustain that life: the production of use values, that is, products for the direct use and survival of the producer and not for commodity exchange, such as food, clothing, and care giving—areas of work that are overwhelmingly the province of women in the gendered division of labor. This retheorization and expansion of the classic Marxist notion of productive labor is what the "German School" of materialist feminist theorists—Maria Mies, Claudia von Werlhof, and Veronika Bennholdt-Thomsen—have called "production of life or subsistence production."[20] For instance, Mies argues that "women's activity in producing children and milk is understood as truly *human,* that is, *conscious, social activity*"—not nature or natural activity—and "has to be understood as a *result* of the patriarchal and capitalist division of labor and not as its precondition" (*Patriarchy and Accumulation* 53–54). To address the issue of labor in the production of body, gender, sexuality, then, means to critically engage the body as both a means of productive labor and itself a site acted on by labor. It opens up the possibility of social struggle over the way the specificities of gender and women's bodies are shaped, used, and exploited by specific historical forms of the division of labor on the basis of ideologically constructed gender differences.

To articulate the unsaid issue of labor in the production of gender questions the usefulness of ludic theories of gender and culture based on a discursive excess, semiotic activism, pleasure, and performance. Will such ludic theories help feminists formulate a historical explanation so that we can develop collective social struggles against the economic exploitation and suffering of women globally—particularly women of color and women in underdeveloped areas in the United States and Europe, and in Hong Kong, Malaysia, Sri Lanka, and elsewhere forced by economic necessity into severely underpaid "women's work" or oppressive forms of unpaid domestic work? Will they help us understand and prevent the "100 million disappeared women"—the global neglect, starving, and killing of girl children and embryos (Kristof C1, C12)—as well as the physical and sexual abuse and economic impoverishment of many of the world's women because of their devalued socioeconomic position in patriarchy? For ludic postmodern feminist theory and cultural studies to fetishize pleasure, desire, and individual libidinal and gender freedom by simply rhetorically displacing—even erasing—the oppressive gender constraints and economic exploitation of patriarchal capitalism is an instance of middle-class myopia, to say the least, which "universalizes" the privileges and relative individual freedoms of the few. (Is it necessary to remind ourselves that nearly all the feminists engaged in debates over theory and cultural studies, regardless of race or nationality, are [upper] middle-class professionals, largely, although not entirely, from North America, Europe, and Australia, and thus part of a minority of the world appropriating the majority of the world's resources and surplus value?) It is not a question of doing away with pleasure, but how do we understand the global relations of pleasure, and make sense of the connections among the liberatory gestures, privileges, and freedoms of the few and the oppression of the many? What is the cost of bourgeois, Eurocentric ludic theories of liberation to all the women (and men) globally in need of radical social emancipation?

> Yes it is bread we fight for . . . but we fight for roses too. . . .
> No more the drudge and idler—ten that toil where one reposes,
> But a sharing of life's glories: Bread and Roses! Bread and Roses![21]

As a first step to developing the theories that can effectively understand and intervene in such social conditions, I believe a resistance postmodern feminist culture studies needs to engage a materialist retheorization of differences as differences-in-relation-to-socioeconomic-systems-of-exploitation and specifically to radically critique cultural practices and significations in connection with the gendered division of labor, particularly in terms of the current global reconfiguration of patriarchal capitalism.

Notes

1. Poststructuralist discursive politics, of course, regards discourse itself to be material in the sense that "language" is material—it has an opacity and density of its own and "means" not simply by the "intention" of the author and speaker but by its own immanent laws of signification. This understanding of "materialism" is idealist: it is transhistorical and refers mostly to the material in the sense of "medium"; it is, in other words, a form of "matterism" rather than materialism. This form of poststructuralist (idealist) materialism—which manifests itself not

only in the matterism of language but also in the poststructuralist preoccupation with (matterism of) the "body"—is subject to the same criticism that Marx made of Feuerbach's idealist materialism: "As far as Feuerbach is a materialist he does not deal with history, and as far as he considers history he is not a materialist" (Marx and Engels 47). By materialism I mean the primacy of women's and men's productive and reproductive practices (labor processes) in the articulation and development of human history. Such a view of materialism also understands "reality" to be a historically objective process: reality exists outside the consciousness of humans—ideas do not have an autonomous existence and thus reality is not merely a matter of desire, dreams, or operation of language. This does not mean that reality, as we have access to it, as we make sense of it, is not mediated by signifying practices, but rather that social relations and practices are prior to signification and are objective in their *effects* on us. The subjugation of women, then, is an objective historical reality: it is not simply a matter of discourses. Transformative politics depends on such a view of reality since if there is no objective reality there will be little ground on which to change that reality.

2. I first articulated the concepts of ludic and resistance postmodernism in a lecture at the conference on "Rewriting the (Post)Modern: (Post)Colonialism/Feminism/Late Capitalism," held at the University of Utah, 30–31 March 1990. A version of the essay is now published as "Writing in the Political: Resistance (Post)modernism" in *Transformative Discourses in Postmodern Social, Cultural and Legal Theory,* a special issue of *Legal Studies Forum.* I also elaborate more fully on the relation of ludic and resistance postmodernism to feminism in my essay "The 'Difference' of Postmodern Feminism."

3. On the debate over the relation of feminism to this (ludic) postmodern "incredulity toward metanarratives" and its displacement of "emancipation" see the collection of essays *Feminism/Postmodernism,* ed. Linda Nicholson, and my critique of the collection and exchange with Nicholson and Nancy Fraser on the issue in *The Women's Review of Books.*

4. Fiske's comments are part of a paper, "Cultural Studies and the Culture of Everyday Life," he presented at the international conference "Cultural Studies Now and in the Future," held at the University of Illinois in 1990 and now published in a massive text titled *Cultural Studies* (see Grossberg et al. 161). This move to substitute affirmation for critique is clearly evident in the majority of papers presented at the conference, which is widely regarded as a watershed in the institutionalization of (postmodern) cultural studies in the United States and included a number of feminist culture critics such as Rosalind Brunt, Donna Haraway, bell hooks, Laura Kipnis, Angela McRobbie, Meaghan Morris, Constance Penley, Elspeth Probyn, and Janet Wolff. In fact, the depoliticization of an oppositional cultural studies was so prevalent during the proceedings that many in the audience (and some of the participants, such as bell hooks) began to protest the erasure of the political not only from the floor but through countermeetings, flyers, and other means—which constituted some of the only sites of political critique during the conference. Scott Heller's report on this protest and debate over the question of the political at the conference appears in *The Chronicle of Higher Education.*

5. This valorization of "pleasure" as liberation and the validation of existing social differences have become so privileged in postmodern discourses and even in much feminism, it is difficult to even question their priority without being read as someone trying to do away with pleasure and difference altogether. But

what I am questioning here is their *uses*, especially the way they are so localized in specific concrete contexts that the underlying socioeconomic conditions—that is, the material relations, particularly the labor relations—producing pleasure and difference are erased. I will take up this issue more fully in the final section of the paper.

6. On the ethical subject of pleasure/*jouissance*, see esp. Foucault, Deleuze and Guattari, and Barthes, and the significant feminist reworking of this issue in Cixous, Irigaray, and Butler.

7. Behind my argument here is Louis Althusser's thesis that "Philosophy is, in the last instance, class struggle in theory" in his *Essays in Self-Criticism*, 143.

8. Largely absent from feminism, the materialist theory of the sign—tracing its genealogy from Marx through Volosinov, Pecheux, and Althusser (in a related articulation of ideological representation)—has had a greater impact on cultural studies, as demonstrated in the work of Stuart Hall (see esp. "The Rediscovery of 'Ideology'"). But under the pressure of ludic textualization and recent post-Marxism in cultural studies, especially the influence of Laclau and Mouffe, the notion of "materiality" itself becomes more rhetorical and discursive (the opacity, sensuousness, and indeterminacy of signifiers), thereby marginalizing, if not completely displacing, the understanding of materiality as the historical forces of socioeconomic relations articulated in and through signifying practices and (labor) relations of difference.

This displacement is especially clear in Kobena Mercer's contribution to the collection *Cultural Studies*, "'1968': Periodizing Politics and Identity," in which she rearticulates the social struggle over signifiers—particularly signifiers of race—in terms of "indeterminacy" and a "radical polyvocality"; this leads to a rewriting of race as a "floating signifier," as Angela McRobbie does when she praises Mercer's (ludic) reunderstanding of the social situation of the sign and uses it to read the "floating signifiers" of "race and sex" in popular culture ("Post-Marxism and Cultural Studies" 727). I have contested Mercer's retheorization of the signifier as a discussant to his paper and critiqued it for omitting the way signifiers are situated in and appropriated by systematic regimes of exploitation and thus are neither historically indeterminate nor simply elements in the possibility of resistance (Grossberg et al. 443).

9. Derrida argues that the very notion of "totality" is logocentric since one cannot have access to such an entity. Totality is, in other words, a rhetorical effect and thus is unobtainable. It is unobtainable because totality is the effect of language, and language is a "field . . . of play," that is, "a field of infinite substitutions . . . that is to say . . . something is missing from it: a center which arrests and grounds the play of substitutions" (Derrida, *Writing and Difference* 289). Totality or totalization, in short, is not possible because there is no center to guarantee its integrity: its claim to truth is undermined by its own centerlessness.

10. Even more likely is the move by many socialist-feminists to displace the socialism in their politics altogether. As Michèle Barrett writes in her introduction to the 1988 revised edition of one of the main texts of materialist/socialist feminism, her *Women's Oppression Today* (a book Barrett considers "could not be written in the same way now" [xxiv]), "the intellectual project of reconciling a feminist and a Marxist understanding of the social world could be said to have been shelved—it was abandoned rather than resolved," and "socialist-feminists," including, to a large degree, Barrett herself, "have become increasingly dubious

about the hyphen in their politics" (xxii–xxiii). One of the leading American socialist-feminists, Zillah Eisenstein, asserts, "I no longer think socialist feminism is an accurate naming of my politics" and argues for a "post-socialist feminism" of specific "coalition politics" ("Specifying US Feminism" 44, 49–50).

11. Another telling example of the ludic feminist delegitimation and exclusion of MacKinnon and interventionist feminism in the name of postmodernism comes from a recent experience of mine. One of my essays on resistance postmodern feminism was rejected by two editors of a special issue on feminism and postmodernism for two main reasons: first, my critique of ludic postmodernism, and, second—significantly—my use of MacKinnon's statistics on rape in developing a materialist postmodern critique of Jane Gallop's ludic feminist celebration of the Marquis de Sade (I have included part of the material in this essay). As the editors said, MacKinnon's statistics "are after all embedded in a highly polemical argument many of whose essentializing premises don't seem at all compatible with yours!" The issue here for resistance postmodern feminism is to question and critique this blanket rejection of radical, interventionist feminist theories—such as those of MacKinnon—as "essentializing" and "totalizing" and to recognize instead the way such exclusion participates in the reactionary ludic postmodern attack on systematic critiques of gender exploitation and oppression.

12. Of course, the current questioning of the importance, even necessity of the struggle against women's oppression is itself a result of the ludic postmodern and feminist erasure of the economic in the name of (upper-middle-class) valorizations of individual pleasures and freedoms. Even such a prominent materialist feminist as Barrett seems to back away from the necessity of "oppression" as a struggle concept for feminism when she opens the introduction to the 1988 revised edition of her book *Women's Oppression Today* by saying, "'Oppression,' too, looks rather crude in terms of current feminist work: does sexual difference *necessarily* mean oppression?" (v). The answer to such a question is, I believe, for the most part yes in a regime of exploitation based on gender/sexual difference, especially the gendered division of labor, if we take into account the specific conjunctions of class and race in which those members of the oppressed gender who participate in the dominant class(es) and race(es)—in the US, for instance, white upper-middle-class women—are accorded relative privilege, power, and gender flexibility, even though they are all still (potentially) subject to oppression, such as economic discrimination and sexual violence. As I have already commented, only those who are largely "free" from economic oppression have the luxury of dismissing oppression and exploitation as the most pressing issues.

13. The binary opposition of male/female is, of course, a historical one, which is the outcome of the contradictions of all exploitative societies. Such "binaries," by the way, will not disappear simply through the discursive deconstruction of "opposition." They will be eliminated only when the socioeconomic conditions producing the contradictions in society are eradicated through the construction of nonexploitative social relations.

14. In addition to the works discussed here, also see such other works on feminism and the body as Eisenstein, *The Female Body and the Law;* Mary Jacobus et al., eds., *Body/Politics: Women and the Discourses of Science;* and Helen Wilcox et al., *The Body and the Text: Hélène Cixous, Reading and Teaching.*

15. The ludic politics of pleasure as liberatory is becoming an increasingly common stance in feminist cultural studies, even at the cost of displacing real

and representational violence against women. See, for instance, Laura Kipnis's apologia for *Hustler* magazine as subversive over against the puritanical ("serious," nonludic) feminism of the antipornography movement. Her piece, "(Male) Desire and (Female) Disgust: Reading *Hustler*," is yet another instance of the largely affirmative approach in the *Cultural Studies* collection.

16. Consciousness raising should not be trivialized as a resistance to conceptuality and rationality, nor, in a reactionary move, should it be reduced to an operation aimed at recovering woman's transhistorical and essential experience. A celebration of transhistorical and nonconceptual experience is as politically damaging to feminism as is a commitment to an equally transhistorical "reason."

17. Ludic feminists have, as a matter of routine, assumed that "reason" is masculine and that Marxism is the embodiment of such masculine reason-ism. Such an assumption is, of course, part of the poststructuralist mythology. Marx and Engels have always argued that "reason" is a "struggle concept"—it is the means for forging concepts that can provide explanatory and transformative critique. They have, in fact, been quite aware of the distortion and misuse of reason. In his famous letter to Ruge (September 1843), Marx specifically addresses the issue, stating that "[r]eason has always existed, only not always in reasonable form" (Tucker, *The Marx-Engels Reader,* 14). Engels, in the opening pages of his *Socialism: Utopian and Scientific,* discusses the way reason was deployed, in the Enlightenment, by "enlightened" philosophers as a device for naturalizing property rights and adds:

> We know today that this kingdom of reason was nothing more than the idealized kingdom of the bourgeoisie; that this eternal Right found its realization in bourgeois justice; that this equality reduced itself to bourgeois equality before the law; that bourgeois property was proclaimed as one of the essential rights of man; and that the government of reason, the Contract Social of Rousseau, came into being, and only could come into being, as a democratic bourgeois republic. The great thinkers of the eighteenth century could, no more than their predecessors, go beyond the limits imposed upon them by their epoch. (Tucker, *The Marx-Engels Reader* 684)

18. Also see Hartsock's critique, "Foucault on Power: A Theory for Women?" in Nicholson.

19. Fuentes and Ehrenreich, *Women in the Global Factory,* 12; also see Enloe, *Bananas, Beaches and Bases,* esp. on the global industry of tourism/sex tourism. Following Mies, I use the concepts "overdeveloped/underdeveloped" instead of "First" and "Third" worlds, in order to indicate the relations between them: "relations" that, as Mies explains, are "based on exploitation and oppression . . . in which . . . one pole is getting 'developed' *at the expense* of the other pole, which is in the process of getting 'underdeveloped.' 'Underdevelopment' . . . is the direct result of an exploitative unequal or dependent relationship between the core-countries" (*Patriarchy* 39).

20. The term "German School" comes from Gail Omvedt's essay on various feminist theories of patriarchy, titled "'Patriarchy': The Analysis of Women's Oppression," 40–41. For the articulation of this retheorization, see esp. Mies, *Patriarchy and Accumulation on a World Scale;* and Mies, Bennholdt-Thomsen, and von Werlhof, *Women: The Last Colony.* For another way of theorizing gender and labor/class, see Harriet Fraad, Stephen A. Resnick, and Richard D. Wolff's

Marxist-feminist analysis of the household and the debate that follows in the special issue of *Rethinking Marxism,* and see Kollontai.

21. Quoted in Sheila Rowbotham from a poem by James Oppenheimer, and "inspired," according to Rowbotham, "by banners carried by young mill girls in the 1912 Lawrence Massachusetts textile strike," 100.

Works Cited

Althusser, Louis. *Essays in Self-Criticism.* London: NLB, 1976.

———. *Lenin and Philosophy and Other Essays.* Trans. Ben Brewster. New York: Monthly Review, 1971.

Austin, J. L. *How to Do Things with Words.* Cambridge: Harvard UP, 1962.

Barrett, Michèle. *Women's Oppression Today: The Marxist/Feminist Encounter.* 1980. Rev. ed. London and New York: Verso, 1988.

Butler, Judith. *Gender Trouble: Feminism and the Subversion of Identity.* New York: Routledge, 1990.

———. "Imitation and Gender Insubordination." Fuss, *Inside/Out* 13–31.

Cixous, Hélène. "The Laugh of the Medusa." Warhol and Herndl 334–49.

de Lauretis, Teresa. "The Essence of the Triangle or, Taking the Risk of Essentialism Seriously: Feminist Theory in Italy, the U.S., and Britain." *Differences* 1.2 (1989): 3–37.

———. "Film and the Visible." *How Do I Look? Queer Film and Video.* Ed. Bad Object-Choices. Seattle: Bay, 1991.

———. "Upping the Anti (sic) in Feminist Theory." Hirsch and Keller 255–70.

de Man, Paul. *Allegories of Reading: Figural Language in Rousseau, Nietzsche, Rilke, and Proust.* New Haven: Yale UP, 1979.

———. *The Resistance to Theory.* Minneapolis: U of Minnesota P, 1986.

Derrida, Jacques. *Glas.* Trans. John P. Leavey, Jr., and Richard Rand. Lincoln: U of Nebraska P, 1986.

———. *Post Card.* Trans. Alan Bass. Chicago: U of Chicago P, 1987.

———. *Writing and Difference.* Trans. Alan Bass. Chicago: U of Chicago P, 1978.

Ebert, Teresa L. "Detecting the Phallus: Authority, Ideology and the Production of Patriarchal Agents in Detective Fiction." *Rethinking Marxism* 5.3 (1992).

———. "The 'Difference' of Postmodern Feminism." *College English* 53.8 (1991): 886–904.

———. "Postmodernism's Infinite Variety" (editor's title). *The Women's Review of Books* 8.4 (January 1991): 24–25. Response 8.6 (March 1991): 5.

———. "Writing in the Political: Resistance (Post)modernism." *Transformative Discourses in Postmodern Social, Cultural and Legal Theory.* Spec. issue of *Legal Studies Forum* 15.4 (1991): 291–304.

Eisenstein, Zillah. *The Female Body and the Law.* Berkeley: U of California P, 1988.

———. "Specifying US Feminism in the 1990's: The Problem of Naming." *Socialist Review* 90.2 (1990): 45–56.

Enloe, Cynthia H. *Bananas, Beaches and Bases: Making Feminist Sense of International Politics.* Berkeley: U of California P, 1990.

Felman, Shoshana. "Women and Madness: The Critical Phallacy." Warhol and Herndl 6–19.

Fish, Stanley Eugene. *Doing What Comes Naturally: Change, Rhetoric, and the Practice of Theory in Literary and Legal Studies.* Durham, NC: Duke UP, 1989.

Fiske, John. "Cultural Studies and the Culture of Everyday Life" and discussion. Grossberg et al. 154–73.

Foucault, Michel. *The History of Sexuality*. Trans. Robert Hurley. Vol. 1. 1978. New York: Vintage, 1980. 3 vols.

Fraad, Harriet, Stephen A. Resnick, and Richard D. Wolff. "For Every Knight in Shining Armor, There's a Castle Waiting to Be Cleaned: A Marxist-Feminist Analysis of the Household" and comments. *Rethinking Marxism* 2.4 (1989): 10–106.

Fraser, Nancy, and Linda Nicholson. "Social Criticism without Philosophy: An Encounter between Feminism and Postmodernism." Nicholson 19–38.

Fuentes, Annette, and Barbara Ehrenreich. *Women in the Global Factory*. Boston: South End, 1983.

Fuss, Diana. *Essentially Speaking: Feminism, Nature and Difference*. New York: Routledge, 1989.

———, ed. *Inside/Out: Lesbian Theories, Gay Theories*. New York: Routledge, 1991.

Gallop, Jane. *Around 1981. Academic Feminist Literary Theory*. New York: Routledge, 1992.

———. *Reading Lacan*. Ithaca: Cornell UP, 1985.

———. *Thinking through the Body*. New York: Columbia UP, 1988.

Gallop, Jane, Marianne Hirsch, and Nancy K. Miller. "Criticizing Feminist Criticism." Hirsch and Keller 349–69.

Garber, Marjorie. *Vested Interests: Cross-Dressing and Cultural Anxiety*. New York: Routledge, 1991.

Gramsci, Antonio. *Prison Notebooks*. New York: Columbia UP, 1992.

Grossberg, Lawrence, Cary Nelson, Paula Treichler, et al., eds. *Cultural Studies*. New York: Routledge, 1992.

Grosz, Elisabeth. "Notes Towards a Corporeal Feminism." *Feminism and the Body*. Spec. issue of *Australian Feminist Studies* 5 (Summer 1987): 1–16.

Hall, Stuart. "The Rediscovery of 'Ideology': Return of the Repressed in Media Studies." *Culture, Society and the Media*. Ed. Marianne Gurevitch et al. London and New York: Methuen, 1982. 56–90.

———. "Signification, Representation, Ideology: Althusser and the Post-Structuralist Debates." *Critical Studies in Mass Communication* 2.2 (1985): 91–114.

Haraway, Donna. *Simians, Cyborgs, and Women: The Reinvention of Nature*. New York: Routledge, 1991.

Harding, Sandra. "The Instability of the Analytical Categories of Feminist Theory." *Signs* 11.4 (1986): 645–64.

Hartsock, Nancy. "Foucault on Power: A Theory for Women?" Nicholson 157–75.

———. *Money, Sex and Power: Toward a Feminist Historical Materialism*. Boston: Northeastern UP, 1985.

Heller, Scott. "Protest at Cultural Studies Meeting Sparked by Debate over New Field." *Chronicle of Higher Education* 2 May 1990: A10–A11.

Hirsch, Marianne, and Evelyn Fox Keller. *Conflicts in Feminism*. New York: Routledge, 1990.

Irigaray, Luce. *Speculum of the Other Woman*. Trans. Gillian C. Gill. Ithaca: Cornell UP, 1985.

Jacobus, Mary, et al., eds. *Body/Politics: Women and the Discourses of Science*. New York: Routledge, 1990.

Jameson, Fredric. "*History and Class Consciousness* as an 'Unfinished Project.'" *Rethinking Marxism* 1.1 (1988): 49–72.
Jardine, Alice. *Gynesis: Configurations of Woman and Modernity.* Ithaca: Cornell UP, 1985.
Kipnis, Laura. "(Male) Desire and (Female) Disgust: Reading *Hustler.*" Grossberg et al. 373–91.
Kollontai, Alexandra. "Sexual Relations and the Class Struggle." *Selected Writings of Alexandra Kollontai.* Trans. Alix Holt. Westport: Lawrence Hill, 1977. 237–49.
Kristof, Nicholas. "Stark Data on Women: 100 Million are Missing." *New York Times* 5 Nov. 1991: C1, C12.
Laclau, Ernesto. "Transformations of Advanced Industrial Societies and the Theory of the Subject." *Rethinking Ideology: A Marxist Debate.* Ed. S. Hanninen and L. Paldan. New York and Bagnolet, France: International General/IMMRC; Berlin: Argument-Verlag, 1983. 39–44.
Laclau, Ernesto, and Chantal Mouffe. *Hegemony and Socialist Strategy: Towards a Radical Democratic Politics.* London: Verso, 1985.
Lyotard, Jean-François. *The Postmodern Condition.* Trans. Geoff Bennington and Brian Massumi. Minneapolis: U of Minnesota P, 1984.
Lyotard, Jean-François, and Jean-Loup Theobaud. *Just Gaming.* Trans. Wlad Godzich. Minneapolis: U of Minnesota P, 1985.
MacKinnon, Catharine. *Feminism Unmodified: Discourses on Life and Law.* Cambridge: Harvard UP, 1987.
Marx, Karl, and Frederick Engels. *The German Ideology.* 3rd rev. ed. Moscow: Progress, 1976.
McRobbie, Angela. "Post-Marxism and Cultural Studies: A Post-script." Grossberg et al. 719–30.
Meese, Elizabeth A. *(Ex)tensions: Re-Figuring Feminist Criticism.* Urbana: U of Illinois P, 1990.
Meese, Elizabeth A., and Alice Parker, eds. *The Difference Within: Feminism and Critical Theory.* Philadelphia and Amsterdam: John Benjamins, 1989.
Mercer, Kobena. "'1968': Periodizing Postmodern Politics and Identity" and discussion. Grossberg et al. 424–49.
Mies, Maria. *Patriarchy and Accumulation on a World Scale: Women in the International Division of Labour.* London and Atlantic Highlands, NJ: Zed, 1986.
Mies, Maria, Veronika Bennholdt-Thomsen, and Claudia von Werlhof. *Women: The Last Colony.* London and Atlantic Highlands, NJ: Zed, 1988.
Miller, J. Hillis. *Theory Now and Then.* New York: Harvester Wheatsheaf, 1991.
Mullarkey, Maureen. "Hard Cop, Soft Cop." *The Nation* 30 May 1987: 720–26.
Nicholson, Linda, ed. *Feminism/Postmodernism.* New York: Routledge, 1990.
Omvedt, Gail. "'Patriarchy': The Analysis of Women's Oppression." *The Insurgent Sociologist* 13.3 (1986): 30–50.
Pecheux, Michel. *Language, Semantics and Ideology.* Trans. Harbans Nagpal. New York: St. Martin's, 1982.
Penley, Constance. "Feminism, Psychoanalysis, and the Study of Popular Culture" and discussion. Grossberg et al. 479–500.
Penley, Constance, and Andrew Ross, eds. *Technoculture.* Minneapolis: U of Minnesota P, 1991.
Rich, Adrienne. *Blood, Bread, and Poetry: Selected Prose, 1979–1985.* New York: Norton, 1986.

Ross, Andrew. *No Respect: Intellectuals and Popular Culture.* New York: Routledge, 1989.

Rowbotham, Sheila. *Women, Resistance and Revolution.* 1972. New York: Vintage, 1974.

Schor, Naomi. *Breaking the Chain: Women, Theory and French Realist Fiction.* New York: Columbia UP, 1985.

Scott, Joan. "Deconstructing Equality-Versus-Difference: Or the Uses of Poststructuralist Theory for Feminism." Hirsch and Keller 134–48.

Trinh T. Minh-ha. *Woman, Native, Other: Writing Postcoloniality and Feminism.* Bloomington: Indiana UP, 1989.

Tucker, Robert C., ed. *The Marx-Engels Reader.* 2nd ed. New York: Norton, 1978.

Ulmer, Gregory L. *Teletheory: Grammatology in the Age of Video.* New York: Routledge, 1989.

Volosinov, V. N. *Marxism and the Philosophy of Language.* Trans. Ladislov Matejka and I. R. Titunik. Cambridge: Harvard UP, 1973.

Warhol, Robyn R., and Diane Price Herndl, eds. *Feminisms: An Anthology of Literary Theory and Criticism.* New Brunswick: Rutgers UP, 1991.

Wilcox, Helen, et al., eds. *The Body and the Text: Hélène Cixous, Reading and Teaching.* New York: St. Martin's, 1990.

Wittig, Monique. *The Straight Mind and Other Essays.* Boston: Beacon, 1992.

Learning Not to Curse, or, Feminist Predicaments in Cultural Criticism by Men: Our Movie Date with James Clifford and Stephen Greenblatt

Judith Newton and Judith Stacey

Portrait of Man With a Book

As *Dances with Wolves,* Kevin Costner's wildly celebrated film, reaches its emotional climax, Smiles a Lot, his proud, young face glistening with reverential tears, returns to Lt. John Dunbar the damaged leather-bound journal in which the latter has recorded field notes on the Lakota tribe from which he and Stands with a Fist, his newly acquired wife, are about to take their poignant departure. Novice film critics, we scribble scarcely legible notes about the musical crescendo and heavenly light that mark this pivotal return of the book from a Native American boy to a white man, noting how the white man's gratitude is mirrored and magnified in a close-up image of his wife's beatified expression. All three—white woman, native boy, and white man—seem gratified by the restoration of this white man's words.

Two Men and Their Books

Our path to this celluloid wilderness had been blazed by other images of natives and of white men with books. During the

© 1993 by *Cultural Critique.* 0882-4371 (Winter 1992–93). All rights reserved.

1991 season of Costnermania the authors of this essay had been reading the work of James Clifford and Stephen Greenblatt in preparation for a collaborative study of the politics of contemporary cultural criticism by US men. The former, Director of the Center for Cultural Studies at the University of California, Santa Cruz, and a historian of ethnography, is a metatheorist of what others have termed "the new" or "postmodern" ethnography; the latter, a founding editor of *Representations* and a literary critic in Renaissance studies, is generally recognized as the central fashioner of an approach to cultural criticism called "new historicism." Both are widely cited as important figures on the frontiers of US cultural studies, that increasingly favored site of discourse in the embattled academy, now frequently identified with the renewed political relevance and multicultural commitments of left/liberal academics.[1]

It was in Clifford's and Greenblatt's books, *The Predicament of Culture* and *Learning to Curse,* both of which sport cover photos of white men with their books,[2] that we found treatments of Native Americans which piqued our curiosity about other white male representations of America's first colonial victims. Although generally wary of Westerns as a field for male dreams, we took our introjected versions of Clifford's and Greenblatt's modes of cultural critique to the movies, where they served as valuable, inspiring, but also, at times, troubling film companions in our critical reception of this Oscar-winning artifact of popular culture, an artifact both touted and condemned, in our local newspapers, as an exercise in the "new politics" of multiculturalism (Grenier; see also Jacobs; Baltake, "Plains" and "It was anything but").

Viewing *Dances with Wolves* through our attempt to simulate Clifford's and Greenblatt's sensibilities, we could produce what we regarded as insightful but also disappointing readings of the film, readings marked by the kinds of insights and disappointments we have often found in Clifford's and Greenblatt's work. Their work, for example, prompted us to readings of the film as a redemptive Western allegory of the kind Clifford finds in the ethnographies that he subjects to his incisive, influential form of cultural critique and as a form of linguistic colonialism of the kind that Greenblatt explores in his complex and likewise influential analyses of Renaissance culture. In a move that the authors of both texts might appreciate, their cultural critique also helped us to read *them*. Through the lens of our enhanced analysis of Costner's film, we were sensitized to ways in which their own work might be said to reinscribe some of the allegorizing and colonizing strategies which they had already enabled us to perceive in *Dances with Wolves*.

Clifford's and Greenblatt's work, however, contributed little to our analysis of the film as a masculine allegory in which, as in much of the cultural criticism they have published so far, gender politics are accommodated but also marginalized and/or contained. This move in relation to gender politics, we will suggest, is complexly related to the racial politics in Clifford and Greenblatt, just as it is in Costner's film. Read in relation to each other, indeed, Costner's film, Clifford's and Greenblatt's recent books, aspects of the current men's movement, the canon war, and some discourse on cultural studies in the United States suggest recurring lines along which gender and racial critique have and have not become part of the "new" politics, multicultural commitments, and reinvented masculinities of left-leaning white men.

Two Women and a "Nagging Text"

We begin this essay with an awkward mixture of trepidation, humility, and hope. Deeply troubled by the orchestrated, full-scale campaign against "PC" (political correctness) inside and outside the academy, our goal is to impede rather than encourage the enemies of "multiculturalism." The anti-PC campaign, which is serving as an ideological shield for racist and sexist assaults on affirmative action and multicultural curricular reforms, indiscriminately positions cultural critics like Clifford and Greenblatt alongside feminists, ethnic studies scholars, deconstructionists, Marxists, critical theorists, and gay and lesbian scholars.[3] It positions as subversive, that is, the very projects many cultural studies advocates subsume under the cultural studies umbrella, and it links them with all other forms of dissidence from the New (or Old) World Order.[4] Indeed, Kevin Costner himself has been attacked, in the pages of *Commentary* and elsewhere, for having reproduced a politically correct, countercultural, quasi-socialist, "anti-white," "new politics" in *Dances with Wolves* (Grenier 26).[5]

Under such Orwellian political conditions, the etiquette of fraternal critique among fellow "subversives" is of no trivial concern. Our goal here is to strengthen oppositional cultural critique, not to undermine it.

But "we," of course, are not fellows, and the etiquette for sororal critique of radical brethren is underdeveloped and fraught.[6] Throughout the 1970s and 1980s white feminists mainly nurtured our own theoretical fields without seeking, or welcoming, much fraternal assistance. In the process we felt free to rake over, appropriate, and critique literature by men for our own pressing purposes. In a political climate as unsettling as the present one, however, cooperative, multivocal alliances are crucial, and these may require, if not kinder and gentler, at least scrupulously constructive forms of criticism. Our goal, like Clifford's and Greenblatt's, is to rewrite stories of cultural difference for a less oppressive future, and to do so we need to rewrite some of the stories of cultural difference we discover in their work. But in critically reading their work and in rereading the film with and apart from them, we hope to produce something closer to a collegial revision than to what Meaghan Morris has identified as that impotent feminist genre—the "nagging text" (15).

As white feminists in women's studies, moreover, we have been humbled by two decades of criticism by feminists of color exposing the exclusions and colonizing gestures of white feminist genealogies and the institutionalization of feminist work in the academy.[7] Like white, middle-class men of the sixties, accustomed to feeling at the center of an important political and intellectual movement, white feminists have been called upon to relinquish privilege within "the feminist movement," within institutions, within women's studies programs, and within "feminist theory."[8] Our hope is that continued reflection upon these contradictions and self-indulgences will foster not less incisive, but less self-righteous critique of white male colleagues with whom we share a commitment to cultural critique, multiculturalism, and a less unjust future.

We are fully aware, finally, that a critic's published work can never encapsulate his/her politics. Oral interviews with Clifford and Greenblatt, conducted after this paper was in draft, suggest a far deeper engagement with gender politics—in relations with students and colleagues, in campus politics, in new research, in domestic life—than is suggested in much of the work they have published so far. Further dialogues have reminded us that their work, like ours, continues to evolve and may now be moving in directions that will render our critique gratifyingly dated. In future essays we plan to focus upon material from these interviews and from interviews with other academic men and to reflect upon the ways that interviews and other forms of ethnographic work challenge and complicate the reflections we offer here upon the mainly textual political trajectories of left-leaning white male critics.[9]

Post-Colonial Cultural Poetics

Clifford and Greenblatt, in our view, are among the most influential and stimulating of these critics. Clifford's distinctive contribution has been to historicize and decode the rhetorical strategies and political effects of Western ethnography. In the essays collected in *The Predicament of Culture* and in *Writing Culture,* the discourse-setting collection of essays he coedited with George Marcus, Clifford has honed a narrative that identifies the collapse of empire as the primary source of anthropological crisis, theoretical ferment, and textual experimentation in the West. Anticolonial struggles and native ethnographers have challenged the legitimacy and the conceptual foundations of the classic anthropological endeavor of representing native societies deemed too weak to represent themselves, while a global world marked by incessant and unequal forms of cultural contact and exchange explodes those coherent and stable concepts of self, other, and culture upon which traditional ethnographies depend.

Clifford regards the neocolonial challenge as the enabling condition for his reflexivity about the textual means through which classic ethnographers crafted their authority and for the kinds of experimental efforts to textualize the syncretic cultural subjects of the neocolonial world that he has done so much to canonize. Thus the post-colonial predicament of culture provides an opportunity for anthropology to reinvent itself as well. Clearing the ground for such renewal, Clifford decodes the textual strategies through which classic ethnographies constructed authoritative cultural accounts that served, however inadvertently, not only to establish the authority of the Western ethnographer over native "others," but also to sustain Western authority over colonial cultures.

Primary among these rhetorical strategies is allegory. Indeed, Clifford insists that ethnographic writing is inescapably allegorical "at the level both of its content (what it says about cultures and their histories) and of its form (what is implied by its mode of textualization)" ("On Ethnographic Allegory" 99). What Clifford believes ethnographers *can* and *should* try to escape, however, is the recurrent allegorical genre of colonial ethnography—the pastoral, a nostalgic, redemptive text that preserves a primitive culture on the brink of extinction for the historical record of its Western conquerors. The narrative structure of this "salvage text" portrays the native culture as a coherent, authentic, and lamentably "eroding past," while its complex, inauthentic, Western successors represent the future. What this structure obscures, Clifford suggests, are the specific historical struggles of peoples caught in contact situations.

Like Clifford, Greenblatt responds to a crisis of representation that challenges the conceptual foundations of his discipline, most particularly in Renaissance studies, where new critical assumptions about the objectivity of the critic, the historical transcendence of the artist, the stability of meaning in free-standing literary texts, and the unity and stability of culture have been especially entrenched. Greenblatt finds in this crisis both a form of loss, in that it challenges familiar forms of power and authority that he, like so many critics trained in the sixties, stood to inherit and as an opportunity to reinvent literary critical practice.[10]

Greenblatt, in contrast to Clifford, does not specifically locate this crisis of representation and authority in a particular set of political developments like the collapse of empire or the development of a global world. In *Learning to Curse,* however, he does insist upon the political entanglements of his own work. For Greenblatt, and for many of his critics, his emphasis upon the syncretic, contestatory nature of identity, texts, culture, and literary criticism; his insistence on reading literary texts in relation to non-literary texts and other phenomena like institutions and political events; his fondness for homologies that link past to present; his interest in power, and, most particularly, his focus on imperialist themes signal a continuation of sixties-style energy (see Cohen; Howard and O'Connor; Wayne; Boose).[11] In "Resonance and Wonder," indeed, the most recent essay in *Learning to Curse,* Greenblatt describes his critical practice as having been "decisively shaped by the American 1960s and early '70s, and especially by the opposition to the Vietnam War" (166–67).

The phrase "learning to curse," which alludes to the linguistic colonization of Caliban in Shakespeare's *The Tempest,* signals a thematic focus on New World imperialism and on imperializing forms of representation, which does recall the political interests and investments of the antiwar sixties and early seventies.[12] Perhaps the central theme of *Learning to Curse,* moreover, is the inescapably colonizing force of all representation. The dramatist, and by implication the literary critic and all who textualize, is metaphorically a colonist: "His art penetrates new areas of experience, his language expands the boundaries of our culture and makes the new territory over in its own image" (24).

If this focus on imperialist themes recalls the politics of the sixties, however, it recalls post-sixties liberation politics as well. For the critique of linguistic colonialism which emerged in the antiwar and student movements and in post-colonial politics, where it was directed for the most part against imperialist governments, was later turned by feminists, black and other ethnic nationalists, and lesbians and gays against the white left/liberal heterosexual male students who had themselves been engaged in the earlier critique. In turning the critique of linguistic colonialism against all who textualize, including the literary critic himself, Greenblatt, like Clifford, might be said to apply it not just to "the usual suspects"—imperialist governments, the establishment, the "fathers" of the 1960s—but, through a series of displacements, to himself, an erstwhile student of the sixties, a "son," who is now a father of "new historicism."[13]

Hollywood Pastoral (or Costner and Custer)

On first viewing *Dances with Wolves* immediately after reading Clifford's essay "On Ethnographic Allegory," we could hardly resist the fantasy that Costner had himself perversely misread this essay as a how-to guide for staging a "salvage text" within a salvage text. Costner plays Lieutenant John Dunbar, the film's white protagonist, a disillusioned Civil War military officer turned lay ethnographer.[14] Alone on the vanishing frontier, Dunbar keeps a journal in which he records the customs, costumes, mores, and language of the Lakota Sioux as well as his own process of personal redemption. The journal inscribes a prototypical instance of what Clifford has called an ethnographic "fable of rapport," and it keys viewers to empathetically witness a full-scale anthropological "gone-native" event in which a former Union military man reinvents himself as a Lakota warrior. Thus, as in the classical tradition of colonial ethnography, Dunbar's textualization of Lakota experience (and Costner's cinemagraphic record of this textualization) aims to rescue their "vanishing primitive culture" from historical oblivion. And in the same ingenious, and, as Clifford's work suggests, inescapable, ethnographic stroke, Dunbar-Costner constructs his own authority as ethnographer-redeemer as well as the triumph of Western technology and artifice over the "authentic," traditional Lakota, who are thereby encoded as incapable of representing themselves.

The much-vaunted, and occasionally disputed, "authenticity effects" achieved in *Dances with Wolves* actually do depend partly on the textual legacy bequeathed by a nineteenth-century lay anthropologist and portrait painter, George Catlin.[15] But they depend even more on the hired counsel of living Native Americans who recall the sort of hybrid, heteroglossic subjects of a postmodern world that James Clifford theorizes far more than they resemble the extinct "authentic" Lakota heroes of the film, Kicking Bird and Wind in His Hair.[16]

We credit Clifford's work with sharpening our awareness that cinematic ethnographer Kevin Costner, a white outsider, had to employ syncretic twentieth-century Native Americans in business suits (and several in Indian renewal movements) in order to successfully misrepresent their "authentic" nineteenth-century ancestors. Under the neocolonial conditions of late-twentieth-century America, Native Americans still lack the power to represent their history by themselves, whether on the screen or in the courts. And so, the protagonist of *Dances with Wolves,* like its producer (the identical hybrid person), is a white outsider.

Native American reviewers had divided reactions to the film that turn on this question of self-representation. Some Native Americans, like Frank Evans and Michael Dorris, condemned the film for stereotyping Indians as "savages" or "ecological saints" while allowing Costner to act out "every white boy's fantasy of being Indian" and for relegating "good Indians—the only Indians whose causes and needs we can embrace" safely to the past (Evans; Dorris). Other Native Americans, like Ed Castillo and Marilou Awiakta, were enthusiastic about *Dances with Wolves*, expressing gratitude to Costner for inviting an unusual level of Native American participation in the cast and crew, for the film's unusual bilingual dialogue, and, of course, for portraying Lakota culture in such positive terms (see Castillo; Awiakta; Valente; Landon). Still others, like Inés Hernández, fully registered the film's (all-too-familiar) colonizing gestures but felt they had been decentered by the Native American actors, who effectively took the movie over, filling the screen with their humor and significant silence.

Our reading of the film, which has its own stakes and limitations, intersects with these readings in different ways. We too were impressed by the film's employment of Native American actors, its sympathy with the Sioux, its use of subtitles, and by the presence and power of Native American actors. At the same time, however, for us, as white feminists, prone to feeling that their race privilege implicates them in the film's colonizing gestures, and as critics recently attending to the images of white men and Native American "others" produced in contemporary cultural critique, a reading of the film that foregrounds its complex and sometimes contradictory colonialism seems more resonant. Costner's positive representation of the Lakota is remarkable in the context of Hollywood's dismal prior record in portraying and employing Indians, but our attention was drawn, nonetheless, to what Frank Evans characterizes as the film's "final form of colonization" (2) and what David Seals aptly dubs the "New Custerism—General George sporting velvet gloves" (637).[17]

Our reading of Clifford's work also encouraged us to perceive *Dances with Wolves* as a colonial ethnography. Costner's depiction of the Lakota as noble savages, for example, struck us as a caricature of the genre of redemptive anthropology, a genre that, no matter how well intended, perennially reinscribes Western domination over natives.[18] In sensitizing us to the narrative structure and effects of such sugar-coated, imperialistic poetics and politics, Clifford's approach to cultural studies makes a contribution that we deeply value. Unnervingly, however, viewing Costner's film from this perspective, we perceived certain unexpected continuities between his and Clifford's treatment of natives.

In a sense, Clifford is busy redeeming natives too, although the natives he prefers to salvage are syncretic, late-twentieth-century survivors and reinventors. If Lieutenant Dunbar absorbs Lakota traits and wisdom into himself, augmenting them with superior Western knowledge (in the form of rifle power), and if Costner redeems the Hollywood Western for liberal neocolonial audiences, Clifford attempts the more difficult task of recuperating the culture, struggles, and texts of hybrid survivors through his own theoretical tools.

Central to Clifford's redemptive project in *The Predicament of Culture* are the Cape Cod Mashpee. The Mashpee, as construed by Clifford, are a cultural inversion of Costner's Lakota Sioux, but they serve analogously to ground an ethnographic allegory. Instead of representing an irretrievable, authentic past, the Mashpee sign Clifford's admittedly utopian attempt to envision multiple routes through modernity to heterogeneous futures. Clifford certainly sympathizes with the courtroom struggle for tribal identity and land rights that is the subject of, or rather the occasion for, "Identity in Mashpee," his partially ethnographic and experimental essay. But he constructs his interpretation of this fraught neocolonial contest not as an intervention on behalf of the Mashpee, but as an intervention in cultural studies. In a world seemingly threatened by global cultural homogenization and technological "progress," the Mashpee stand for the reinvention of cultural difference. Their court battle provides a complex discursive site which Clifford, as "positioned observer," reads from a self-consciously distant, theoretical vantage point.[19]

Clifford views the trial as "an experiment in translation" between cultures (*Predicament* 289). Embedded in this translation, however, is a contest between history and anthropology, between written and oral texts, which Clifford, as a historian of anthropology, is unusually well positioned to resolve. His solution (ironically, of course, achieved through *writing*) is, appropriately enough, a syncretic one that fuses and renovates both disciplines. Clifford constructs and deconstructs alternative narratives about cultural identity that were presented to the Boston jurors: "History I" is Clifford's recounting of the version of Mashpee history presented in the successful legal case against Mashpee claims to tribal identity; Clifford represents this as a flawed, linear, primarily *historical* account based exclusively on written documents. "History II" Clifford presents as a better, but still inadequate, more *anthropological* account which the Mashpee lawyers culled from a mixture of oral and written evidence. This narrative, in Clifford's view, suffered not only from the constraints of adversarial courtroom rules, but also from a flawed concept of continuous culture. Having partially cast the struggle in these disciplinary terms, Clifford finds that it was anthropology's concept of culture that proved more fragile in the trial: "This cornerstone of the anthropological discipline proved to be vulnerable under cross-examination" (323). Clifford's redemptive role is to historicize and re*write* that concept in a manner that reinvents cultural difference for post-colonial society; thereby, Clifford's work offers to rescue the endangered enterprise of ethnography which he has so perceptively criticized and chronicled.

Linguistic Colonialism or Tatanka/Buffalo: Same Difference

If reading Clifford prompted us to construct *Wolves* as an ethnographic allegory, reading Greenblatt supplied us with critical tools for further deconstructing the liberal humanist assumptions that ground this allegory and that obscure its colonizing tendencies. Like Greenblatt's own work, *Dances with Wolves* might profitably be read as a 1990s reinvention of sixties-style political critique. Although the film is set in the period of the Civil War, the battle scenes with which the film opens recall nothing so much as Vietnam, a conflict seemingly without purpose, in which officers are incompetent and out of touch with what is going on, and acts of intended suicide are construed as heroism. Like so many young men of the Vietnam period, Lt. John Dunbar attempts to cut his ties with this bankrupt establishment, the US government and its military, which are, once again, engaged in imperialist conquest—this time of Native American land. In so doing he throws in his lot with the ostensible enemy, the Lakota Sioux.

Dunbar's rejection of his structural relation to US imperial power is located in and guaranteed by his class position, a position that is most centrally represented by his literacy and education, by the fact that he is, for most of the film, a man writing a book. Writing is the record but also the sign of Dunbar's ability to see beyond his culture's racist constructions of cultural difference: "Nothing I had heard about these people was correct." It is this book-writing student of Sioux culture who enters into a brotherhood with Sioux males and in the process disowns imperialist agendas. This escape from complicity is further guaranteed by a series of contrasts that the film constructs between this textualizing middle-class male and a series of dirty, badly dressed, physically unhealthy, illiterate, lower-class white male figures who become increasingly identified with the brutalities of imperialist power. The distance between these figures and the middle-class Dunbar is recurrently signaled, in fact, by the vulgarities they perform in relation to his text. There is the crude, slovenly mule-driving guide, for example, who farts and then quips to the earnest, scribbling Dunbar—"put that in your book." And there is the lower-class soldier who scornfully wipes his ass with a page torn from Dunbar's journal.

In the meantime, Dunbar himself becomes increasingly clean, well groomed, and well dressed, qualities which the film identifies with the nineteenth-century Sioux but which struck us as more redolent of twentieth-century middle classes. In becoming like the Sioux, therefore, Dunbar becomes, not a bicultural subject, but what he regards as his own true self. Thus, after learning that his adoptive Sioux relatives had renamed him "Dances with Wolves," he writes, "I knew for the first time who I really was." In the end, despite Costner's obvious sympathy with Native Americans, the Sioux are rewritten as the white hero, who bears their shared virtues into the future. Dunbar's superior literacy and technology, of course, smooth the way for this colonizing translation.

Having recently read Greenblatt's *Learning to Curse,* we were particularly sensitized to the colonizing potential of the film's easy equations between education, belief in a common humanity, non-complicity, and progress. In "Learning to Curse," for example, textualization of the "other," most particularly by "educated" and "humanist circles," is identified not with transcendence of imperialist agendas, as it is in Costner's film, but as a central site on which colonizing processes move forward (19). Greenblatt, moreover, is particularly incisive about the ways in which not only racist constructions of cultural difference—the notion, for example, that Native others have no language or culture—but also liberal constructions of cultural sameness—the notion that Native others are like "us"—may be turned to colonizing purposes. The "sympathetic" and "seductive" assumption that Native inhabitants of the New World were like Europeans and "comfortable in (their) own modes of thought" may not have caused "the horrors of the Conquest, but it made those horrors easier for those at home to live with" (30).

Costner's film, of course, does reject several stereotypical notions about Native Americans, some of which date back to the sixteenth century—the idea that Native Americans have no family life or political organization, for example, or that Native Americans are sexually degenerate. *Dances with Wolves* also respectfully invokes cultural difference in exposing non–Native American viewers to the experience of hearing Lakota spoken and of having to rely on subtitles for obviously broken translation. At the same time, however, the film ultimately collapses cultural difference into cultural sameness by suggesting that the two languages translate into each other—Tatanka/Buffalo, same difference.

The humanist implications of this suggestion, increasingly manifest in the film, that languages are transparent, that there is a common reality and humanity, facilitate Dunbar's brotherhood with the Sioux, but they also prepare the ground for Costner's rewriting of the Sioux as his white hero and as a figure for himself. At the end of the film Dunbar and Kicking Bird speak one language, English, Dunbar's own, while Dunbar is given permission—through the return of his diary by a Native American boy—to represent Lakota culture and values, now transparently reinscribed in Dunbar's text and in himself. As in Renaissance culture, where, as Greenblatt observes, Europeans rehearsed their encounter with the peoples of the New World through their constructions of the legendary "wild man," the "wild man" appears at the end of Costner's film to be an upper-class white man who has gotten lost (*Learning to Curse* 21). We have met the other and he is us—those of us, that is, who are literate, white, middle-class males.

It would come as no surprise to Greenblatt, we imagine, that his work on the colonizing force of representation and of liberal humanist assumptions provides tools for reading his own textualizations. A major feature of his work, after all, has been to identify homologous relations between seemingly unconnected cultural sites. Thus, despite his emphasis upon the inescapably colonizing force of all representation, Greenblatt too suggests that textualization can put distance between us and colonizing activities. In contrast to Costner, of course, whose presentation of cultural difference is collapsed into a celebration of cultural sameness in the end, Greenblatt locates himself between these two modes of constructing the other, as like us and as different. This ability to hold sameness and difference in suspension, moreover, is identified with resistance to assimilation by dominant forms of power.

In "Filthy Rites," for example, Greenblatt first locates this capacity in the nineteenth-century Zuñi, whose ritual dance is read as a form of mocking white colonizers, acknowledging submission, and producing powerful medicine. This balance of unlike elements in Zuñi ritual defies "hierarchical organization," and "in this indifference to unity, this refusal of conceptual integration, we may grasp one of the sources of the Zuñis' dogged resistance, to this day, to assimilation" (*Learning to Curse* 64). In the title essay, "Learning to Curse," a similar capacity to sustain the simultaneous perception of likeness and difference, "the very special perception we give to metaphor," is located in Shakespeare, whose *Tempest* tests our capacity to sustain metaphor in relation to colonial themes (312).[20] The same capacity, however, is most powerfully located in Greenblatt himself, whose literary critical mode throughout these essays is characterized by the practice of establishing homologies between different cultures and cultural phenomena, homologies attended by rigorous attention to the ways in which these phenomena are the same and different.

Like Clifford's, then, Greenblatt's meditation on imperialist themes focuses upon the reinvention of a discursive practice, representation of native others. One might quarrel here with this focus, as tending to narrow the field of colonizing practices being considered, but it is Greenblatt's own representation of native others that seems most problematic. In contrast to Clifford's essay, where syncretic others are refigured along with ethnographic authority, in *Learning to Curse* native others tend to disappear. Despite the careful identification of "culture" with the oral as well as the written, the private as well as the public, Greenblatt's essays here concentrate, for the most part, on delivering readings of public written texts and, through them, of the educated, publishing (and in Renaissance culture, elite male) colonizers. There is much less of a focus on offering, say, constructions of or speculations about the cultural practices of oral, often illiterate colonized others.[21] Culture, therefore, tends in practice, if not in theory, to be most richly represented by the productions of elite white men.[22] Since Greenblatt makes little use of his characteristic homologies to link native others in the past with native others in the present, native others in this book appear to exist almost entirely in the past and to leave almost no impact on "culture" as it is constructed here. Inevitably, "most of the people of the New World will never speak to us. That communication, with all that we might have learned, is lost forever" (32).

Learning Not to Curse

It is because of the critiques that Greenblatt and Clifford enable us to make of their own work that we are far from wishing to denigrate their projects. If in both *The Predicament of Culture* and *Learning to Curse* the representation or thematization of native others is also an occasion for establishing the author's or white elite men's cultural authority, Clifford and Greenblatt provide powerful tools for scrutinizing their own authorizing moves, for uncovering narratives of salvage and the ways in which privilege, in the words of Elizabeth Spellman, finds "ever deeper places to hide" (183). In thinking through this essay, indeed, we have tried to turn these tools against ourselves. For our project too has redemptive agendas. It seeks, for example, to find space for feminist authority in male-centered cultural studies and space for male authority in feminist cultural work. To what degree do we seek to enhance our own authority in this critical reading of Clifford's and Greenblatt's representations of native others? In making this critique we too evoke and displace the same others at least partially for our own ends. Few among us can claim clean hands, and in critically reading Clifford and Greenblatt we hope to become better readers of our own indulgences and dodges.

We also value Greenblatt's and Clifford's genuine contributions to envisioning multicultural and less unjust futures, for academic and lay concepts of cultural difference and sameness sorely need reconstruction, and not just for the sake of conceptual currency. The image of a culture, David Seals reminds us,

> is as important, especially in this high-tech world of instant global telecommunications, in the perception of it, or of a race of people as whatever lies in the *actual* truth of that culture. Indians have often been victims of stereotyping—Custerism, I call it—and this reduction of the image of a people kills as surely as any real-life, Wounded Knee–type massacre. (635)

In the wake of the demonization of Khadafy, Noriega, and Saddam Hussein, and the "orientalizing" of Arabs, the lethal consequences of reductive images in the New World Order should be all too obvious. And closer to our academic "home," the reactionary media epithet, "PC thought police," applied indiscriminately by the media, and by some of our colleagues as well, to all who criticize the Eurocentric humanities curriculum, makes crucial the forging of cooperative, multivocal alliances among all of its targets. Working alliances, however, as opposed to theoretical or mythical ones, require something more than a compelling cause. They require the acknowledgement and working through of tensions and divisions. As we turn our gender glasses first on Costner's film and then on Clifford's and Greenblatt's work, we hope to foster, not hamper, resistance to the reactionary discourses now dominating the decline of the twentieth century.

Iron John Dunbar

Gendered as well as native "others" are subjugated in *Dances with Wolves,* where masculinist and imperialist representational strategies are mutually dependent. Costner's movie, to be sure, does evince a superficial patina of awareness and sympathy with feminist criticism of cinematic representations of women. The film, for example, does not portray women primarily as sexual objects, or as frail or foolish. Indeed, in a promotional video trailer that hypes the film for potential cable television audiences, Costner recounts his victory over conventional Hollywood standards in casting a woman "with lines in her face" for the role of the white woman, reared by the Sioux, who becomes Dunbar's linguistic translator and bride. Likewise, the filmscript challenges gender conventions in its character-naming strategies and elsewhere. Lieutenant Dunbar becomes the nature dancer of the film's title, while his future bride who "Stands with a Fist" also shoots with a rifle—and with courage and accuracy. And while the Lakota wife of Dunbar's mentor and double, Kicking Bird, is more stereotypically named "Black Shawl," she displays wisdom and more than quiet strength.

If *Dances with Wolves* does not portray women rapaciously or disrespectfully, however, it scarcely portrays women, especially Native American women, at all. As in the conventional Western genre that the film attempts to invert, women are utterly tangential to its overt narrative interests, interests which have to do with the reinvention of the white hero's masculinity in relation to activities conventionally associated with men—hunting, waging war, governing a community, and bonding with other males. Yet Costner's film, to give it credit, makes a point of reinventing masculinity in relation to women as well.

Native American women, for example, though minimally represented in the film, provide hints of a gender order in which the contributions of women are more overtly validated than in nineteenth-century, white, middle-class culture. Although they do not hunt, for example, we do see them at work skinning hides. Although excluded from tribal council, native women speak at community gatherings, where they are accorded honor by the men (and by the camera as well). Black Shawl gives her husband,

Kicking Bird, direct criticism and pointed advice.[23] These hints of self-assertion, status, and power on the part of women suggest a set of domestic relations that Dunbar will enter into as he assimilates to Sioux culture. But white men and women, we are to learn, are not the same as Native Americans.

Stands with a Fist, for example, is assertive too, as her name indeed suggests, but her assertiveness is directed toward Native American women and men and not toward her white suitor. Her other moments of agency, moreover, either serve to facilitate men's relation to each other (as in her translating activities for Dunbar and Kicking Bird) or they mark her as more comfortable than Native American women with Western male technology (as when she, not Black Shawl, shoots a Pawnee warrior with one of Dunbar's rifles). As an evocation of the feminist new woman, moreover, Stands with a Fist is ultimately rewritten as that familiar woman, a submissive wife. For at the end of the movie when Dunbar proposes to leave the Sioux, Stands with a Fist assures him, "You made a decision; my place is with you; I go where you go."

This recoding of spunky frontier woman as adoring wife is facilitated by the fact that Native American women are relegated to the background of this film and by the fact that self-assertion on their part often acts to foreground the white heroine. (Both instances of Black Shawl's critical advice to Kicking Bird are interventions on Stands with a Fist's behalf.) The traditional recoding of the white heroine, who, as the lone female survivor of the film, represents the only "new woman" with whom the future must engage, is also facilitated by Costner's extended focus on Dunbar's political and personal reinvention of himself in relation to the male Sioux, the official cultural "other" in this film, and by ethnocentric evocations of cultural difference between Dunbar and Native American men. For throughout the film the white, middle-class hero is represented as less harshly patriarchal than Native Americans.

Dunbar, for example, arrives at the Sioux camp tenderly cradling the unconscious woman in his arms, but angry, suspicious Wind in His Hair retrieves her from the white intruder by dragging her by her arm and dumping her in the care of Lakota women. In this first transfer scene, as in several later scenes with

Kicking Bird, Lakota men are portrayed as more authoritarian and less civil to women than Dunbar, and it is Dunbar's implied racial superiority in this domain that justifies the domestication and later the transfer of patriarchal rights from native Kicking Bird back to white Dunbar. Thus when Stands with a Fist falls in love with Dunbar, white audiences have been well prepared to agree with the Lakota villagers that "it makes sense. They are both white."

If racial superiority is evoked in the service of traditional gender relations, however, Dunbar's superior performance of patriarchy, in turn, prepares the way for the colonizing transfer of the future to this white hero. The film, in this respect, evokes the more polarized and more extreme codings of the Gulf War, in which Western men were represented by the US government and its censored media servants as both liberators and protectors of women, while native male others were represented as callous and patriarchal or, in the case of Saddam, as rapists of a feminized Kuwait. At the same time, those privileged objects of Western male liberation, female soldiers, were turning up on the frontier of "Indian country" only to be studiously recoded in the media, as in *Dances with Wolves,* as mothers and wives. This gender coding of the war, of course, helped paper over real divisions between US white men and men of color both in the war and as citizens in the New World Order, an order which they are ostensibly to inherit.[24]

Despite its patriarchal politics, however, *Dances with Wolves,* like some strands of the men's movement today, contends that "men can change."[25] Castillo accurately locates the chief source of the movie's popularity in the audience appeal of Dunbar's character, "precisely because he is a 1990s man, not an 1860s white man" (19). Echoing elements of the men's spiritual movement, a la Robert Bly, the movie suggests that traditional forms of masculinity wound, and even castrate, men. Like the wounded boy in Bly's masculine mythology, Iron John, John Dunbar enters into the wilderness of the frontier to be healed among other men—the male Sioux. "Going native," he may be seen as getting in touch with the "wild man" within, a process most dramatically suggested by his ecstatic fireside dance, which evokes the contemporary phenomenon of men's drumming societies.[26] Castillo notes that "powerful drum beats rhythmically signal a deeper transformation of Dunbar as he joins in the rhythm of the earth and perhaps harks back to a race memory of his own neolithic ancestors" (19).

Reading the film as a modern Native American man committed to contemporary Native struggles, Castillo probably perceives political advantage to the cultural association of Native Americans with ecological values.[27] We can appreciate this view, but as Euro-American white feminists, whose reading strategies have been influenced by feminists of color, we cannot overlook subtle dimensions of colonial discourse intermingling with male chauvinism in Costner's postfeminist masculine fantasy. For Costner's 1990s man contains feminist threats to white male hegemony not only by maintaining patriarchal power relations but by selectively absorbing feminine traits, just as he does male Native American ones. While his stolid, unfluid woman stands with her fist, Dunbar becomes the sensitive, communicative, and playful yet also virile man, shaving his facial hair, wearing Sioux jewelry and dress, and becoming more beautiful than the heroine in every frame.[28]

This gender recoding is consistent with a recent report on network programming strategies for "Children's TV, Where Boys Are King." ABC, for example, has dropped all children's programs with female central characters, because boys refuse to watch these, while girls will watch male leads, and to compensate for the absence of female leads, the networks now "give the male characters attributes considered to be 'female'" (Carter Al). Costner makes a similar cooptive concession to white feminism when he syncretically reinvents Dunbar as embodying the best of white femininity and native masculinity. Costner, that is, while reinscribing gender and racial superiority, also seems, wistfully, or defensively, to have displaced onto white men those far more visible processes of cultural reinvention recently undertaken by feminist, lesbian and gay, Native American, and other racial and ethnic liberation movements. White men can change, as *Dances with Wolves* demonstrates, but individual, psychological change, while welcome, is hardly enough. Authority for some groups is "easily compatible with the expression of soft and tender emotions" (Segal, *Slow Motion* 284) as with other signs of cultural reinvention, like "the dream of limitless multiple embodiments," which Susan Bordo calls the "*dance* from place to place and self to self" (145). What is required, of course, is a greater challenge to patriarchal power relations than that of performing them with greater sensitivity and better grace.

Feminist Predicaments

Of course, neither Clifford nor Greenblatt succumbs to simplistic masculine allegories about rediscovering the wild man within. Nonetheless, it unsettles us to find more sophisticated marginalizations and/or displacements of feminist and other forms of cultural reinvention in most of their published work. Clifford directs and teaches in a vanguard cultural studies program and campus where the presence of feminist scholars is unusually prominent. Greenblatt teaches in a department where feminist scholarship is also strong. Both scholars, moreover, not only are overtly sympathetic with feminism and its intellectual contributions to ethnography and literary criticism, but also have demonstrated their own capacity for feminist analysis, as in Clifford's discussion of the male gaze that William Carlos Williams turns on the disparaged figure of "Elsie" and Greenblatt's analysis of *Martin Guerre.*

Disappointingly, however, in *The Predicament of Culture* and in *Learning to Curse,* both authors still marginalize feminist contributions to cultural criticism even though their own projects might be strengthened by including the kinds of emphases which have consistently characterized feminist work—emphases on the investigation of familial life and other nontextual cultural practices outside the officially "public" sphere. Clifford, for example, might have buttressed his argument for a syncretic understanding of Mashpee cultural identification had he pursued the possibility that Mashpee women bore disproportionate responsibility for negotiating that hybrid identity. In a passing reference, Clifford mentions the prevalence of intermarriage during the late eighteenth century between Mashpee women and freed black slaves, which was "encouraged by a common social marginality and by a relative shortage of men among the Indians and of women among the Blacks" (297). Greater attention to the history of Mashpee kin and gender arrangements might have strengthened the case for

Mashpee tribal status as well as Clifford's case for cultural reinvention because women may have been the primary cultural carriers of the continuous tribal identity that the Mashpee lawsuit sought to establish or the primary cultural reinventors and syncretists for their "tribe." Greenblatt, as various of his critics have observed, tends in practice if not in theory to equate culture with a discursive field defined by the published texts of elite white men. This representation of culture might be broadened by the more extensive employment of strategies which have marked the work of feminists and of ethnic studies men—the insistence on a larger definition of the discursive domain, one that takes into greater account heterogeneous cultural spaces, the oral, the nonliterate, the familial.[29]

A similar tendency to foreground the texts and activities of male public spheres informs Greenblatt's and Clifford's textual relations to feminist work. Both, for example, have tended to confine their references to feminist labor to the literal margins of their texts, placing them in parenthetical comments and footnotes, where they fail to revise otherwise androcentric metanarratives, genealogies, or characterizations of what constitutes a discursive field. Clifford, for example, makes an explicit decision to bracket gender (and class) analysis while exploring "emergent possibilities" represented by "Natives." He sets out in "The Pure Products Go Crazy" to liberate Elsie from symbolic exploitation by William Carlos Williams, who has submerged her particularity into the general decaying condition of modernity. Clifford instead asks Elsie to stand for marginalized, silenced groups—"'Natives,' women, the poor,"—and the syncretic possibilities of postmodernity he hopes they represent. Ironically, however, Clifford's decision to bracket Elsie's gender and class locations reduces her to a monological script of race-ethnicity, even though, in a footnote, he registers awareness of literature by feminists that demonstrates systematic interrelationships among ideological constructions of race, gender, and class.[30]

Greenblatt, too, has been roundly and sometimes harshly criticized, both for his exclusions and for his use of feminist insights.[31] *Learning to Curse* provides further ground for feminist critique. If in Clifford's revisionary ethnography few feminists are cited as among those up against the predicament of culture, in *Learning to Curse,* feminists are marginally alluded to as persons who seem not to have gotten things, particularly fluid and syncretic things, right. Thus, in a footnote to "Resonance and Wonder" Greenblatt notes that "the discourse of the appropriating male gaze is itself in need of considerable qualification" (183). This may be true, but largely feminist work on the male gaze is critiqued here without citation or even identification as feminist. In the same essay, moreover, feminists seem foregrounded among those whose gaze is problematic: "[A] criticism that never encounters obstacles, that celebrates predictable heroines and rounds up the usual suspects, that finds confirmation of its values everywhere it turns is quite simply boring" (168). Like Stands with a Fist, feminist new women seem implicitly rewritten here as an even more familiar feature of the cultural landscape, not the adoring, but the nagging wife.

In Greenblatt's *Learning to Curse,* therefore, as in Clifford's *The Predicament of Culture* and in some of the discourse on cultural studies as a whole, feminist work by women, despite its multiple reinventions of itself over the last thirty years, is, at best, marginally represented as experimental or is presented as fixed. Cultural criticism by men, however, along with the author's personae, often appears syncretic, fluid, postmodern, or playful. Thus, Clifford depicts himself as a rootless, syncretic Westerner, while Greenblatt enacts the "lie" of any single narrative of himself by imposing and reimposing not identities but critical positions. In *Learning to Curse,* indeed, where he adapts and critiques multiple critical approaches and engages a whole catalogue of cultural themes, Greenblatt seems a figure for US cultural studies itself, with its multiple themes, syncretic borrowing, and perpetual critique of all critical positions.[32] Self-characterizations such as these may challenge traditional masculine authority and suggest a refreshing capacity for change, but they imply unsettling polarities with the representations of feminist scholars presented in these works. Feminist scholars, that is, sometimes appear to be standing stolidly with their fists while male cultural critics are fluidly dancing with wolves.

Predicaments of Cultural Studies

More troubling analogies may be at hand in the texts of some male cultural critics who represent cultural studies as the fluid, syncretic repository of the best of what has been thought and said since 1968, for like *Dances with Wolves* these representations have the potential to marginalize and/or absorb the discourse of the other into a common, and dominant, language.[33] Indeed, an essay on cultural studies published in 1985 maintains that feminist studies, Black studies, and American studies have failed and that cultural studies now stands alone on the political frontier (Giroux 473). In this formulation, cultural studies becomes the lone voice in the wilderness, having absorbed the voices of those who did not get it right, arguing for "the necessity of a counter-disciplinary praxis" and "introducing the notion of the resisting intellectual as an educational formation necessary to restore academics to their roles as intellectuals" (Giroux 473). It is disturbing that syncretism and multiplicity appear here not as conflicting and identifiable voices but as a new, improved discourse, as one heteroglossia for all of us.

The reinscription or reinvention of a specifically white masculine authority and privilege which accompanies the efforts by some male cultural studies critics to reinvent "real world" politics for their work may be difficult to see because of the way "politics" is often coded. "Politics," that is, may be coded, the way it is in Costner's film, as a critique of imperialist, other world ventures. Any criticism of white male authority, meanwhile, is carried on as a textual repositioning of the self vis-à-vis distantly colonized (male) others. Introducing a special issue of *Cultural Studies* on "Chicano/a Cultural Representations," for example, Rosa Linda Fregoso and Angie Chabram find it ironic that the ubiquitous image of "the other" in much postmodern cultural criticism is so abstract, despite the physical proximity of so many tangible "others" to postmodern or white male cultural studies theorists:

> As Raymond Rocco points out, "they are no longer out there, but are instead an integral part of the theorist's everyday life, serving their food, driving their cars, cleaning their homes or offices." And it is doubly ironic that we remain an abstraction

> when we are now in fact challenging their theoretical formulations as well. (210)

Anxiety about direct confrontations seems one likely source for these ironies and contradictions. Representing visions of distant male "natives" may appear a safer "Field of (Men's) Dreams" than representing more proximate "others."[34] This caution is all the more ironic, of course, given the "political anxiety" of many cultural studies scholars and their insistence on looking at the power relations which construct present critical discourse.[35]

The new war on "political correctness," however, in offering an opportunity for "humanists" to gain a "real world political relevance in which the left finally has a cause not only against academic conservatives but against statist ones also" (Marcus, "A Broad(er) Side" 8), offers the possibility for reinventing relations between domestic others as well, between left-leaning men, white feminists, feminists of color, and US antiracist men of color in the academy. It is crucial, however, that sufficiently complex narratives emerge about what is at stake and who the interested parties are. The emerging battle, for example, is sometimes figured in relation to a political paradigm which no longer seems adequate to our construction of present political realities. Debate about the canon, according to George Marcus, "reproduces the fiction of the old categories (left and right) and has great nostalgic appeal. There is a conservative, orthodox authority which various liberal/left positions can resist" ("A Broad(er) Side" 8). Race and gender divisions which position the left/liberal allies in this struggle rather more complexly are obscured by the reassertion of this sixties-style political paradigm in the nineties wardrobe of cultural studies.

We would not have written this piece, however, if we did not believe that different narratives of our political histories and alliances were possible. One aim of this essay, indeed, is to shift our own discursive strategies, to enter into a differently constructed dialogue with a wide spectrum of our male colleagues, one which involves the sort of criticism that also includes appreciation and fosters exchange. We are aware that in shifting strategies we will please very few. We will inevitably be read, depending on the "positionalities" of our readers, as having been too critical or too kind, as having given male colleagues too much credit or too little, as having acted like the feminist police or like deferential wives, as having positioned ourselves, once again, inside a nagging text. Shifting strategies, however fashionably postmodern, is not a comfortable, reassuring, or ingratiating move.

Alliance, however, would seem to require a willingness to experiment, to be tentative, and to encounter risk, lessons we are learning as we work with our colleagues of color to build a multicultural women's studies program on our campus. The voice we present here, moreover, is only one of many that might be registered, just as our focus here on domestic others is one of many and is meant not to displace but to augment the post-colonial focus that Clifford and Greenblatt favor. Resistance to the monovocal, after all, is what Clifford and Greenblatt advocate, and hearing the discourses of "the 'Other'—of all the others" is the announced aim of cultural studies as it is sometimes currently defined (Brantlinger 3). Both seem key to the political alliances we really need, alliances that, in practice as well as in theory, are polyvocal, syncretic, and reflective, alliances which help us to hear and to see the "other" and in the process help us to investigate that spot the size of a quarter, which, as Virginia Woolf points out, we cannot see on the back of our own heads.

Fields of Dreams

Clifford and Greenblatt were not with us when we unenthusiastically accompanied male relatives to *Field of Dreams,* an earlier Costner movie. Had they been, they could have enhanced our understanding of its allegorical properties, while we would have urged them to attend equally to its masculinist script. Then bell hooks might have inspired us further to decode the liberal, hierarchical race relations between Costner and the retired black reporter he conscripts to realize his baseball fantasy. In a genuinely multivocal alliance with critical friends like these, we might resolve some predicaments in cultural criticism and better weather the right-wing assault on all of us.

Notes

We want to thank the following for helpful suggestions on this piece: Emily Apter, Wini Breines, Bob Connell, Rosa Linda Fregoso, Maggie George-Cramer, Susan Gerard, Julie Haase, Ines Hernandez, Tom Laqueur, Louis Montrose, Mike Rogin, Roger Rouse, Debby Rosenfelt, Kamala Visveswaren, and Judy Walkowitz.

We also wish to thank James Clifford and Stephen Greenblatt for their forthright and generous responses to an earlier draft.

1. See Giroux et al. On some of the perceived tensions between new historicism and cultural studies see Kuenzli; Veeser.

2. The men on Clifford's cover are, however, black men masquerading as white ethnographers, an image that conveys a self-consciously critical and ironic stance toward the politics of racial and colonial relations.

3. These categories are in fact complexly overlapping. They are retained in much anti-PC discourse although this discourse constructs members of each category as subversive in the same way. They are also retained in much academic discourse where their usefulness as categories seems increasingly problematic.

4. Examples of the voluminous media attacks on campus "PC" include Bernstein, Taylor, Will ("The Derisory Tower") and the *Newsweek* cover story provocatively entitled "Thought Police." President Bush made the PC issue the focus of his commencement address at the University of Michigan in May 1991; see Dowd. Not in the popular media, but particularly vicious, is Epstein. Numerous essays have analyzed and responded to this campaign, but these have received far less attention in the popular media. See, for example, Martinez; Wiener; Beers; Carton; Graff. Two new organizations, Teachers for a Democratic Culture and Union of Democratic Intellectuals, have formed to counter the offensive spearheaded by the National Association of Scholars and right-wing think tanks and foundations.

5. While Costner's recent movies and starring roles, including *Robin Hood* and *JFK,* might suggest a liberal political orientation, Costner refuses to discuss his political views and is a recurrent dinner and golf companion of President Bush. For an illustrative expression of his reluctant, ambiguous political views, see Wuntch.

6. One, not entirely successful, attempt to initiate a dialogic approach to such a discourse was Jardine and Smith. Boone provides a sensitive critique of that volume's formulation of the subject as men *in* feminism and attempts to carve a less polarizing frame for male feminism.

7. Among the most influential of these critiques have been hooks, *Feminist Theory;* Moraga and Anzaldúa; Hull, Scott, and Smith; Asian Women United of California; Anzaldúa; and Mohanty, Russo, and Torres.

8. The quotation marks suggest the problematic status of these terms, which have, in the past, very often been equated with white feminist politics and scholarship.

9. An initial discussion of these issues appears in Newton and Stacey.

10. Among those forms of power, for example, is that of identifying and celebrating a "numinous literary authority" that appeared to "bind and fix the energies we prize, to identify a stable and permanent source of literary power, to offer an escape from shared contingency" (Greenblatt, "Circulation" 3).

11. Cultural studies is also sometimes characterized as a resurgence or rein-

vention of sixties-style political energy or modes of thought. See Brantlinger (25); Marcus ("A Broad(er) Side" 8).

12. On the cover of *Learning to Curse,* which bears the portrait of an elite white man holding a book, the phrase does not appear to refer to native others but, if anything, to the critic himself. Perhaps cursing has to do here with the burden of being elite, a representor, a colonizer of others. Perhaps it has to do with the burden of understanding how elite cultures operate. One review of the book reads the phrase in this light. See McLeod.

13. "The usual suspects" is a phrase from *Learning to Curse,* 168.

14. For a paper that intersects at some points with our own, see Padget.

15. The costumes were modeled on the drawings in Catlin. According to Edward D. Castillo, Catlin's drawings were of formal and ceremonial Sioux attire that *Dances with Wolves* inaccurately presents as daily garb.

16. For example, Doris Leader Charge, a linguist at Sinte Gleska Indian College in South Dakota, translated the screenplay's dialogue into Lakota and coached the "authentic" Lakota actors, "none of whom spoke Lakota fluently." The role of Kicking Bird was played by a Canadian-born Oneida, that of Wind in His Hair by an Omaha, while the Lakota who played Chief Ten Bears is also a folk singer and activist. See Castillo.

17. Although not himself a Native American, Seals is a South Dakota resident and author deeply immersed in and identified with contemporary Indian cultures and struggles, particularly those of the Lakota. His essay quotes divided reactions from his Lakota friends to Costner and the film.

18. Clifford explicitly criticizes the elegiac view of vanishing Indians in "Identity in Mashpee" 284; also see Clifford, "On Ethnographic Allegory." *Dances with Wolves* has also been criticized for exploiting Lakota culture and people to enhance Costner's authority and coffers at their expense. See Seals and Harrison.

19. "Overall, if the witnesses seem flat and somewhat elusive, the effect is intentional. Using the usual rhetorical techniques, I could have given a more intimate sense of people's personalities or of what they were really trying to express; but I have preferred to keep my distance" (*Predicament* 291).

20. This reading of *The Tempest* has been attacked by "anti-PC" forces. See Will. See also Greenblatt's response, "Literary Politics."

21. For an example of this approach, see Davis; see also Newton for a comparison and contrast of Davis and Greenblatt.

22. See Porter for a detailed and rigorous reading of these tendencies.

23. Awiakta notes this aspect of the movie, 70–71.

24. For compatible feminist analyses of the Gulf war, see the symposium "Watching the War," esp. Jeffords.

25. For some recent reflections on men and change, see Segal, "Can Men Change?" and Connell, "The Big Picture." See also Segal, *Slow Motion;* Connell, *Gender and Power.* For an overview of various strands of the "men's movement," see Clatterbaugh.

26. See Adler et al. For an account of the wild man and of Bly's other contributions to the spiritual wing of the men's movement, see Clatterbaugh.

27. We are grateful to Linda Collins for suggesting this association to us.

28. On the general phenomenon of "sensitive men" in current Hollywood movies, see Maslin. On related deconstructions of masculinity in mass culture, see Modleski; Hanke; and Segal ("Can Men Change?").

29. Porter makes a similar argument.

30. We are, of course, not the first feminists to object to these practices. White feminists have launched several challenges to Clifford's explanation for excluding feminists from the *Writing Culture* conference and volume that has come to define what ethnographic poetics "are." See, for example, Mascia-Lees, Sharpe, and Cohen; Gordon; Lutz. Feminists of color have broadened this critique; see hooks, "Culture to Culture"; Fregoso and Chabram.

31. See, for example, Boose; Waller; Neely; Newman.

32. For a reading of Greenblatt that sees nothing redeeming in his "self-referentiality," see McLeod's review of *Learning to Curse,* 102. McLeod reads Greenblatt's storytelling, playful self as a form of "self-centeredness" that goes hand in hand with the "denial of ideological responsibility" (101–2).

33. Several recent essays on feminism and cultural studies cite the marginalization of feminism and feminist theory in cultural studies discourse. See Schwichtenberg; Rakow; Long; Radway. Meaghan Morris discusses and disrupts the analogous marginalization of feminism in postmodernist discourse more broadly.

34. The interviews of male cultural critics that we have begun conducting have already begun to challenge and complicate this thesis.

35. See Rooney. On the political nature of cultural studies, see Nelson.

Works Cited

Adler, Jerry, et al. "Drums, Sweat and Tears." *Newsweek* 24 June 1991: 46–53.

Anzaldúa, Gloria, ed. *Making Face, Making Soul = Haciendo Caras: Creative and Critical Perspectives by Women of Color.* San Francisco: Aunt Lute Foundation, 1990.

Asian Women United of California, eds. *Making Waves: An Anthology of Writings By and About Asian American Women.* Boston: Beacon, 1989.

Awiakta, Marilou. "Red Alert! A Meditation on 'Dances With Wolves.'" *Ms.* Mar.-Apr. 1991: 70–71.

Baltake, Joe. "It was anything but 'Costner's Last Stand.'" *Sacramento Bee* 26 Mar. 1991: F1 +.

———. "Plains of Magic." *Sacramento Bee* 21 Nov. 1990: Scene 1 + 5.

Beers, David. "PC? B.S." *Mother Jones* Sept.-Oct. 1991: 384–87.

Bernstein, Richard. "The Rising Hegemony of the Politically Correct." *New York Times* 28 Oct. 1991: D4.

Boone, Joseph A. "Of Me(n) and Feminism: Who(se) Is the Sex That Writes?" *Engendering Men: The Question of Male Feminist Criticism.* Ed. Joseph A. Boone and Michael Cadden. New York: Routledge, 1990. 11–25.

Boose, Lynda E. "The Family in Shakespeare Studies; or—Studies in the Family of Shakespeareans; or—The Politics of Politics." *Renaissance Quarterly* 40 (1987): 739–41.

Bordo, Susan. "Feminism, Postmodernism, and Gender-Skepticism." *Feminism/Postmodernism.* Ed. Linda J. Nicholson. New York: Routledge, 1990. 135–56.

Brantlinger, Patrick. *Crusoe's Footprints: Cultural Studies in Britain and America.* New York: Routledge, 1990.

Carter, Bill. "Children's TV, Where Boys Are King." *New York Times* 1 May 1991: A1 +.

Carton, Evan. "The Self Besieged: American Identity on Campus and in the Gulf." *Tikkun* 6.4 (1991): 40–47.

Castillo, Edward D. "Dancing With Words: Reflections on the Shadow Catcher Kevin Costner." *Film Quarterly* 44.4 (1991): 14–23.

Catlin, George. *North American Indians.* 1844. Ed. Peter Matthiessen. New York: Penguin, 1989.

Clatterbaugh, Kenneth. *Contemporary Perspectives on Masculinity: Men, Women, and Politics in Modern Society.* Boulder: Westview, 1990.

Clifford, James. "On Ethnographic Allegory." *Writing Culture: The Poetics and Politics of Ethnography.* Ed. James Clifford and George E. Marcus. Berkeley: U of California P, 1986. 98–121.

———. *The Predicament of Culture: Twentieth-Century Ethnography, Literature, and Art.* Cambridge: Harvard UP, 1988.

Cohen, Walter. "Political Criticism of Shakespeare." *Shakespeare Reproduced: The Text in History and Ideology.* Ed. Jean E. Howard and Marion F. O'Connor. London: Methuen, 1987. 18–46.

Connell, R. W. "The Big Picture—a Little Sketch. Changing 'Western' Masculinities in the Perspective of Recent World History." *Theory and Society,* forthcoming.

———. *Gender and Power: Society, the Person and Sexual Politics.* Stanford: Stanford UP, 1987.

Dances with Wolves. Dir. Kevin Costner. Tig Productions/Orion Pictures, 1990.

Davis, Natalie. "Boundaries and the Sense of Self in Sixteenth-Century France." *Reconstructing Individualism: Autonomy, Individuality, and the Self in Western Thought.* Ed. Thomas C. Heller, Morton Sosna, and David E. Wellbery. Stanford: Stanford UP, 1986. 53–63.

"The Derisory Tower." *New Republic* 18 Feb. 1991: 5–47.

Dorris, Michael. "Indians in Aspic." *New York Times* 24 Feb. 1991: E17.

Dowd, Maureen. "Bush Sees Threat to Flow of Ideas on U.S. Campuses." *New York Times* 5 May 1991: A1.

Epstein, Joseph. "The Academic Zoo: Theory—In Practice." *Hudson Review* (1991): 9–30.

Evans, Frank. "'Dances' trips on its image." *Sacramento Bee* 13 Jan. 1991: *Encore* 2.

Field of Dreams. Dir. Phil Alden Robinson. Universal, 1989.

Fregoso, Rosa Linda, and Angie Chabram. "Introduction. Chicana/o Cultural Representations: Reframing Alternative Critical Discourses." *Cultural Studies* 4 (1990): 203–12.

Giroux, Henry, et al. "The Need for Cultural Studies: Resisting Intellectuals and Oppositional Public Spheres." *Dalhousie Review* 64 (1985): 482.

Gordon, Deborah. "Reflections on Gender in *Reflections.*" *Gender in the Field: The Politics of Cultural Description, 1967–1990.* Ann Arbor: U of Michigan P, forthcoming.

Graff, Gerald. "The Nonpolitics of PC." *Tikkun* 6.4 (1991): 50–52.

Greenblatt, Stephen. *Learning to Curse: Essays in Early Modern Culture.* New York: Routledge, 1990.

———. "Storm over 'The Tempest.'" *California Monthly* 102.1 (Sept. 1991):46.

———. *Shakespearean Negotiations: The Circulation of Social Energy in Renaissance England.* Berkeley: U of California P, 1988.

Grenier, Richard. "Wolves in Sheep's Clothing?" *San Francisco Examiner* 31 March 1991: 26.

Hanke, Robert. "Hegemonic Masculinity in *thirtysomething.*" *Critical Studies in Mass Communication* 7 (1990): 231–48.
Harrison, Eric. "For Lakota 'Dances' Can't Keep Wolf from the Door." *Los Angeles Times* 29 July 1991: A1 +.
Hernández, Inés, personal conversation.
hooks, bell. "Culture to Culture: Ethnography and Cultural Studies as Critical Intervention." *Yearning: Race, Gender, and Cultural Politics.* Boston: South End, 1990.
———. *Feminist Theory from Margin to Center.* Boston: South End, 1984.
Howard, Jean E., and Marion F. O'Connor. "Introduction." *Shakespeare Reproduced: The Text in History and Ideology.* Ed. Jean E. Howard and Marion F. O'Connor. London: Methuen, 1987.
Hull, Gloria, Patricia Bell Scott, and Barbara Smith, eds. *All the Women Are White, All the Blacks Are Men, But Some of Us Are Brave: Black Women's Studies.* Old Westbury: Feminist, 1982.
Jacobs, Joanne. "And now, it's 'Indian chic.'" *Sacramento Bee* 8 Apr. 1991: B7.
Jardine, Alice, and Paul Smith, eds. *Men in Feminism.* New York: Methuen, 1987.
Jeffords, Susan. "Protection racket: The 'rape' of Kuwait." *Women's Review of Books* July 1991: 10.
Kaplan, E. Ann. "Cultural Studies, Film and Discursive Constructions." *Cultural Studies.* Ed. E. Ann Kaplan and T. Brennan. Forthcoming.
Kuenzli, Rudolf. Introduction. *Cultural Studies and the New Historicism.* Spec. issue of *The Journal of the Midwest Modern Language Association* 24.1 (1991): 1–2.
Landon, Susan. "In Another's Man's Moccasins." *Sunday Journal [Albuquerque]* 16 Dec. 1990: A1 +.
Long, Elizabeth. "Feminism and Cultural Studies." *Critical Studies in Mass Communication* 6 (1989): 427–35.
Lutz, Catherine. "The Gender of Theory." American Anthropological Association Meeting. Chicago, Nov. 1991.
Marcus, George E. "A Broad(er) Side to the Canon: Being a Partial Account of a Year of Travel Among Textual Communities in the Realm of Humanities Centers & Including a Collection of Artificial Curiosities." Unpublished essay.
Martinez, Elizabeth. "Willie Horton's Gonna Get Your Alma Mater." *Z Magazine* July-Aug. 1991: 126–30.
Mascia-Lees, Frances E., Patricia Sharpe, and Colleen Ballerino Cohen. "The Postmodernist Turn in Anthropology: Cautions From a Feminist Perspective." *Signs* 15 (1989): 7–33.
Maslin, Janet. "Give Him a Puppy. And Get the Lady a Gun." *New York Times* 21 July 1991: 1+.
McLeod, Bruce. Rev. of *Learning to Curse. Journal of the Midwest Modern Language Association* 24.1 (1991): 100–03.
Modleski, Tania. *Feminism Without Women: Culture and Criticism in a "Postfeminist" Age.* New York: Routledge, 1991.
Mohanty, Chandra Talpade, Ann Russo, and Lourdes Torres, eds. *Third World Women and the Politics of Feminism.* Bloomington: Indiana UP, 1991.
Moraga, Cherrie, and Gloria Anzaldúa, eds. *This Bridge Called My Back: Writings by Radical Women of Color.* 2nd ed. New York: Kitchen Table, 1981.
Morris, Meaghan. *The Pirate's Fiancee: Feminism, Reading, Postmodernism.* London: Verso, 1988.
Neely, Carol Thomas. "Constructing the Subject: Feminist Practice and the New Renaissance Discourses." *English Literary Renaissance* 18.1 (1988): 5–18.

Nelson, Cary. "Always Already Cultural Studies: Two Conferences and a Manifesto." *Journal of the Midwest Modern Language Association* 24.1 (1991): 24–38.
Newman, Karen. *Fashioning Femininity and English Renaissance Drama*. Chicago: U of Chicago P, 1991.
Newton, Judith. *Starting Over: Feminism and the Politics of Cultural Critique*. Ann Arbor: U of Michigan P, forthcoming.
Newton, Judith, and Judith Stacey. "Ms.representations: Postmodern/Feminist Dilemmas in Studying Men." Meeting of the Society for the Study of Social Problems. Pittsburgh, Aug. 1992.
O'Connor, Alan. "The Problem of American Cultural Studies." *Critical Studies in Mass Communication* 6.4 (1989): 407.
Padget, Martin. "Film, Ethnography, and the Scene of History: 'Dances with Wolves' as Participant Ethnography." U of California at Berkeley Film Studies Conference. Berkeley, Feb. 1992.
Porter, Carolyn. "Are We Being Historical Yet?" *South Atlantic Quarterly* 87.4 (1988): 743–86.
Radway, Janice. "Antidisciplinary Logic of Culture Studies." Modern Language Association Meetings. San Francisco, Dec. 1991.
Rakow, Lana F. "Feminist Studies: The Next Stage." *Critical Studies in Mass Communication* 6.2 (1989): 209–15.
Rooney, Ellen. "Discipline and Vanish: Feminism, the Resistance to Theory, and the Politics of Cultural Studies." *differences* 2 (1990): 14–28.
Schwichtenberg, Cathy. "Feminist Cultural Studies." *Critical Studies in Mass Communication* 6.2 (1989): 202–08.
Seals, David. "The New Custerism." *Nation* 13 May 1991: 637.
Segal, Lynne. "Can Men Change? Masculinities in Context." *Theory and Society*. Forthcoming.
———. *Slow Motion: Changing Masculinities, Changing Men*. London: Virago, 1990.
Spelman, Elizabeth V. *Inessential Woman: Problems of Exclusions in Feminist Thought*. Boston: Beacon, 1988.
Taylor, John. "Are You Politically Correct?" *New York* 21 Jan. 1991: 33–41.
"Thought Police." *Newsweek* 24 December 1990: 48–54.
Valente, Judith. "For the Sioux, life is as hard as the Dakota hills." *Sacramento Bee* 1 April 1991: B6+.
Veeser, H. Aram. "Re-Membering a Deformed Past: (New) New Historicism." *Journal of the Midwest Modern Language Association* 24.1 (1991): 3–13.
Waller, Marguerite. "The Difference It Makes." *Diacritics* 17 (1987): 2–20.
"Watching the War: Seven Perspectives." *Women's Review of Books*. July 1991: 4–13.
Wayne, Don E. "Power, Politics, and the Shakespearian Text: Recent Criticism in England and the United States." *Shakespeare Reproduced: The Text in History and Ideology*. Ed. Jean E. Howard and Marion F. O'Connor. London: Methuen, 1987. 47–67.
Wiener, Jon. "What Happened at Harvard." *Nation* 30 Sept. 1991: 384–87.
Will, George. "Literary Politics." *Newsweek* 22 Apr. 1991: 72.
Woolf, Virginia. *A Room of One's Own*. 1929. New York: Harvest, 1981.
Wuntch, Philip. "Garrison's case weak, Costner says." *Sacramento Bee* 3 January 1992, final ed.: 18.

"Day After Tomorrow": Audience Interaction and Soap Opera Production

Jennifer Hayward

> You'd think a hospital would know what protein is. I ask for protein and they give me cornflakes. No wonder everybody's sick.[1]

In the lines quoted above, Palmer Cortlandt (the leading capitalist patriarch of the soap opera *All My Children*) succinctly argues one side of cultural studies' continuing debate over the function of mass culture. In this view, the culture industry (like the hospital café) supplies its own choice of, for example, televisual "food" to the starving masses, ignoring audience needs and opinions completely. Forced to fill up on empty calories, the viewer consequently suffers (like Palmer's daughter Nina, for whom he seeks protein) from diabetes. The inability to control blood sugar levels is a suggestive metaphor, recalling the plethora of arguments which, beginning in the early nineteenth century and continuing through our own, castigate producers of popular fiction for force-feeding a vacuous or even dangerous textual "diet" to a voiceless, passive audience.

© 1993 by *Cultural Critique*. 0882-4371 (Winter 1992–93). All rights reserved.

But it is important to acknowledge the limitations of such metaphors. Soap opera, like other cultural texts, requires active participation on the part of viewers. At the very least, a series of choices must be made: which soap to watch, while doing what, with whom. Just as Palmer's legendary impatience leads him to ignore the hospital's complex nutritional regimen as well as the fact that cornflakes were not his only available choice, so disdain for mass culture both produces and results from ignorance of the complexity of viewer/text relations.

In this essay, which forms part of a larger work on the history of mass serial fiction, I explore the narrative and televisual codes soap producers have developed; the active role soap audiences play in interpreting these codes; and the interaction between the two, as soaps, thoroughly enmeshed in the social and economic network, respond—in some of their manifestations and in limited ways—to the desires of audiences. My approach responds to recent work (by Tzvetan Todorov, Jane Feuer, Steve Neale, and Robert Allen, among others) that pressures the limits of genre,[2] extending the term outward to include "both sides of the camera," the expectations and actions of audiences as well as purely formalistic categorizations. As Todorov argues:

> In a given society, the recurrence of certain discursive properties is institutionalized, and individual texts are produced and perceived in relation to the norm constituted by that codification. A genre, whether literary or not, is nothing other than the codification of discursive properties. (17)

A genre functions, then, as a "horizon of expectations," so that, for example, texts marketed serially tend to attract audiences who have already enjoyed other serials. Conversely, audience expectations guide producers in the kinds of texts they create and the marketing strategies they employ. Audience desires and expectations are not, however, static; they shift with cultural, historical, political, and economic contexts. Robert Allen explains that

> genre theorists have until fairly recently presumed that their classification of the world of literature was also based on features objectively and indisputably existing in the text itself . . . [but g]enre describes not so much a group of texts or textual

> features as it does a dynamic relationship between texts and interpretative communities. (44)

A similar point has been made, in relation to television, by John Fiske, who contends that "[t]here is no text, there is no audience, there are only the processes of viewing" (57).

In what follows, I will briefly outline the history of soap operas before proceeding to address questions of audience interaction with soap narrative, televisuals, and production. I draw most of my examples from ABC's *All My Children* and *One Life to Live*.

Serial History

> —Today's the big day, huh?
> —Oh, every day is a big day here in Pine Valley.[3]

To begin with, a brief history of soap-as-commodity will be useful. The daytime drama phenomenon is a technocratic development of techniques initiated over a hundred years before radio soaps began, when nineteenth-century advances in printing and mass production technologies combined with increased literacy rates to change the printed text from luxury to commodity, while shifting its audience from elite patron to mass consumer.

Soap creators like Agnes Nixon and Bill Bell credit Charles Dickens with most successfully developing techniques of attracting—and holding—a mass market. Like soaps, his novels incorporated a large (40+) cast of characters; multiple subplots intercut within each part-issued installment, both to increase suspense and to ensure that the interests of a wide range of readers are engaged; an unanswered question, a dilemma, or some other anxiety-producing situation at the end of each installment, to stimulate desire for the next; and a focus on contemporary social issues, especially social injustice and familial or interpersonal relations.

In 1922, early radio producers convinced manufacturers that radio was an ideal advertising medium, which impelled demand for vehicles to "carry" advertisements. Daytime listeners were initially considered an "undesirable market"; but food and soap manufacturers like General Foods, Kellogg, and Procter and Gamble eventually realized that their products, though consumed by a diverse population, were purchased primarily by a particular subsegment—mothers of families, a.k.a. housewives. Both advertisers and networks perceived their target audience as afflicted with a short attention span and low intelligence, and therefore sought daytime programming guaranteed to catch, and hold, the attention of even the most distracted listeners.

The first soap opera (defined, in that era, as a serial aimed at a female audience and marked by a domestic setting, an emphasis on emotional and interpersonal concerns, and a continuing narrative) is credited as Irna Phillips' *Painted Dreams* (1931), which followed the activities of a strong, courageous woman, Mrs. Moynihan, and her daughters; immensely successful, it inspired a plethora of installment dramas. Starting in 1951, existing soaps made the transition to television—which necessitated important changes in serial form.

First, television's added visual dimension allowed for a greatly expanded cast, since viewers could now identify characters by appearance as well as voice; larger casts produced more involved plots, which in turn demanded lengthened segments. The initial fifteen-minute episodes were extended to half an hour in 1956 and to a full hour for most soaps by the late seventies.

Second, radio and television segments are free. Once the initial investment in a set has been made, there is no direct cost per episode; profits depend upon advertising revenues. This marks an important departure from earlier serials: readers of nineteenth-century part-issued novels, for example, had to pay a per-unit cost, thus enforcing a direct link between the consumers exercising "free choice" and the text they chose to consume. The airwaves elide this direct economic relationship. The text is no longer the commodity; it is the *audience* who generates profit, when packaged in units of a thousand and sold, or "delivered," to advertisers. A complex network of ratings systems attempts to convince both current and potential advertisers of the effectiveness (measured in viewers reached and influence obtained) of their investment; networks, the middlemen in this transaction, have an enormous economic stake in maintaining high ratings day after day, week after week.

Soap setting, characters, format, even subject matter are inextricably intertwined with the economic imperatives of soaps. For example, soap scenes usually center on a dyad or triad because intimate conversation is infinitely cheaper to tape than group or action scenes, and can be set in any one of a number of small, reusable sets that fit easily into the studio. While clearly economically determined, this interiority enhances daytime's "women-centered" atmosphere, since its dyadic structure and familiar setting necessitate a primarily emotional and interactive, rather than action-oriented, narrative.

In the beginning, of course, soaps *were* women-centered, both created and consumed almost exclusively by women. Daytime's consequently low prestige meant that it was shunned by male media professionals; on the other hand, women trying to break into the media business sometimes had no choice but to work on daytime.[4] While men moved onto soap production teams as the form became more profitable, soaps remained unique both in positively portraying strong women and in being a form produced primarily *by* women: those forced into soaps in the early days are now in control of the production process and have begun to redress gender imbalances by hiring and training other women—who then move up through the network and continue the legacy. The creator, producer, associate producer, head writer, and all but one of the "stable" of outliners and dialoguers, as well as one of the four directors and several director's assistants and technical crew (female technical trainees are still hard to come by), of *All My Children* are female. A production assistant described the apparently unique experience of being in a TV editing room when putting an episode together and realizing that all the people involved, from head writer to technical crew, were women.

In recent years, technological developments—notably the advent of video recorders—have changed the narrative structure and production values of soap operas to some extent. The fact that viewers can now record shows (according to its network, *AMC* is the most-taped show on television) means increased pressure to compete for overall viewer-hours against prime-time shows and cable as well as other soaps. This leads to soap appropriation of the pacing, style, suspense, and high production values of prime-time adventure series and soaps, TV movies, and MTV. VCR technology has also affected demographics, since working viewers can catch up on shows in the evening.

Through all these changes, soaps have retained one constant: they exist for profit and therefore institutionalize the impossibility of *ever* achieving narrative resolution. Tune in tomorrow, same time, same place—the soap slogan makes visible its economic imperative. Earlier serials encouraged audiences to return week after week or month after month until the story was complete. Soaps invite their audience to return day after day, *forever*. They surpass Dickens by institutionalizing what Peter Brooks calls the "logic of the excluded middle" (168) of melodrama, or what Tania Modleski characterizes as a generic "placing of ever more complex obstacles between desire and fulfillment, which makes anticipation of an end an end in itself" (88). Even more importantly for my argument, networks seeking to keep huge audiences faithful over years and even decades gradually incorporated at least the form of audience response into their production process, as will be discussed in a subsequent section.

While I will argue, at the end of this essay, that soaps' increasing recycling of themes, plots, and characters reflects larger cultural shifts—in expectations about consumption, for example, and in awareness of limits—its structure is clearly influenced by its production and consumption context. Predicated upon the impossibility of closure, ending not with narrative resolution but with a new set of questions, soaps are perfect consumer texts, keeping the real commodity—potential consumers for advertised products—always already in place.

Narrative

> As twisted and sick as it is, he's going to have to be told the whole story.

Soaps as a genre have recognizable themes and codes, most of which can be traced to the Dickensian techniques outlined above. According to Robert Allen, the standard soap themes are family interrelations, romantic triangles, money and its relationship to power, and social issues; I would add a recent focus on self-reflexivity. The narrative codes by which these themes are realized are normative resistance to closure, producing attenuation of events instead of the temporal compression of most other narrative forms; episodic structure of six distinct "acts," each separated by commercial breaks and ending on a note of indeterminacy; cutting, within each act, from one to another of three or four scenes involving distinct characters and story lines; and construction of an interior world and of a complex network of character interrelations.

On the largest temporal and structural level, soap operas run three or four miniature Scribean "well-made plays" simultaneously—on two levels, by continuing ongoing "well-made" story lines from episode to episode, and by encapsulating, within each individual episode, a complete dramatic experience, including exposition, complication, and crisis. However, there is a crucial difference. While the conventional drama includes a conclusion of some kind, each soap scene, "act," and episode ends just before—or during—the climactic moment, leaving resolution forever postponed.[5] In addition, soaps provide not just one but several ongoing story lines, carefully balanced to satisfy very different levels of interest—romance, humor, intrigue, suspense—and to unfold at different rates, so that the crisis of one subplot is juxtaposed with the exposition or complication of another.

In October 1991, for example, *AMC*'s climactic story involved Natalie Chandler's psychotic twin sister, Janet, who—having flung Natalie into a well months ago, impersonated her and married Natalie's fiancé Trevor—was finally discovered to be an impostor and had therefore taken Trevor's niece hostage. Almost every episode ended with the psychotic Janet waving a gun in the terrified Hayley's face, threatening instant oblivion. Viewers who cared about Hayley (or who wanted to check out the special effects of a shooting—a more likely attraction, since Hayley had been voted "Most Annoying New Character" by viewers) would return next day—to watch, yet again, the resolution's postponement.

Although there *are* small, temporary conclusions in soap opera (Janet seemingly safely locked behind bars, a long-separated couple blissfully reunited, a racist thug successfully prosecuted), viewers know, above all, that consummation of an affair, a plotline, or a murder will always be disrupted: diegetically by old lovers, new passion, fatal disease, multiple suspects; structurally by the successive levels of subplot, commercial, interepisodic, and weekend interruptions. During commercial or interepisodic gaps in the text, the refusal of narrative satisfaction ensures audiences' eternal return, since *lack* of resolution intensifies the desire aroused by soap situations.

This formulaic narrative disruption signals an insistence upon the inevitable interposition of obstacles between Self (character/viewer) and Other (love object/text). Significantly, such fissures are usually predicated upon language: false information or inaccurate interpretation. Characters who fail at interpretation by trusting someone who betrays them, for example—or, alternatively, by believing a false witness and therefore failing to trust someone who is loyal—usually experience, and articulate, a temporary paralysis. To reinvoke Natalie's dismal scenario—flung into a well by her twin months ago and only rescued at the end of the summer ratings sweep by the gothic Dimitri Marrick—poor Natalie desperately attempts to interpret (false) "evidence" that her true love Trevor has embraced Janet-as-Natalie without noticing the essential difference beneath superficial appearance. Dimitri, endlessly staring into Nat's eyes while telling her how devastated she must be by Trevor's apparent betrayal, does not help the process of conducting an "objective" reading of events; his words invade her perception of reality, until she finally succumbs to the paralysis caused by "discovering" that what she had considered the center of her life was never there at all. "Nothing matters anymore, anyway," she repeats, abandoning her life to Dimitri's control.

And we the viewers—having been dragged through Trevor's summer-long anguish as well as Natalie's—experience firsthand the radical disjunction between appearance and reality, word and world. We had been promised the wedding of the year and the Nick-and-Nora repartee of Nat and Trevor; now we have relentlessly sincere Dimitri to contend with instead, not to mention a Nat whose acting style appears to have been strongly influenced (and not for the better) by the tricks she has acquired to play a psychotic twin as well as her original character.

It is crucial, however, to stress that soap viewers, far from being "tricked" into expecting a climax that never arrives, profoundly enjoy the extended suspense, which has been refined to an art over years of serialization. As cult filmmaker David Lynch remarked about *Twin Peaks,* a show that at least temporarily attested to the incredible power of the soap genre in producing an international media experience,

> It's human nature . . . to have a tremendous letdown once you receive the answer to a question, especially one that you've been searching for and waiting for. It's a momentary thrill, but it's followed by a kind of depression. And so I don't know what will happen. But the murder of Laura Palmer is . . . It's a complicated story. (qtd. in Pond 26)

Making explicit the pragmatics behind *Twin Peaks'* narrative strategy, Lynch simultaneously provides a possible solution to the show's eventual failure. Besides the soap opera, *Twin Peaks'* other strong generic influence was the murder mystery, and "Who killed Laura Palmer?" became the question obsessing not just viewers but virtually all the *characters* within the show. Because the focus had remained so fixed for the first eight or ten episodes, by the time Lynch and Frost began attempting to diversify their portfolio the new plotlines seemed gratuitous, even annoying. The "complicated story" was not complicated enough; depression could not be dispelled.

True soap operas, on the other hand, fully aware of the depression following narrative conclusion, diffuse that disappointment by interweaving multiple *and equally weighted* plot strands. Disjunctive romances like the Natalie/Trevor disaster are balanced, denied, even partially recuperated by simultaneous subplots featuring characters whose romantic/infantile merging of self and other seems (for a time at least) blissfully undifferentiated: in this particular case, Nat and Trevor's romance is juxtaposed with a new love affair (Dixie/Craig) and the recycling of an old, and immensely popular, passion (Erica/Jack). (As Opal Cortlandt so self-reflexively says, this is "Jackson–Erica: The Sequel.") Soap narrative structure as well as soap character relations, then, vividly embody that vexed relation to the Other that produces the "radical oscillation between contrary emotions" (certainty/doubt, excess/lack, triumph/despair, love/hate) and positions (subject/object, victim/victimizer, exhibitionist/voyeur) which characterizes both subjects trapped within Lacan's Imaginary order (Silverman 158) and actors trapped within a melodramatic script. And radical oscillation describes not only the relations of subplots and characters to each other but also those of viewers to their text.

Televisuals

> Opal: Jackson–Erica: The Sequel. On its way, and better than the original. The principals are set, the scene is set, all we need now is a little action and the cameras will roll.
>
> Erica: Well it is that action part that's a little tricky, Opal.

The issue of televisual spectator positioning has recently received some much-needed critical attention. E. Ann Kaplan says of MTV that

> the spectator has the illusion of being in control of the 'windows' of television whereas in fact the desire for plenitude that keeps him/her watching is, in this case, forever deferred. The TV is seductive precisely because it speaks to a desire that is insatiable—it promises complete knowledge in some far distant and never-to-be-experienced future. TV's strategy is to keep us endlessly consuming in the hopes of fulfilling our desire. (4)

Of all TV forms, soaps are arguably the most skilled at deploying this strategy of seduction. Viewers use the discourse of addiction: they are hooked, have to get a fix, go through withdrawal, are in *AMC* ecstasy. Clearly soaps work, as Kaplan says MTV does, to arouse some need that can be satisfied only by—more soap. But what exactly is the mechanism by which this desire is aroused?

To complement the narrative strategies discussed above, soaps work, visually, through a distillation of Hollywood conventions pushed to their hermeneutic limit. Since they are taped in cramped studios with limited budgets and extremely limited production time, soaps must *mean* as economically as possible, restricting visuals to one or two camera positions and one small set per scene. Camerawork is highly coded, delivering well-established cues to viewers trained to read them. As Bernard Timberg argues in "The Rhetoric of the Camera in Television Soap Opera," "Like the visibility of the purloined letter in Poe's short story, the very obviousness of the cinematic codes of soap opera keeps people from thinking about them and thus makes them more effective in doing their job: to shape and direct the audience's point of view" (166).

Soaps rely almost exclusively on a long shot to set the scene, tracking in to alternate between variations on the standard two-shot, and ending each scene with a closeup to catch every nuance of a character's reaction to the usual cliffhanger. An intensification of classic cinema's reaction shot, this shot becomes temporally extended to a sometimes disconcerting extent at the end of each "act," or group of three or four scenes between commercial breaks. This much-mocked soap "freeze" is actually highly functional in creating soap meaning. Like the cinematic close-close, it invites viewers to attend to an actor's reaction, to imagine his or her thoughts. As Timberg expresses it, the camera's slow truck-ins and "elegiac movement" toward a character's face have "the effect of bringing the viewer closer and closer to the hidden emotional secrets soap opera explores: stylized expressions of pity, jealousy, rage, self-doubt" (166). We are so close, this shot tells us, that we *must* be almost inside the character's mind and therefore must know what is happening there.

However, while actors do occasionally manifest the emotions Timberg describes, in most cases they are actually trained to keep the expression intense, but neutral, projecting strong, concentrated, *impenetrable* emotion.[6] What is fascinating about the soap version of reaction shots is their strategic purpose. Since it is so difficult to read—and thus impossible to predict—exactly what a character will do or say next, the freeze's intense neutrality fosters doubt and suspense, which in turn ensures that viewers stay tuned through the commercial break. So the freeze has a dual and seemingly contradictory purpose, functioning both to pull us into empathy by zooming, as Timberg elegantly describes it, almost into the actor's thoughts and to push us to objectivity by "making strange" the contours of a face so minutely scanned, forcing the realization that in fact we cannot possibly enter this Other's thoughts.

This paradoxical function signals a larger ambivalence reverberating across soap televisuals. On one level, soap techniques work to create intimacy with the characters. The camera literally pulls us into each scene, positions us at eye level with the actors, situates us inside living rooms, kitchens, and bedrooms, enabling us to share with certain characters knowledge unavailable to others. We hear the most intimate details of characters' lives—people who have become familiar over years or even decades, to the extent that viewer letters claim to have known them longer than many friends, longer than some family members.

On another level, familiarity pairs with estrangement. Though pulling us into the action, soap televisual techniques have the peculiar effect, not of establishing viewer identification with one character (as cinematic point-of-view shots do) or of effectively inserting the viewer into the scene as *voyeur,* but of maintaining a certain distance between viewer and text. We remain a little outside every scene, quite literally: the cinematic shot/countershot or glance/object editing that sutures viewers into one point of view is practically unavailable to the soap director, since it requires too many camera positions and too many takes. Most soaps are shot from the "fourth wall" of a long row of three-sided sets packed into an urban studio; like a theater audience, then, we remain cut off from the action and cannot be inscribed into it by seeing through any one character's eyes. This leaves a large gap, a space that inserts the viewer into the narrative, but with a difference. We are positioned within the gap, but—crucially—are *not* assigned a specific, voyeuristic perspective.

And soap narrative reinforces this objectivity. We see all sides of a story. As I write (July 1992), ABC's *One Life to Live* has tackled an extraordinarily complex exploration of homosexuality and AIDS. Having spent weeks building the teen story line most soaps develop over school holidays to attract students on vacation, *OLTL* now plunges viewers into the problems faced by one of the most popular teens, Billy, as he "comes out" to his closest friends, to a local minister, Andrew Carpenter—and, indirectly, to us. As usual, we follow all sides of the story as they develop: Billy's terror of his snobbish and dictatorial parents; their terror of homosexuality; Billy's friends' reactions, both positive and negative, public and private. We simultaneously track teen troublemaker Marty, following her to various covert vantage points as she spies on Carpenter and plots against him; the camera then pulls back to allow us to catch *her* reaction. And finally, we watch Carpenter as he prepares and delivers a funeral service for a parishioner who died of AIDS: he urges the importance of AIDS education in schools, lashes into the upper classes who ignore the epidemic because of class- and race-based imagined "immunity," announces the fact that his own brother died of AIDS, and publicly pins the red badge of HIV awareness onto his surplice.

These independent subplots begin to converge when Billy's parents, already falsely "warned" that Andrew is gay by jealous Marty, spot the Reverend (who has been counseling Billy) holding the boy's shoulders and looking into his eyes . . . Tune in tomorrow. A witch-hunt seems imminent.

In developing these complications, the camera does occasionally position itself "over the shoulder" of a character—as when we "spy" with Marty on the Reverend or on Billy—and this exception to the general rule of nonidentification with any one character makes sense, pragmatically. The voyeuristic character, Marty in this case, positions herself outside the set in order to observe without being noticed; in so doing, she enters the blank 180° of space usually reserved for cameras, sound equipment, crew, and viewers. Interestingly, though, even in this type of situation we are not encouraged to identify with the voyeur; the camera's privileged objectivity usually reasserts itself by pulling back at the end of the scene, to catch the spy's own reaction to what she or he has heard.

So each character involved knows only a small part of the total whirlpool of events; "we," represented by the camera, know all, and what is more, we *know* that we alone are privileged. Like the freeze that ends most "acts," this creates an interesting interpretive confusion. We are privileged to see and hear the most private moments, a voyeurism even more intimate, because more familial/familiar, than that of cinema. At the same time, we are *more* privileged than the characters and thus distanced from them.

This paradoxical relation to narrative and televisuals, which can be seen to inflect soap opera from its smallest elements (the freeze on a character's face) to its largest (the ways soaps are structured), also inflects all television shows to a greater or lesser extent. It is important to emphasize the very different feel of televisual, as opposed to cinematic, spectatorship. First, the camera positioning, production values, scene construction, even acting style are much "smaller" and more intimate in television. Second, the viewing context is very different. Dominated by the vast screen above, surrounded by darkness and strange bodies, the cinemagoer's viewing experience is both spectacular and specular. Glancing at a small screen, surrounded by familiar objects and people, the television watcher has a viewing experience both intimate and distracted. He or she virtually exchanges glances with the smaller-than-life-sized actors, watching them within the private space of the home rather than in a public theater; if others are present, they may or may not be watching (but in either case will probably be talking over, wandering in front of, and otherwise distracting his or her attention from) the television—a small, familiar piece of household furniture. Perhaps most importantly, viewers have power over the images. As Ann Kaplan points out in the passage quoted above, this feeling of control over the "windows" of television is to some degree illusory. Nevertheless, viewers can certainly choose, at any time, to "channel-surf," mute, or turn off the set.

In his *Visible Fictions,* John Ellis discusses the distinction between cinema and television, citing differences in both visual qualities and viewing contexts to show that television "engages the look and the glance rather than the gaze, and thus has a different relation to voyeurism from the cinema's" (128). In the closeup, for example, cinema iconicizes vast, godlike actors; television explores a face scaled to approximate normal size and located close to the viewers' own eye level, producing equality—even intimacy—as opposed to the "distance and unattainability" (130–31) imposed by the size and positioning of the cinema screen. The cost of this intimacy is that "the voyeuristic mode cannot operate as intensely as in cinema" (137–38).

In "Narrative Form in American Network Television," Jane Feuer draws on and extends Ellis's discussion, stressing the psychological positioning of the viewer in each form and arguing that the dominant model of a "cinema apparatus" does not work for television, whose implied spectator is not "the isolated, immobilized pre-Oedipal individual described by Metz and Baudry in their metapsychology of the cinema, but rather a post-Oedipal, fully socialized family member" (103).

By exploring TV's familial give and take, the distraction inherent in the activity, and the nondiscrete "flow" of televisual life, Ellis and Feuer underline the crucial role viewers play in making televisual meaning. Unlike the "cinematic apparatus," the physical qualities of the TV set itself push us into awareness of the activity of *watching*, thus unplugging the rapt voyeurism films can produce. In the case of soap opera, our distance from the highly emotional stories unfolding on the small screen is enforced by its size, by the distractions of the household, by the refusal of a single perspective, and above all by the relentless interruption of commercial breaks. Again the paradox: "we," represented by the camera, are temporarily privileged as "objective" viewers who see all, know more than any of the characters. Sometimes. At other times we know less, particularly during commercial or episodic gaps in the text.

Audiences and Power

> Love is glorious, but it's fleeting. Whereas money is forever. Money is power.
>
> "I want to thank, most of all, the fans—because without you none of this would be happening. And we all know that."[7]

Soap fans have long been considered passive victims, entangled in an ideologically sticky web of narrative and televisual brainwashing. Phenomenal in emotional investment as well as in sheer numbers, fans write letters to their shows, cluster outside the studios from early morning till evening, waiting for the actors to emerge, threaten to stop watching if their suggestions are ignored. It is easy to understand how outside observers, stunned by this overwhelming allegiance, could misinterpret it.

Oprah Winfrey, in a show devoted to untangling soaps' mystique (5/91), echoed the popular misconception that soap viewers become unable to distinguish between soap excess and real life when she solemnly informed her panel of "soap addicts" and her audience that

> [i]t's all really kind of acting. Don't—everybody realizes that, right—that it's all really acting. But that's still okay?

One of her "addict" panelists, a woman named Vicky, responded,

> That's wonderful. That's what makes it so much fun.

Oprah, looking confused, replied,

> Uh-huh. That it's— that— 'Cause you know it's— Do you find yourself worrying about their problems sometimes, Vicky?

And Vicky patiently answered,

> Beyond our conversations with the day's soap opera, my daughters and I—we're trying to figure out things, but I don't worry about them, no.

This exchange underlines one of the most important and least understood aspects of soap pleasure: texts become an ongoing narrative game, in which viewers puzzle out clues and meanings. Pretending to take soap events as real is part of "what makes it so much fun."

Vicky's comments also imply a crucial function of serials: they provide communities, both extradiegetically in bonds formed with other viewers and diegetically in extended familiarity with characters. Almost every long-term viewer I have spoken with has stressed one or both of these aspects as an integral part of soap pleasure. The historical timing of soaps' incredible popularity, which exploded in the postwar years as America became increasingly geographically mobile and extended families increasingly fragmented, confirms the importance of the stable "family" provided by soap communities. Soaps also function to open lines of communication between viewers. Soap-talk clearly strengthens

Vicky's relationship with her daughters; how much more crucial, then, for workmates or neighbors who may have no other common interests. Early soaps provided a shared community and a neutral field of discussion for housewives isolated in their respective homes and nuclear families; contemporary shows serve a similar function for college students, office workers, NBA and NFL teams, while also providing a forum for communal exploration of divisive social issues. Given soaps' explicit commitment to "socially relevant" story lines, a daily show discussed by so many disparate people and raising issues of AIDS and HIV, racism, homelessness, addiction, the importance of voting and instructions for registration, etc., can have a powerful impact on society. Soaps act out social issues in a space apparently free from consequences, thereby offering low-threat opportunities for discussion of politically charged issues.[8]

While much work remains to be done, recent ethnographic exploration suggests that what might be called a "vulgar Frankfurt" vision of mass audiences as cultural dupes (a vision which Oprah Winfrey, for example, echoes in fearing that soap audiences are unable to separate reality and fiction) is much too simple. My own analyses of the contents of the bags of letters sent in to every soap, and conversations with soap fans, suggest a much more active involvement with the processes of fiction making.

The following paraphrases of *AMC* fan letters attest to the confidence of these viewers that their voices will be heard, a confidence that, for me at least, is one of the most compelling arguments in favor of the serial genre.[9] Letters harangue the show's producers, suggesting that they get the wheels rolling and give the devoted and very disappointed fans what they want. In reference to the recently split soap couple Travis and Erica, for example, a writer asks producers how, after watching these two on the monitors (this fan is clearly aware of the monitor installed in executive offices, allowing Big Brother to spy on rehearsals) and observing their "chemistry," they can persist in splitting the couple.

Fans also complain about the predictability of certain characters, as in a two-page, single-spaced, typed letter concerning Palmer Cortlandt (who has a fascinating predilection for keeping young female relatives all to himself) which points out that soap writers first gave him Nina to torment, then Julie, now Melanie, and that viewers are getting bored. This letter writer goes on to imagine the plotting possibilities of Palmer's death; and to reassure producers that if they want the actor to stay on the show, they can always (since they don't seem to mind being predictable) bring him back to life, or give him a long-lost recently discovered twin.

Another letter asks *AMC* writers to please pull the plug on the couple Melanie and David, who give new meaning to "boring"—adding that the Jeremy-Marissa story line is an equally weak link, but then Jeremy's story lines always are. In conclusion, this viewer asks that Jeremy's story receive less airtime—fans are already suffering enough with Melanie and David.

There are also, of course, praises for the show, fans who want to let producers know what they particularly enjoy. Interestingly, most of these letter writers see themselves as spokespeople, explicitly referring to a viewing community—phrases like "my friends and I," "the majority of viewers I know," "I and all my friends who watch" are common. A black writer praises the Cliff/Angie interracial story line, which exposes the problems interracial couples face as well as the racism of the '90s; she cites the approbation of a black viewing community in Atlanta, saying that it discusses the story line and finds it fairly realistic.

Letters often close with thanks for the interest they feel the show takes in their opinions. Almost all those viewers who bother writing to the show (admittedly, a small percentage of the total audience—though the minimum number of letters received, 1,200 per month, is not inconsiderable) are both articulate and sophisticated, demonstrating awareness of the role of production factors in determining story lines. They have a strong stake in articulating opinions about "their" show; many apparently expect to have a voice in its creation. The only correspondence that did not demonstrate some degree of awareness of the production process and the economic factors underlying soap fictions was brief notes requesting autographed pictures.[10]

Unlike many critics, networks are forced to study the ways audiences actually use soaps in daily life—when they tend to be watched, for example, in what contexts, with whom, for how long. Networks also have to acknowledge audience involvement in the interpretation, uses, and even creation of the shows they watch. In the soap world, all aspects (creation, production, advertising, consumption) interact. To produce a profitable show, networks must increase advertising revenues; increasing revenues requires keeping ratings up; high ratings imply satisfied viewers; viewer satisfaction demands a compelling show, which means networks must keep close tabs on what viewers consider compelling.

To facilitate this, networks hold "forums" in which they invite panels of fans to view an upcoming episode and to discuss their reactions to characters and story lines while producers and writers note responses, which are then brought into weekly soap-planning sessions. Each show also has a fan mail department where letters are analyzed quantitatively and qualitatively; producers and writers study a monthly report detailing the number of letters each actor received, the number of letters the show received, an abstract of particular suggestions regarding each story line and couple, and a synopsis of attitudes toward the show. If strong reaction occurs in favor of or opposition to a story line, couple, or character, writers will alter planned scripts accordingly. For example, when actor Billy Husfey left *OLTL* due to contract disputes, ABC received 45,000 letters requesting his return and quickly rehired him, an affirmation of viewer power soon splashed across soap-mag headlines.

Active fandom, which has made viewers increasingly aware of soap opera as constructed text,[11] has influenced form in forcing producers to make the shows themselves increasingly self-conscious about soap as a genre. Many now incorporate generic commentary; for example, one-liners on the absurd coincidences of the genre abound, as when *AMC*'s Erica Kane, hearing about the fabulous fortuity of Natalie-in-the-well being stumbled on by the handsome, wealthy, and available Bachelor #1, Dimitri Marrick, comments, "Well my goodness, lucky Natalie. She falls into a well, she finds the only singles well in America."

An obvious structural example of soap self-parody is *OLTL*'s soap-within-a-soap, "Fraternity Row." In June of 1989, *OLTL*'s soap-star heroine, Megan, began fueling up for the Daisy Awards, in which she competed against stars from such top-rated daytime dramas as "All Or Nothing," "The Wild and the Wealthy," and my personal favorite, "Day After Tomorrow." The Daisy show aired on June 29, the same day as the Daytime Emmy awards. It was hosted by Robin Leach. Many viewers reported the Daisys to be infinitely better produced than the Emmys, with more interesting costumes and choreography and superior entertainment value. As an added bonus, Daisy viewers were treated to behind-the-scenes glimpses of Megan locked in a meat freezer by Spring Skye, her competition for Best Actress.

Lynn Joyrich, who believes that feminists can recuperate television in ways similar to those in which cinema has been legitimated as subject for serious scholarly attention, argues that

> [f]ilm melodrama has been able to call attention to the contradictions in our class and gender system through its use of formal conventions which stand as ironic commentaries on otherwise conventional narratives. By reading TV melodramas against the grain and providing our own ironic commentaries, feminist criticisms may continue to bring out the contradictions of the TV age. . . . Such work might then make more apparent the sites of stress and contradiction in postmodern culture, its construction and deconstruction of the terms of gender and consumption, so that the boundaries thus drawn may be stretched in new directions. (147)

Joyrich rightly calls for critics to provide ironic commentaries on televisual texts; however, most critics of soap opera ignore the fact that such arguments have informal parallels among both audiences and producers, who are now very much aware of soaps' reputation for social relevance[12] and of its potential for irony or parody; shows already provide their *own* commentaries. Soaps take their responsibility for dealing with sites of social stress and contradiction very seriously. In addition to humorous self-reflexivity, most interact extratextually with contemporary news, current events, and urgent social issues, as discussed earlier. Many of these episodes included hot line numbers flashed on-screen during the show, or public service announcements like the one running before *AMC* in February 1992, featuring the show's teen members (a black teen, Terrence, was beaten into a coma by racists) urging talk, not violence, in settling racial issues.

Of course, soap opera's social responsibility and self-ironizing commentary do not mean that the form has become the only self-conscious, nonideological text going. Far from it. It is interesting, for example, that "over-the-top" or intentionally parodied soap characters are generally either wealthy, powerful, and snobbish, or lower-class buffoons. The middle classes—which networks still perceive as their primary audience—are generally treated "straight." And soaps' reprehensibly few minority characters invariably receive kid-glove treatment, their story lines handled with a desperate seriousness that underlines the urgent need to incorporate more varied perspectives on all races across the media.

Also, despite soap producers' very real interest in viewer opinion and viewers' very active role in choosing how to use texts in their daily lives, it is important to emphasize that however much audiences may influence a particular text, control over the production agenda remains firmly in the hands of the networks, producers, and advertisers. ABC production executives have told me, for example, that while networks do monitor audience response and opinions carefully, strong negative response to a story line does not necessarily alter it. If viewers are engaged enough to respond angrily, they're engaged enough to keep watching. Only when *no* response comes in will axes definitely fall. So, again, the relation between soap texts and soap audiences is a double-edged one. While soap opera does seem to be one of the few mass cultural forms where viewers feel at least some degree of power over the fictions they consume—a confidence that producers insistently (though how sincerely remains open to question) support—the kind of power they wield is a highly mediated one. By investigating ways in which networks respond to audience desire, and working to expand them, we encourage a more actively hegemonic mass-cultural production.

Conclusion

> Look, it's up to you. Can you accept the status quo for a while longer, or should we just end things right now?

In the past ten years Tania Modleski, Robert Allen, Sandy Flitterman-Lewis, and others have reclaimed the previously denigrated soap opera as a viable and valuable narrative form. Two factors enabled this relative legitimization: feminist recuperation of condemned "women's fiction" and (in a move politically influenced by feminist rewriting of the canon) institutionalization of mass culture within the academy. Modleski cites Horace Newcomb, who suggests that daytime drama's televisual and narrative conventions "represent in some ways the furthest advance of T.V. art" (87). Soap focuses on interiors, personal relations, small moments; its narrative space is far better suited to the small screen so intimately inserted into our private lives than are, say, adventure series.

Modleski proposes a focus on exactly those qualities that make the genre an alternative pleasure directed at women (87). Discussing soaps' fantasy-fulfilling function, she explains that

> it is important to recognize that soap opera allays real anxieties, satisfies real needs and desires, even while it may distort them. The fantasy of community is not only a real desire (as opposed to the "false" ones mass culture is always accused of trumping up), it is a salutary one. As feminists, we have a responsibility to devise ways of meeting these needs that are more creative, honest, and interesting than the ones mass culture has supplied. Otherwise, the search for tomorrow threatens to go on, endlessly. (108–09)

Her approach here speaks for the compelling Marxist/feminist modification of the Frankfurt School's cultural imperialism. She not only insists on the valuable qualities of the existing form but asserts our power to change and improve it.

I would like, though, to revise the "we" with responsibility to transform televisual texts. Power lies in the hands, not just of feminist academics, but of audiences themselves: the nonworking women often perceived as the typical soap audience as well as the large numbers of professional women, adolescents, unemployed, people of color (20%), and men (30%) who form its actual audience. Because of its serial production process, enormously high rate of output, and vast audiences, soap opera is of necessity collaboratively created, incorporating ideas from many different sources. Monitoring—and at least partially responding to—audience desire is a crucial part of production. This is not just network hype: changing demographics led directly to increases in minority characters and inscription of issues like drug addiction, interracial couples, and homosexuality long before these became hot tickets at Hollywood box offices. In a mediated, negotiated way, then, soaps provide a space for audience interaction with the production process.

The deep interpenetration of fictional themes and everyday lives that has marked serial fiction as a genre from Dickens's time to the present also makes soap opera a powerful forum for exposure and debate of social and political questions; serial history inscribes a narrative of the absence, elision, stereotypical inclusion, and gradual visibility of populations marginalized by race, class, gender, and sexual preference. Thematically, soaps act out historical moments in the political economy of sex, race, and class roles within cultural production.

Of course, showing a popular black character as victim of sex and race discrimination in the workplace does not affect civil rights legislation; neither does showing that an abortion is, for many reasons, the best possible choice for a character mean that the Supreme Court will uphold reproductive rights. But soap opera's multiple perspectives on highly charged issues makes the form capable of providing that first step toward increased tolerance of Others: a forum for public discussion of the issues involved. Generic televisual codes, which refuse the subject/object positioning structuring classic Hollywood cinematography by constructing the viewer as simultaneously voyeur and participant, possessor of knowledge and investigator, increase soaps' potential for exposing all sides of any issue.

There is another way in which soaps represent Newcomb's "furthest advance of T.V. art." The narrative of serial development over the past 150 years—taking on new themes, characters, messages, even media in response to the demands and available technologies of successive ages—provides important lessons about cultural adjustments to changing material conditions. The obvious parallel to be drawn between serial narrative economies and ecologies and environmental ones is that serials teach a relentless consumerism that can never be satisfied. That is not, however, the parallel I am suggesting. There is another story told by serial development: a story of limits, reusability, recycling. Serial fictions—and, interestingly enough in view of our present environmental predicament, contemporary soap operas most of all—are in some ways the most "honest" of texts, in that they make no secret of the paucity of plots, character types, and situations available to them. Soaps ask: What if we were to have the same plots, only a few of them, at our disposal forever? What if the number and type of characters were limited? What if, admitting this, we made no attempt to hide the fact? Could we make narrative strange, could we make it new, could we bear to keep watching forever? Soaps say yes. Nothing is lost, nothing is wasted, all returns—that is one of its messages.

However, there is a flip side to serial recycling. Like "real-life" history, soap history is subject to rewriting at the hands of those in power. Characters are killed off arbitrarily as a consequence of contract disputes; an actor leaves the show, and his or her character—who has been a mainstay for years—suddenly mutates to a different appearance and personality; characters written out years earlier inexplicably return. Perhaps the most widely publicized (but certainly not the most sensational) of these soap revisions is the *Dallas* dream, by which a year's worth of television events were retrospectively relegated to the status of a single night of Pam Ewing's REMs.

Are producers betraying their obligation to viewers by careless recycling of worn-out plots and resuscitation of characters long abandoned to the garbage-barges of television history, even if this comes at the cost of a "forgetting" of soap history that is of crucial importance to long-term viewers? Or is it exactly this recycling that puts soap at the forefront of mass-cultural production, as one of the first forms to parallel material and cultural recycling by admitting the existence of limits (of plot, character configurations, identities) and the cultural relativity of "truth"? Do viewers actually enjoy the narrative ecology of soap opera, taking pleasure in its cyclical revisions of what has always already occurred?

As usual, Erica Kane will have the last word. Her most recent seduction—an attempt to recycle a previously trashed romance with Jackson Montgomery—takes place under the auspices of Pine Valley's campaign to block the aptly named "Mar View" landfill. Learning that Jackson is on the anti-landfill committee, Erica suddenly realizes how deeply she cares about our planet. As they work together on a fundraising campaign, she articulates her seduction of Jack through an impassioned defense of environmentalism (her rhetoric is so convincing that it eventually sweeps Erica herself away on its green tide and she becomes an authentic, and effective, social activist, but that's another story). Leaning toward Jack, Erica stares into his eyes and breathes, "[T]he solution is so simple . . . and absolutely life-affirming, you know what I mean? Because most people feel that they are so small and insignificant. But the truth is that every one of us has the ability, within us, together, we have it in us to absolutely change the world." While speaking, Erica becomes increasingly passionate. She has convinced herself: she *can* rekindle her relationship with Jack; she *can* stop the landfill from destroying Pine Valley. The two goals become fused. Showing us how serial recycling intersects with both narrative ecology and the narrative of twentieth-century ecology, Erica makes environmentalism sexy.

And what's more, she is right. If Erica Kane, over-the-top soap seductress, can convincingly explain the importance of the environment not only to Jack but to sixty million Americans—and if, more importantly, mass concern with the environment can spur the ABC writing team to incorporate green story lines (however cynical their motivation) that impel more mass concern as audiences discuss the show—surely this means that we, not just "viewers" but participants in cultural production, can acquire still more of a voice. Surely this means we *can* change things.

Notes

1. Unless otherwise noted, this and all subsequent offset quotations are selected from episodes of *All My Children* aired 1991–1992.
2. While work on genre is ongoing across the media, the most innovative developments have occurred with respect to film and television studies.
3. These and all subsequent offset quotations are selected from recent *All My Children* scripts.
4. Discussing early soaps, James Thurber coined the term "wheelchair syndrome" to denote the alarming predilection of soap men to become crippled, paralyzed, blinded; symbolic castrations that "excused" the threatening strength and centrality of women on these shows—and maybe avenged the women who had been forced to work on them?

5. Hence Marcia Kinder's suggestion that the "open-ended, slow paced, multi-climaxed" soap form is "in tune with patterns of female sexuality" (qtd. in Modleski 98)—though I think it is important to move beyond essentialist explanations of serial narrative appeal, especially given the fact that the soap audience is now 30% male.

6. Classes for new or would-be soap stars teach the "freeze" technique, among other soap-specific skills.

7. Spoken by David Canary (who plays twin brothers Adam and Stuart Chandler on *AMC*) when accepting *Soap Digest*'s Outstanding Lead Actor award, 1/10/92.

8. This function was unwittingly acknowledged by the press coverage of the Anita Hill/Clarence Thomas case: repeatedly, and derogatorily, labeled a "soap opera," the case did in fact serve the discursive function of actual soaps, making issues of race and sexual harassment the focus of nationwide debate. Unfortunately, the "hearings" were not a space free from consequences.

9. Many thanks to the head of the viewer mail department, who volunteered to waylay a number of letters (after quantitative and qualitative analysis by the department) and forward them to me.

10. To determine letter writers' awareness of *AMC* as constructed text, I looked for references to the distinction between the actor and the character he/she portrays; the importance of actors' contract negotiations, soap opera conventions, and competition with other soaps in determining story lines; and awareness of viewer power—as rulers of the ratings—over *AMC* writers and producers.

11. One of the most interesting activities of fandom is the intertextual game of following both a show and the numerous media sources, and using knowledge of actor hirings, firings, contract disputes, ratings, etc., to predict plot moves within the soap itself.

12. Or what were initially know as "Agnes Nixon stories"; Nixon created the groundbreaking ABC shows *All My Children* and *One Life to Live.*

Works Cited

Allen, Robert C. "Bursting Bubbles: 'Soap Opera,' Audiences, and the Limits of Genre." *Remote Control: Television, Audiences, and Cultural Power.* Ed. Ellen Seiter et al. London and New York: Routledge, 1989. 44–54.

Brooks, Peter. *The Melodramatic Imagination.* New York: Columbia UP, 1985.

Ellis, John. *Visible Fictions.* London and Boston: Routledge and Kegan Paul, 1982.

Feuer, Jane. "Narrative Form in American Network Television." *High Theory/Low Culture: Analysing Popular Television and Film.* Ed. Colin MacCabe. Manchester: Manchester UP, 1986. 101–13.

Fiske, John. "Moments of Television: Neither the Text, Nor the Audience." *Remote Control: Television, Audiences, and Cultural Power.* Ed. Ellen Seiter et al. London and New York: Routledge, 1989. 56–78.

Joyrich, Lynn. "All that Television Allows: TV Melodrama, Postmodernism, and Consumer Culture." *Camera Obscura* 16: 129–54.

Kaplan, E. Ann. *Rocking Around the Clock.* New York: Methuen, 1987.

Modleski, Tania. *Loving With a Vengeance: Mass-Produced Fantasies for Women.* New York: Methuen, 1982.

Pond, Steve. "Shades of Change." *US* 28 May 1990: 20–26.

Silverman, Kaja. *The Subject of Semiotics.* New York and Oxford: Oxford UP, 1983.

Timberg, Bernard. "The Rhetoric of the Camera in Television Soap Opera." *Television: The Critical View.* Ed. Horace Newcomb. New York: Oxford UP, 1987. 164–78.

Todorov, Tzvetan. *Genres in Discourse.* Trans. Catherine Porter. 1978. Cambridge: Cambridge UP, 1990.

SOCIAL THEORY

A BIBLIOGRAPHIC SERIES

The series includes bibliographies on the work of individual social theorists and topical bibliographies in social theory.

Bibliographies on **HABERMAS, DERRIDA, FOUCAULT, LACAN, BLOCH, ADORNO, LUKACS, BENJAMIN, BAKHTIN, ARENDT, KRISTEVA, HEIDEGGER, IRIGARAY, CIXOUS, LYOTARD, BAUDRILLARD, GRAMSCI,** Deconstructionism and Feminist social theory.

$15/ea. bibliography
$45/prepaid subscription/4 bibliographies/ea. year

REFERENCE AND RESEARCH SERVICES
511 LINCOLN STREET
SANTA CRUZ, CA 95060 USA

Please urge your university library to add these bibliographies to the reference collection.

The *Homme Fatal*, the Phallic Father, and the New Man

Margaret Cohen

> "You know a dame with a rod is like a guy with a knitting needle."
>
> —a gangster from *Out of the Past*

Mutatis Mutandis

The femme fatale, the phallic mother, and the new woman: we know this trinity from a now-classic body of feminist analysis on classic film noir. I rescript its gender in my title because I am interested in the transformation of classic noir's gendered division of investigation visible in the most recent neo-noir. Multiple thrillers of the past few years transport us to the seamy side of big cities by night, to follow a disjunctive narrative unfolded in shadowy sequences filled with strangely distorting camera angles, where an observer, often a detective, delves into how life really is beneath the veil of the nuclear family and uncovers social deviance confounding sexuality and criminality into one. Striking, however, is

© 1993 by *Cultural Critique*. 0882-4371 (Winter 1992–93). All rights reserved.

the fact that the distinction between investigating "eye" and investigated object no longer breaks down across clear gender lines.

In such films as *Blue Steel, Internal Affairs,* and *Sea of Love,* a male investigator no longer tracks a femme fatale across a gender divide. Rather male and/or female investigators uncover the object of their investigation as criminally and sexually deviant men. Thus, in *Sea of Love* a cynical, alcoholic detective (Al Pacino) is on the track of a seeming femme fatale (Ellen Barkin), whom he suspects of using personals ads to lure men to their death. He discovers, however, that she is instead an innocent victim whose madly jealous ex-husband is knocking off all the men she tries to meet to rebuild her life. In Kathryn Bigelow's *Blue Steel,* the opposition of investigator to criminal sexuality along a gender divide dissolves in an even more explicit way. A hardened, divorced, bourbon-drinking male detective, Nick Mann, is on the trail of a psychopathic killer, and his investigation is focused in part on a female rookie cop, Megan Turner (Jamie Lee Curtis), with whom this killer is obsessed. Turner has been dating a man who, while he seems to be a sensitive, Jewish commodities trader on Wall Street, is by night a psychopath and goes off on a killing spree when he sees Turner kill a robber her first night on the job. Mann and Turner come to share the burden of the investigation, and when the killer gets Mann after the latter and Turner have had sex in her apartment, she must finish the killer off herself.

The breakdown of film noir's gendered division of investigation extends to recent thrillers bathing in noirish ambiance. In discussing *The Grifters* (1990), Pauline Kael draws attention to the modification it works on classic noir of most interest to me: "[F]ilm noir is enriched by two competing femmes fatales" (128). But two femme fatales are not better than one: such doubling empties the femme fatale of her authority by evincing confusion as to what traits she should display. And in many of these films, the femme fatale is replaced by dangerous men, sexually magnetic or/and deviant. In *Bad Influence,* a young yuppie man discovers the mysteries of Los Angeles by night with the help of a dark handsome man of ambiguous sexuality whom the yuppie must eventually kill. *Silence of the Lambs* portrays two deadly men, one a psychopathic psychoanalyst-cannibal, and the other a psychopathic transvestite who skins his women victims because he fantasizes that he may one day change sexes (would this be into some new kind of femme fatale?). The investigation is once more carried out by a woman rather than a man, or rather by a young, rookie, female FBI agent, Clarice Starling (Jodie Foster), both spurred on and misled by a hardened, non-emotive, male FBI bureaucrat (Scott Glenn). The investigation reveals to Starling social deviance where criminality and *masculine* sexuality turn out to be one and the same. In addition, it opens her eyes to the creepiness of masculine sexuality more generally, even in its ideologically acceptable forms.

What contemporary social anxieties are at stake in the recent breakdown of classic noir's gendered division of investigation (the breakdown, I should stress, is very recent; as *Body Heat* illustrates, ten years ago the femme fatale was alive and well)? I will focus here on an example of the trend that does not serve up this breakdown as fragmentary remains. Rather, Mike Figgis's *Internal Affairs* (1990) provides a larger-than-life alternative to the femme fatale in what we might call an *homme fatal:* the corrupt cop, Dennis Peck, played by Richard Gere. A figurative lady killer and literal man killer, Peck both embodies the Law (as cop) and transgresses it (as gangster), both belongs to a domestic setting (as father) and is a sexualized object of desire. Most importantly, he makes no difference between intimacy and work. (The choice of Gere as actor is significant in this respect, for Gere has a history of playing male objects of desire, and, specifically, those who use their sexuality as a business tool; in *American Gigolo,* he plays a masculine version of another traditional female sex-object role: the high-class call girl.)

Feminist analysis of classic noir has suggested the femme fatale as a phantasm produced when psychic conflict intersects with contradictions on the collective social plane. Ann Kaplan well sums up the tangled psychosocial nexus that the femme fatale is understood to mediate throughout discussions of the genre: "The film noir as exemplified by *Double Indemnity* stresses precisely the ordering of sexuality and patriarchal right, the containment of sexual drives with patriarchy as Symbolic Order. Thus there is a sense in which film noir could be seen to close off the ideological contradictions of patriarchy" (4). Sylvia Harvey locates the social component to this nexus in precise historical terms. Remarking that the film noir was first put into place during and immediately following the Second World War, she observes that in it

> the normal representation of women as the founders of families undergoes an interesting displacement. For it is the strange and compelling absence of "normal" family relations in these films that hints at important shifts in the position of women in American society. Among these changes must be listed the temporary but widespread introduction of women into the American labor force during World War II, and the changing economic and ideological function of the family that parallels the changing structure and goals of an increasingly monopolistic economy. (25)

When Linda Williams discusses the generically mixed *Mildred Pierce,* she adduces an additional historically specific social factor to which classic noir responds. If Bert Pierce is "passive and inactive," it might not be only because he is a wartime slacker but also "as the result of a discouraging Depression economy" (25).

How might such arguments be updated *mutatis mutandis* to the femme fatale's younger brother? Rather well, I propose—the homme fatal crystallizes contemporary social anxieties around material and ideological threats to a traditional gendered division of labor, and particularly around the figure of the new man.[1] If the homme fatal is the new man run amok, can his psychological appeal also be designated by regendering feminist analysis of classic noir? What would it mean to posit the psychic lure of the homme fatal as residing in the phantasm of the phallic *father?*

The Homme Fatal

Dark, deserted streets, the headlights of a police car. From the opening sequence, *Internal Affairs* places us in the nighttime world that film noir uses to reveal the underbelly of ideological life. The investigating "eye" would seem to be star cop Dennis Peck and the object of investigation an innocuous one-family house. Leading us through its dark corridors, Peck takes us to a bedroom where we discover a tiny TV playing cartoons, a stash of drugs, and (a discovery that will take on great resonance in light of the film's subsequent narrative) a sleeping couple.

But soon Peck himself will be under investigation by young, ambitious, yuppie Hispanic cop Raymond Avila. Avila sees Peck as his big break in the Bureau of Internal Affairs. Peck has the reputation for being the best cop on the force, and his superiors resist the investigation: if he bends the rules a little, he brings in a lot. Our initial impressions of Peck confirm this reading of his character. When, in the opening drug bust, one of his young buddies flies off the handle and shoots a fleeing suspect (dressed in a Yale sweatshirt), Peck helps him out of a tight spot. Placing a knife in the dead man's hand, Peck arranges things so the killing will appear justified. Yes, a little playing with the rules, but it seems to come from Peck's fatherly concern for the younger, inexperienced cops with whom he works.[2] Our first glimpse of Peck's private life, too, supports this view of him as someone who bends the rules from the bigness of his heart. He would seem to be a concerned biological father to several different families at once. He handsomely supports his multiple ex-wives, whom we watch wandering in and out of his kitchen chatting with his current wife, everyone the best of friends. He would seem to take a hand in raising his family, as well. We first discover him at home giving breakfast to his kids while his wife sleeps in. Even in this scene, Peck seems affected with the urge to father everyone around. Sitting around the Cap'n Crunch are not only two of Peck's kids from different marriages, but a young buddy, Van Stretch, whose wife has kicked him out and who is already in trouble with Avila and the Bureau of Internal Affairs.

But the more we find out about Peck's own internal affairs, the more we realize this impression is only a veneer. Peck turns out to be at the center of concentric circles of corruption, including such activities as drug smuggling, prostitution, and mercenary murder. While this certainly makes him a gangster, his business methods align him in important ways with classic film noir's femme fatale. Peck has no qualms about employing his sex appeal, making no distinction between, on the one hand, affective relations and sex, and, on the other, money—between the sphere of intimacy and business. Binding everyone he works with to him through affective blackmail, his blackmail takes one of two forms, depending on the sex of the individual involved. If it is a woman, he has sex with her, and if it is a young cop, he plays a physically affectionate father (there is a marked homo-erotic undertone to these relations: Peck is both physically affectionate and physically brutal with his young buddies in a visibly sensuous way). Morality or a concern for others turns out to be entirely absent from Peck's economy; we gradually discover the mainspring of Peck's actions to be only a furthering of his own affairs. Thus, that Peck's young buddy Van Stretch is married to Penny Stretch, his money-laundress (a function which, significantly, would have been allotted to a male character in classic film noir), makes no difference to Peck. He fathers the one and has sex with the other, and when Van Stretch, under pressure from Avila and the Bureau of Internal Affairs, shows signs of "rolling over" on him, Peck has no qualms about wiping Van Stretch out. In a chilling sequence, Peck has sex with Penny Stretch while she is on the phone pleading with her distraught husband not to do anything about Peck until the couple have seen each other; we then see Peck and Van Stretch on the beat together, and watch Peck having Van Stretch shot. The assassin fails to kill Van Stretch completely and Peck is forced to finish off the job himself. Cradling Van Stretch's head in what seems to be an embrace, he strangles him, then returns to cradling him at the moment that the other cops appear on the scene (Fig. 1).

For Peck, the home and the Force, women and men, wives, mothers, buddies, and children merge into one undifferentiated arena where he can pursue the aggrandizement of his power.[3] This collapse of intimacy, notably sex, into business is a crucial operating strategy of the femme fatale. As Walter Neff from *Double Indemnity* puts it, reflecting retrospectively on the disaster that such a collapse effects: "I didn't get the woman and I didn't get the money." In his experience of this collapse as disaster, Neff is not alone; if the fusion of intimacy and business is one of the femme fatale's favorite operating strategies, it is also the key to the social menace that she portends. Repeatedly, classic noir teaches that a collapse of the distinction between business and intimacy is disastrous, ending in the destruction of everyone involved.

If Peck carries on business like the femme fatale, his unsound methods amount to a similar zero profit by the end. He

Fig. 1. The *Homme Fatal* at work. From *Internal Affairs*. Photo courtesy Paramount Pictures.

ultimately destroys everyone he seemed to be helping, not only his surrogate sons, the young cops he is fathering, but also the women that he sleeps with and his own family. And for Peck, as for the femme fatale, the punishment fits the crime. Peck transgresses the boundaries separating private intimacy from the public sphere; his home is, appropriately, destroyed by the eruption of the public force, the Law, into it. He tells us in his last monologue: "I went to my house. My wife was crying, my children were crying; they were being interrogated by my buddies . . . I knew them all; I can never go back there." In comparing Peck's methods of operating to those of the femme fatale, we must eventually answer the question of whether they are agents of similar ideological work. But I leave this question open until we have understood the social specificity of the homme fatal in more detail.

It may be objected to my comparison of Peck and the femme fatale that their transgressions in relation to the home differ on one important point. While the femme fatale is rarely a mother, the homme fatal is an undeniable father, indeed almost too much a father, as he gets in trouble in part because he does not confine his fathering to a nuclear family. But I wonder if Peck's fatherhood in fact separates him from the femme fatale as much as it at first might seem. For while the femme fatale is hardly ever linked to maternity (when she does come into contact with children, either her husband's or her own, it is an unmitigated disaster), critics have compared her to a very special kind of mother. The "dame with a rod" packs the lure/menace of the phallic mother, and this likeness has been used to explain the masculine psychological imperative operative in the habitual bad end to her career. Thus, Lucy Fischer writes of Elsa Bannister in Orson Welles's *Lady from Shanghai:* "[W]hile Elsa's characterization as femme fatale has been read by some critics as a demystification of woman's traditional idealization, it can be read as the flip side of the coin—with dread standing in for overvaluation" (44). And I wonder whether the devastation sparked off by the homme fatal's deviance could derive from the fact that he, too, pushes some sort of psychological panic button? How would the concept of the phallic mother travel across gender lines? Might the menace of Dennis Peck have to do with what I am tempted to call the phallic *father?*

The Phallic Father

The phallic father: at first glance, the concept seems an empty tautology.[4] The father is father, after all, by virtue of possessing the phallus; he is always by definition a phallic father.[5] But the phallus is also, as Lacan has taught us, the privileged signifier of lack. No one can have the "real" phallus, not the father exercising the phallic function any more than the mother; as Slavoj Žižek puts it, "[T]he phallic signifier is, so to speak, an index of its own impossibility" (157). We enter here the domain of Lacan's analysis of the inseparable link between the phallus and the Symbolic order: "The phallus is the privileged signifier of that mark in which the role of the logos is joined with the advent of desire," Lacan writes ("Signification" 287). And "this moment of cut is haunted by the form of a bloody scrap—the pound of flesh that life pays in order to turn it into the signifier of the signifiers, which it is impossible to restore, as such, to the imaginary body; it is the lost phallus of the embalmed Osiris" ("Direction" 265).

The lost phallus of the embalmed Osiris: might not Lacan give us here a paternal equivalent to "that very special penis," the maternal phallus, that the fetishist keeps alive?[6] This would be a phantasm which is tautological in an affectively significant fashion, evincing, to echo Žižek on Lacan's concept of the *sinthomme,* a paradoxical attempt to preserve "the impossible junction of enjoyment with the signifier"—impossible because "the signifier dismembers the body . . . evacuates enjoyment from the body" (Žižek 123). What if someone fantasized that the father had both the symbolic phallus and also the imaginary phallus on whose very loss symbolic authority depends? Translated into the sphere of family romance, might this be the phantasm of a father who took his pleasure from the very subjects which his Law simultaneously placed out of his reach?

What would be the consequences for someone who imagined the existence of the phallic father? Above all, it seems to me, a troubled relation to the Law. The phallic economy is not one where two phalluses are better than one, at least not these particular two phalluses. Lacan has suggested that the only good father is a dead father; in his myth for the origin of society out of the primal horde, Freud, too, posits the radical separation of the living "violent and jealous father who keeps all the females for himself" from the dead father whose killing is necessary to the creation of the Law (141). It thus seems highly disturbing to try to sustain that the father could be simultaneously dead and alive. To do this, one would have to posit the existence of a father who enforces the Law while he does not conform to its dictates, a situation which would seem to undermine the authority of the Law itself. The phallic father, that is, threatens the moment of Oedipal passage and, along with it, threatens such founding social notions as the incest taboo, as well as a division of sexuality according to a binary gender divide. One could imagine that a subject suffering under the delusion of the phallic father would get stuck in this moment, if not regress to a state even before.

That the phallic father undermines the authority of the Law is certainly suggested by the character in *Internal Affairs,* who misrecognizes himself as phallic father. Peck has substituted his own will to power for the Law whose uniform he wears. The genesis of Peck's misrecognition is not hard to surmise. Peck is the son, who, when acceding to the position of the Law, discovers that the emperor has no body beneath the police blue. The gap between imaginary and symbolic phalluses opens up, and it is a gap to whose temptations Peck succumbs. Peck mistakes the symbolic nature of the Law for proof that the Law is "empty," a fiction that he can use to his own ends. Peck, that is, tries to have it both ways: he wants to use the "empty" power of the Law and believes that it does not exist. But the fact that the emperor has no body is not only an index of the Law's symbolic power; it is the precondition for this power. No imaginary phallus, no matter what size, can fill out the empty blue. Having fundamentally misrecognized the Law by thinking that it is "only" imaginary, Peck runs the risk that his own misrecognition will come back to haunt him. And it does, in the form of agents internal to the Law, Avila and Wallace, his female partner, its emissaries from the Bureau of Internal Affairs.

But disabusing Peck of the fiction that he is the phallic father would seem to be more than all in a day's work for the male half of the investigating team. Avila, the private eye, becomes unusually obsessed with destroying Peck to the exclusion, as his wife complains, of everything else and, notably, genital, heterosexual sex. The phallic father, that is, is a figure highly compelling to Avila, and for Avila, too, it threatens the power of the Law, although in a somewhat different way. Peck observes of Avila's highly invested, panicked response to him: "You're such a baby, Raymond, buttons all over you. I push the buttons." What are these buttons but the undomesticated, pre-Oedipal drives, as the figure of the phallic father causes Avila to regress? The aggressive character of Avila's erotic response is common in a situation of regression.

If Avila's invested response to the phallic father leads us to surmise that this figure plunges him deep into the zone of infantile fantasy, the closing sequence of *Internal Affairs* supports this suspicion. In it, Figgis films the death of Peck as Avila's version of the primal scene. We watch Avila spying on Peck at night, peering through half-open blinds into a bedroom where Peck and a woman are on a bed. But Avila peers not into his parents' bedroom but rather his own, and he does not discover a father and a mother having sex. Rather, Avila sees Peck, wounded in the foot, sitting on his bed and asking a favor from Avila's kneeling wife,

Kathleen. (At this point, we have repeatedly watched Avila shadow Peck with voyeuristic fascination, as Avila pursues the suspicion [we never are quite sure of the extent of its validity] that Peck is seducing Kathleen—the woman, that is, whom Avila neglected in order to pursue Peck.)

The primal scene fantasized with the phallic father is, then, somewhat different from the Oedipal primal scene, confirming that the phallic father threatens to undo the incest taboo. With horror and fascination, Avila watches the phallic father try to take back "all the females for himself," threatening the generational prohibition associated with the Oedipus complex by settling on the woman belonging to the son. (Once formulating the notion of Peck as phallic father, I am better able to explain the strange queasiness that I experience in watching the scene where Peck talks business with a buddy while his little daughter, not his wife, plays at serving tea while he holds her and strokes her hair.) Ultimately unable to stand this seduction, Avila bursts into the room to destroy the phallic father, and we notice the strange content of the moment which catalyzes his response. Avila enters on the scene not when Peck lays a hand on Kathleen, but rather when Peck asks Kathleen to help him take off his boot, thereby exposing his bleeding foot. Which, we wonder, does Avila fear/hope for more: that he will discover castration as an imaginary spectacle or that Peck will be shown to possess the missing "bloody scrap," the lost paternal Thing? Žižek writes, if "some objects (those which are too close to the traumatic Thing) . . . intrude into the fantasy-space, the effect is extremely disturbing and disgusting" (120). "It's just a buddy movie about two guys shooting each other in the crotch," a scientist countered heatedly when I presented this film at an interdisciplinary forum, suggesting that *Internal Affairs* might be the vehicle of phantasmic ideological work. While, in fact, we never do know where Avila shoots Peck (at one moment in the remainder of the scene, after Avila has shot Peck a first time, Peck comments, "That's very good Raymond. You think he was aiming for my foot?"), the scientist unerringly gave voice to the menace that Avila feels. In shooting the phallic father, Avila transforms him back into a dead father, the position the father is supposed to hold.

But if the mistake leading Peck to misrecognize himself as

the phallic father is clear, why should Avila collude in this misrecognition? Why does he not simply have Peck arrested when he got the hard goods on his financial dealings, or, indeed, at multiple points along the way? Why does everything culminate in a traumatic showdown in Avila's bedroom, much to the horror of Avila's wife? Which is a way of asking, what psychic pressure might lead Avila to collude in Peck's mistake? An answer to this question takes us to the psychosocial imperative to which such a phantasmic projection responds.

The Panic Button

When commenting on how the signifier evacuates enjoyment, Žižek remarks: "[T]his 'evacuation' . . . is never fully accomplished; scattered around the desert of the symbolic Other, there are always some leftovers, oases of enjoyment, so-called 'erogenous zones', fragments still penetrated with enjoyment" (123). His remark recalls Avila's buttons, leading us to ask whether these oases of enjoyment are always experienced as pleasurable. Might they not, in certain conditions, be terrifying, particularly if the subject felt the order of the phallus to be under attack? And is not Avila precisely in such a position, as, more specifically, he repeatedly confronts social situations where the ideological link joining symbolic and imaginary phalluses threatens to come undone?

Both at home and in his job, Avila experiences a situation destabilizing a traditional gendered division of labor. At home, he confronts a wife who is a yuppie with a job at The New Museum for Contemporary Art. Out to accumulate power in the art world, she does so with an active use of sexualized intimacy that Avila considers uncomfortably close to their own. Significantly, when we first see the Avilas at home, it is in a sequence where Avila expresses anxiety about this behavior. "Did you have to kiss everyone at the party?" Avila asks his wife." "It's my job," Kathleen answers, to which Avila responds, "It's *my* job." The ambiguous referent of that "it" whose dominion Avila wants to claim can be resolved in several ways. Most obviously, it refers to sexualized intimacy, which, Avila asserts, belongs not at work but rather in the home (although Avila's choice here of the word "job," while witty, challenges the very distinction between job and home he invokes it to support). In addition, however, the referent "it" can refer to aggressive sexual behavior: the fact that Kathleen is doing the kissing, as well as kissing everyone. In this case, Avila expresses discomfort with her aggressive display of sexuality, a form of behavior traditionally coded as masculine, and certainly not the province of the good wife. In either case, Avila makes his discomfort with his wife's passage into traditionally unfeminine forms of behavior apparent, or, we might also put it, with the fact that she accumulates and employs phallic power, without herself being a man. That Avila is uncomfortable about women accumulating phallic power is intensified by the fact that he confronts such a situation at work. It is, after all, as he tells his wife in this scene, a woman cop who is assigned the role of initiating him into the Law. And while it takes him a few more scenes to realize that this woman is a lesbian, the realization cannot but further threaten to unmoor the symbolic from the imaginary phallus. It reveals the agent responsible for initiating him into the Law as a figure whose own sexuality obviously cannot be confined within a phallic economy.

Both on the job and at home, then, Avila finds himself in a situation where the collusion of symbolic and imaginary phalluses threatens to come undone. And might not such a situation hit the panic button of a subject with an investment in this collusion, particularly when he crosses into zones of illicit pleasure that the Law has not managed to erode? Avila's first confrontation with Peck, when he goes to question Peck about Van Stretch's drug problem, is revealing in this context; it occurs one hot night in a seedy section of Los Angeles. Avila finds Peck hanging out at a sleazy fast food stand with some prostitutes who serve as his "snitches." One more experience, that is, where the collusion between symbolic and imaginary phalluses becomes confused, as the man in the uniform of the Law haunts, to ambiguous purpose, the "oases of enjoyment" in the urban desert. When Peck proceeds to offer one of these prostitutes to Avila, Peck underlines his imbrication in illicit pleasure despite the fact that he is dressed as the Law. Is it coincidence that Peck chooses a prostitute who blurs notions of sexual identity? A beautiful woman with a markedly androgynous cast to her features, she leaves a strong impression on Avila, later making her way into his hallucinations.

In such a world, where the coupling of imaginary and symbolic phalluses is under attack from all directions, might not a subject with an investment in this coupling become distressed? And might not the phallic father be a phantasmic response to this distress, both a projection of it and an attempt to ward it off? The phallic father would be then an apotropaic construction, as Freud put it in his essay on the Medusa's head. To refuse the gap yawning between symbolic and imaginary phalluses, what better response than to hold up an example where both occur at once? But in hallucinating the paradoxical notion of the phallic father (in human existence at least, many of the gods enjoy precisely this privilege), Avila hits upon a construct which runs counter to its goal. As we have seen, he enters into a phantasm problematizing the Oedipal passage, and thereby the phallic function, more thoroughly than the situation of panic which led him to it. That the phallic father, Peck, breaks the Law which he seems to embody is not coincidental but rather a consequence of the notion of the phallic father itself.

American Yuppies and the Gendered Division of Labor

The phallic father, I have suggested, is the response of a subject (with an investment in the coupling of symbolic and imaginary phalluses) to a situation where this coupling threatens to come undone. And *Internal Affairs* is noteworthy in grounding this phantasm in recent social transformations, specifically those which transgress a traditional gendered division of labor. I would like to pass, that is, from a psychological description of the panic that *Internal Affairs* represents to the social factors that it implicates in this panic. Already we can see one factor: Avila's projection is catalyzed by his problems dealing with women's entrance into positions of professional power, a consequence of feminist efforts in the past twenty years.

Internal Affairs isolates an additional factor contributing to the uncoupling of symbolic and imaginary phalluses, and hence to Avila's distress: the rise of a form of labor that does not fit neatly into liberal-capitalist society's dominant ideological mapping of social space. I refer here to the growth of the service sector of the economy, which is touched on repeatedly in the film. If Avila and Kathleen both work, Avila displays aggression over the fact that Kathleen's work involves a sexualized intimacy which Avila understands as suitable to the home. Her work, that is to say, involves that quintessential yuppie activity of networking, and Kathleen and Avila's dress, lifestyle, and social interaction code them as yuppies throughout the film (how they manage to support this yuppie lifestyle on the double salaries of a cop and a gallery-like museum assistant the film neglects to explain). That it is Kathleen's networking which Avila finds so anxiety provoking is significant. Networking is one of the most celebrated examples of yuppie activity which deviates from the paradigm of production that provides the founding ideological model for the extraction of surplus value in liberal-capitalist society; insider trading exemplifies this activity in more nefarious form. In light of Avila's identification with yuppie culture, his job of spying, a convention of film noir, also resonates as an instance of yuppie labor ("You're talking about one of the most *productive* guys on the force," Peck's superiors comment when protecting Peck from Avila's shadowing eye).

Engaging in work that violates the dominant liberal-capitalist paradigm for labor, yuppies are not alone. Yuppies occupy the upper end of the service sector that constitutes an increasingly large part of the US economy. And, his superiors' opinion notwithstanding, Peck's socially deviant business shares important features with the nonproductive labor epitomized by the yuppies. Like Katherine's networking, and Avila's spying, Peck's illicit affairs constitute a form of activity where the distinction between public business and private life threatens to collapse.[7] The collapse between public and private threatened by Peck and the yuppie couple must be differentiated from the collapse portended by the operating strategies of the femme fatale. But first, it is necessary to explain in more detail how the rise of the service industry produces psychological panic—what threat does it pose to the collusion of imaginary and symbolic phalluses?

Yuppie labor and, more generally, the service industry of which it is the tip prove something of a conundrum for the ideological categories that liberal-capitalist society has long used to map social space. From its inception, this society has drawn a founding ideological divide between private, intimate, affective activities, notably of reproduction, carried on in the home, and rational activities of visibly economic content, notably of production, performed in a publicly accessible sphere. The divide is, more generally, part of a system of sliding binary oppositions constitutive of liberal-capitalist ideology. Among these oppositions, we might single out politics/the private; outside/inside; the *res publica*/the home; male space/female space; men's work/women's work; production/reproduction; production/consumption; business/leisure; reason/sentiment; publicity/privacy; publicity/intimacy. The terms of these pairs are not coherent; it is imperative to the complexities of ideological work that a tremendous amount of slippage among them obtains. In particular, as is visible from even the pairs that I have chosen, there is slippage around the problem of how to categorize economic production.[8] For the economic realm is understood in bourgeois-liberal society as at once public and private, a category that cannot be comfortably placed on either side of liberal society's binary structuring of its ideological space. While not overtly concerned with politics, the realm of economic activity does not belong only to private life, and this becomes all the more the case once capitalism moves out of its early phase where the production of surplus value is often pursued on the level of the individual household. Historically, the ideological solution has been to break the economic up into two sides, those aspects of it carried out in public spaces (production) and those activities carried out in the home (reproduction/consumption). And both pairs of oppositions (production/reproduction and production/consumption) relay along the ideological network via the gendered division of labor.

But the recent rise of the service sector, a form of public production resembling activities previously mapped as occurring in the home, puts pressure on this solution. In threatening the ideological distinctions between the business of the public sphere and the affairs of the home, the service industry threatens other binary oppositions in the network as well. Above all, it threatens the distinction between production and reproduction and hence the distinction between men's and women's work. If the latter were to collapse, what would become of the Oedipal scenario, at least as we know it? In what imaginary constellation would the symbolic phallus finds its support? We return to *Internal Affairs* and to the unmooring of the collusion between symbolic and imaginary phalluses so frightening to Avila. Not only the rise of women to positions of social power, I am suggesting, but the rise of the form of labor that he in fact practices intensifies Avila's panic. Indeed, it is Peck's words "you selfish yuppie" that push Avila's buttons one last time: "You do not feel because you do not have kids. You don't know what it's like. You'd go around the world for them. Everything changes when you have kids . . . you selfish yuppie." Peck's closing words trigger Raymond into shooting Peck rather than turning him over to the Law.

Isolating the service industry's pressure on liberal ideology as a key social contradiction mediated by the phantasm of the homme fatal, we also arrive at an important difference in the ideological pressures at issue in classic and contemporary film noirs. For while classic film noir responds to the entrance of women into the work force during the Depression and the Second World War, it also mediates the principal economic transformation putting pressure on liberal-capitalist ideology during the era of classic noir: the rise of the consumer economy. In this rise, the production/consumption opposition is the principal liberal binary opposition under attack—although once one pair in the tangled mess is invoked, the slippery remainder tumbles in as well. And it is this opposition above all that the femme fatale's unsound business methods threaten to erode. Who can forget Phyllis Dietrichson and Walter Neff's illicit meeting among the commodities in the supermarket or Cora's home restaurant revenues soaring as a result of her crime?[9]

Whose Work (the New Man)?

If liberal-capitalist ideology has historically consolidated itself through struggle around a network of allied binary oppositions, the binary opposition of gender difference is a founding pair in this network, and hence also a crucial site of dispute. Historically specific to *Internal Affairs* is, however, the fact that femininity is not the terrain where the battle lines are drawn. This contrasts not only with classic film noir but also with a long history of the strategic use of femininity by liberal-capitalist ideology. Thus, the bourgeoisie first consolidated its values against the aristocracy by representing aristocratic society in feminine-effeminate terms.

That masculinity is the site of contemporary ideological struggle is a point that Sasha Torres makes in an insightful reading of *thirtysomething*. "The unanswered and persistent question for the show," Torres asserts, "is masculinity, not femininity. *thirtysomething* knows, or at least thinks it knows, where women's 'place,' spatially and affectively, is; what it doesn't know is where men fit in" (92). Torres links the show's difficulty representing men to "the stresses placed on the nuclear family by the sexual division of labor and by the gendered construction of sexuality" (99). I would agree completely, only emphasizing that the problem derives from the specific articulation of this division as a result of changing gender roles and the changing nature of the relations of production in the past ten years.

Commenting on the way in which *thirtysomething* deals with the stresses placed on the nuclear family, Torres reads it as functioning according to the long-standing strategies of melodrama: using representations of private life to stabilize and dispel social anxieties. As a cinematic form, melodrama has traditionally been addressed to a feminine audience, but Torres underlines a crucial transformation that *thirtysomething* works on the usual Hollywood gendering of the genre; *thirtysomething* is a melodrama that "wants to harness melodrama's therapeutic potential through its insistently insular concern with family, but chafes against the form's association with femininity" (90). It is "therapeutic, male domestic melodrama," Torres argues, suggesting a "structure of disavowal" which enables the show to perform its ideological work (102). This brings me to a final question: in whose service is the ideological work of *Internal Affairs?* Discussing *Mildred Pierce,* Williams opposes the melodramatic "day-time woman's filmic discourse of Mildred's own story" to "the noir male discourse of a dangerous nocturnal underworld" (13). If Torres reads *thirtysomething* as appealing to an audience that is not usually the primary addressee of melodrama, can the same be said of the most recent neo-noir?

To discern *Internal Affairs*'s ideological agenda, it is helpful to recall the contemporary social resonances of the types of masculinity embodied by both Avila and Peck. Although Avila confronts women accumulating traditionally coded male power, he is trying, at least when we first meet him, to respond to these challenges in politically correct fashion. Avila is the enlightened new man, accepting women as equals, both in the home and on the job. But this acceptance is tenuous; we have discussed Avila's difficulty coming to terms with his wife's job from the moment they are in their home. Throughout the film, we will watch his marriage disintegrate around the problem of balancing job and home life, as Avila regresses into "old man" macho jealousy. So, too, while he initially accepts his lesbian partner as his superior, he will quickly take control. The turning point in their relation occurs when Avila takes the Law into his own hands, trying to get Van Stretch to roll over in return for going free. "You are not authorized to make this deal. It's a violation even to offer it," Wallace tells Avila. "I am the senior partner." Further, she tries to call Raymond on what is really at issue in his obsessional interest in Peck: "Well I've got another idea. Why don't you and Dennis Peck both pull 'em out and I'll decide which one's bigger?" Far from retracting his deal, however, Avila reacts by assertively taking control. In doing so, he imitates Peck's misrecognition, taking his own possession of the imaginary phallus for authority to decide on the content of the symbolic Law. And the spectacle of the imaginary phallus rampant would seem to cow even Wallace, whose lesbianism initially could be construed as allowing her to escape a phallocentric economy. We will subsequently see Avila snap at Wallace, who is shown sitting in secretarial position, typing, when he enters the office steamed up after a fight with Peck: "I want you to run complete backgrounds on him—mortgages, loans, bank checks, everything." "What do you say?" Wallace counters, but Avila is already out of the room, and it will take him a moment to return with "please."

Avila is, then, a new man trying but failing to make the grade. And Peck displays traits of the new man as well. While Avila is dealing with the problems of accepting women at work, Peck is dealing with the new man's new access to the domestic sphere. Torres observes, "[M]asculinity in the 80's is being modified in the direction of allowing men easier access to their parental yearnings" (101). From his initial appearance to his closing soliloquy, Peck repeatedly gives voice to these yearnings. But Peck is a new man where the new man is revealed as a ruse of masculine control. When unleashed in the domestic sphere as well as on the job, Peck shows himself to have the power to absorb all the power, leaving no place for women at all (nor for men, for that matter).

For what ideology does the new man become a ruse of masculine control? Let me rephrase this question by recalling Jacques Alain-Miller's distinction between imaginary and symbolic identification as Žižek uses it to discuss representation as a vehicle of ideological work. "To put it simply," Žižek writes of a rather complicated distinction that merits lengthier discussion than I can give it here, "imaginary identification is identification with the image in which we appear likeable to ourselves, with the image representing 'what we would like to be', and symbolic identification, identification with the very place *from where* we are being observed, *from where* we look at ourselves so that we appear to ourselves likeable, worthy of love" (105). And, Žižek continues, "the question to ask is: *for whom* is the subject enacting this role? Which *gaze* is considered when the subject identifies himself with a certain image?" (106). Turning to the realm of ideological products, Žižek uses this distinction to emphasize the importance of isolating not only what a particular representation imitates but also the viewpoint which it solicits, invokes. Thus, discussing Chaplin, and, in particular, Eisenstein on Chaplin's "vicious, sadistic, humiliating attitude towards children," Žižek observes: "The question to ask here, however, is from which point must we look at children so that they appear to us as objects of teasing and mocking, not gentle creatures needing protection?" (107). Žižek proposes that "the answer, of course, is *the gaze of children themselves*" (107). Or, again, "at the opposite extreme, we find the Dickensian admiration of the 'good common people', the imaginary identification with their poor but happy, close, unspoiled world, free of the cruel struggle for power and money. But (and therein lies the falsity of Dickens) from where is the Dickensian gaze peering at the 'good common people' so that they appear likeable; from where if not from the point of view of the corrupted world of power and money" (107). Following in the line of Žižek's analysis, let me rephrase my previous question about the homme fatal: not for whom does the new man turned homme fatal represent "what s/he would like to be"? but rather, *from where* is the new man turned homme fatal being observed? *from what place* do we look at the new man turned homme fatal so that he appears likable and, relatedly, so that we appear likable to ourselves? (Thus, to follow Žižek on Dickens, the corrupted world of power and money likes itself all the better for the existence of the "'good common people.'")

The best answer to this question is that proposed by *Internal Affairs* in the form of the character who devotes his time on screen to the fascinated observation of Peck. Avila cannot tear his eyes from the spectacle of the new man run amok. Watching Peck's monstrous career, the failing new man watches the career of someone who was all too successful in the domestic sphere that the new man is solicited to engage. But Avila discovers that this success, rather than dismantling phallic power, extends it over both the sphere of private intimacy and public life. Peck's career provides Avila with consolation for his own failures. In comparison to the monstrous career of Peck, the failures of the failing new man become innocuous and, paradoxically, confirm Avila as the new man that he failed to be. Displaying his weakness, Avila relinquishes phallic power and hence proves that he is a new man. Peck's career also could solicit the viewpoint of the "old man," who finds consolation for his lack of interest in the new man in the devastation brought about by Peck. Compared to such destruction of the home, the old man's "petty" tyranny in it looks innocuous, although it is harder to imagine the old man as either needing consolation for the shape of his masculine identification or so attuned to the monstrous face that *more* masculine power might display. In both cases, however, neo-noir's homme fatal is not the new man seen from a feminist point of view. Rather, consonant with traditional, "crime-related, film noir masculine concerns" and despite some shifts in gender identification, the ideological addressee of *Internal Affairs* remains primarily masculine (Williams 13).

Transformations in gender roles undeniably provoke panic not only for new and old men but for *all* subjects invested in the collusion between imaginary and symbolic phalluses. Nonetheless, the pleasures of *Internal Affairs* should not blind us to the fact that consolation for the new man's failure is a bit premature. In terms of the pleasures of *Internal Affairs,* there is, that is to say, a crucial residue in the panic of ideological projection. Of what does it consist? With this question we arrive at one of the most vexing issues confronting contemporary efforts to position representation at the nexus of psychic, social (i.e., economic-political-ideological), and aesthetic modes of production. Is the residue to be located in the plurality of subject positions resisting the dominant ideology, non-nuclear families, lesbian authority, men gaining access to their paternal yearnings, even if these subject positions are destroyed or shown to be fatal at the end? Is the residue to be located in the way *Internal Affairs* gives access to transgressive and dangerous desires, be they the zones of criminal pleasure uncovered in the trajectory of the *homme fatal* or the narrative pleasures of the trajectory itself? Is it to be located in the fact that the film not only projects an ideological phantasm but brings the social conditions responsible for its production to view? Is it found in those moments when the film disrupts the dominant codes of Hollywood cinema; moments such as the Godardian sequence when Avila, spying on Peck having lunch with his wife, has his view continually obstructed by passing traffic in a scene that unsutures the naturalized relation of sight to sound, drawing attention to the fundamental hermeneutical uncertainty of the image?

All these questions are a way of asking whether the residue is to be theorized according to a dialectics of resistance and cooptation—the dialectics of the good, the bad, and the beautiful. While modes of analyses authorized by identity politics valorize representation for elaborating "good" political alternatives to dominant ideology(ies), generally on the level of content, the avant-garde wing of the Marxist tradition has long valorized the resistant power inherent in a work's aesthetic dimension, whether the aesthetic at issue is the beauty of high art or the pleasure of low. But, as too much critical writing of the later 1980s demonstrates, this evaluation will remain purely speculative unless we recognize that it fundamentally shifts the methodological terrain from critical analysis of ideological production to sociological investigation of its reception.

My own inclination would be not to move toward sociology

but rather to remain at that uncomfortable nexus of the psychic, social, and aesthetic where so much remains unexplored. In particular, if I have tried to isolate material shifts resulting in the psychosocial phantasm of the *homme fatal,* I am left wondering about the historicity of that type of phantasm itself. While Althusser declared that ideology, like the unconscious, is eternal, this declaration in no way negates the historicity of ideological forms. Specifically, the constructs of the *homme fatal* and the *femme fatale* situate us under the historically local regime of what Walter Benjamin termed the phantasmagoria.[10] Revising Marxist theory with the help of psychoanalysis in his work on Paris in the later 1930s, Benjamin employed the term to identify the phantasmic projections of subject positions within liberal-capitalist society, which, far from empty reflection, bring the obscured and overdetermined workings of material processes to collective view. Benjamin turned to psychoanalysis because the paradigm was itself a product of the society he used it to explain; it thus satisfied the dialectical imperative that he understood to regulate the relation of theory to its object. He was particularly fascinated with the privilege that cinematic media enjoyed in making the phantasmagorias of liberal-capitalist society palpable from this society's inception (the literal spectacle coining the term with such a powerful figurative afterlife was a popular magic lantern show in the wake of the French Revolution).[11] The *homme fatal* of *Internal Affairs* is a latecomer in a long parade.

Why should the phantasmagoria be a dominant form of liberal-capitalist ideological projection? How does one characterize its phenomenal appeal in historically specific terms; why should it have a privileged relation to cinematic spectacle? This questions, too, the historicity of that residue which is so difficult to name. Finally, then, it is to look for one more missing piece in Benjamin's overarching but never completed project to write the history of the senses under capitalism.

Notes

1. Anxieties concerning AIDS also contribute to the recent crystallization of masculine sexuality as the locus of deviance. I suspect, however, that this anxiety

is a catalyzing but not a sufficient factor in such crystallization. For we must ask what social changes are powerful enough to transform a long-standing tradition tying the nexus of sexuality and disease to encounters between married men and dangerous single women. In nineteenth-century urban bourgeois culture, the unmarried woman, usually the prostitute, bore the responsibility for venereal disease, irrespective of how the actual transmission of syphilis and gonorrhea occurred. On this subject, see, for example, Alain Corbin's *Les Filles de noce.* Significantly, this strategy is employed in one of the first Hollywood films concerned with AIDS to come to general notice, *Fatal Attraction,* with the important modification that the single woman is an ambitious career woman, the nexus sex-disease hence being linked to the deformations that feminism works on women.

2. Mike Davis discusses the history of brutality associated with the Los Angeles police force in *City of Quartz: Excavating the Future in Los Angeles.*

3. The refusal to differentiate between intimacy, notably sex, and business distinguishes Peck from the Hollywood Mafia Don, to whom he bears some resemblance. While the Hollywood Don presses the family into his service, he never confuses business and sex (the fathers of Mafia families, unlike the brothers and sons, have learned how to control their sexuality and relegate it to that most private space of their home). The Mafia Don's tools of manipulation are the indisputably masculine weapons of authority, physical strength, and wealth, not the traditionally feminized weapons of affect-sex. Consequently, far from threatening the integrity of the home, the Don reinforces it, ordering it with the authority of his patriarchal eye. He is a father who obeys and supports the symbolic order, as contrasted to the phallic father, whom I will shortly discuss. In this respect, the Don embodies the dominant liberal-capitalist phantasm of an ordering paternal power that the nuclear family too often in reality fails to display.

4. Elizabeth Stewart has drawn my attention to Harold Bloom's use of this expression in "Freud: Frontier Concepts, Jewishness and Interpretation." Discussing "'A Child Is Being Beaten,'" Bloom makes the following highly suggestive remarks:

> The unconscious sense of guilt, we are informed, is punishment both for the genital relation fantasized to the father, and for the regressive substitutes that avoidance of the relation breeds in us, women and men alike. Freud, perhaps on one level, intended the literal or *phallic father* [my emphasis] as the fantasy object, but the mythological profoundity of the notion of the drive sets such literalism apart. (146)

5. The phallic father should not be confused with the Don Juan figure, who, as Julia Kristeva observes, remains entirely a son. Kristeva asks, "[W]ould the seducer not be the phallus itself?" But she goes on to qualify her statement: "Isn't Don Juan, in the last instance, entirely possessed by someone himself? By the Father? . . . What does the seducer want? The father's punishment" (191–92).

6. Jean-Joseph Goux uses Lacan's reading of the Osiris myth to raise the "historical and epistemological" question of "the difference between the ancient and the modern, even postmodern, phallus" (45). Goux summarizes the myth, retold by Plutarch, as follows:

> The god Osiris is killed by Typhon who dismembers his corpse into pieces which he then scatters in all directions. Osiris's faithful com-

> panion, Isis, patiently retrieves the fourteen pieces to reassemble and reanimate them. However, there is one part of Osiris's body which she cannot find: his virile member. To replace this missing piece which is irretrievably lost, Isis erects a simulacrum which she orders everyone to honor. (41)

7. In this context, it is also significant that one of Peck's big jobs in the film (and ultimately the site of his downfall) is to arrange the killing of the parents of one Steven Arocos. Arocos wants his parents dead because they are business partners who, he feels, do not do business in a modern way. By this he means that they do not engage in unscrupulous, speculative exchange where circulating capital has come unmoored from its support in production: "They don't get it. They won't borrow, they won't diversify, they have no idea how to conduct business today," Arocos tells Peck. "They're just not bad enough," his wife adds, as Peck caresses her under the table.

8. On this subject, see, for example, Poovey.

9. I am indebted to Daniel Klotz for this observation, as well as for multiple insightful comments on *Internal Affairs.*

10. On Benjamin's understanding of the phantasmagoria, see my *Profane Illumination.*

11. On the historical origins of the phantasmagoria, see Castle.

Works Cited

American Gigolo. Dir. Paul Schrader. Paramount, 1980.

Bad Influence. Dir. Curtis Hanson. Epic, 1990.

Bloom, Harold. "Freud: Frontier Concepts, Jewishness and Interpretation." *American Imago* 48.1 (1991): 135–52.

Blue Steel. Dir. Kathryn Bigelow. Vestron/Lightning Pictures, 1990.

Castle, Terry. "Phantasmagoria: Spectral Technology and the Metaphorics of Modern Reverie." *Critical Inquiry* 15.1 (1988): 26–61.

Cohen, Margaret. *Profane Illumination: Walter Benjamin and the Paris of Surrealist Revolution.* Berkeley: U of California P, 1993.

Corbin, Alain. *Les Filles de noce: misère sexuelle et prostitution: 19e et 20e siècles.* Paris: Aubier Montaigne, 1978.

Davis, Mike. *City of Quartz: Excavating the Future in Los Angeles.* London: Verso, 1990.

Double Indemnity. Dir. Billy Wilder. Paramount, 1944.

Fatal Attraction. Dir. Adrian Lyne. Paramount, 1987.

Fischer, Lucy. *Film Tradition and Woman's Cinema.* Princeton: Princeton UP, 1989.

Freud, Sigmund. *Totem and Taboo.* London: Hogarth, 1955. Vol. 13 of *The Standard Edition of the Complete Works of Sigmund Freud.* 24 vols. 1953–66.

Goux, Jean-Joseph. "The Phallus: Masculine Identity and the 'Exchange of Women.'" *differences* 4.1 (1992): 22–34.

Harvey, Sylvia. "Woman's Place: the Absent Family of Film Noir." *Women in Film Noir.* Ed. E. Ann Kaplan. London: British Film Institute, 1978.

Internal Affairs. Dir. Mike Figgis. Paramount, 1990.

Kael, Pauline. Review of *The Grifters. New Yorker* 19 Nov. 1990: 122–33.

Kaplan, E. Ann. Introduction. *Women in Film Noir.* Ed. E. Ann Kaplan. London: British Film Institute, 1978. 1–5.
Kristeva, Julia. *Histoires d'amour.* Paris: Denoël, 1983.
Lacan, Jacques. "Direction of Treatment and Principles of Its Power." *Ecrits: A Selection.* Trans. Alan Sheridan. New York: Norton, 1977. 226–80.
———. "The Signification of the Phallus." *Ecrits: A Selection.* Trans. Alan Sheridan. New York: Norton, 1977. 86–102.
Poovey, Mary. *Uneven Developments: The Ideological Work of Gender in Mid-Victorian England.* Chicago: U of Chicago P, 1988.
Sea of Love. Dir. Harold Becker. Universal, 1989.
Silence of the Lambs. Dir. Jonathan Demme. Orion, 1991.
Torres, Sasha. "Melodrama, Masculinity, and the Family: *thirtysomething* as Therapy." *Camera Obscura* 19 (1989): 88–106.
Williams, Linda. "Feminist Film Theory: *Mildred Pierce* and the Second World War." *Female Spectators: Looking at Film and Television.* Ed. Deidre Pribram. London: Verso, 1988. 12–30.
Žižek, Slavoj. *The Sublime Object of Ideology.* London: Verso, 1989.

Nonstop to Nowhere City? Changes in the Symbolization, Perception, and Semiotics of the City in the Literature of Modernity

Klaus R. Scherpe

A loss of regularity, validity, and authority has the effect of promoting a vague, all-encompassing mode of expression. By the same token, a loss of orientation on the part of the triumvirate of genres (the epic, lyric poetry, and drama) relative to its position in classical poetics meant that the sense of the epic, the lyric, and the dramatic had to be newly secured in terms of language. For Goethe and Friedrich Schlegel, the leading voices of this debate in Germany, this meant the need for a new anchoring in language, an anchoring that would function as the "natural form" of literature, as archetype and anthropological standard.

Perhaps this most poetical reminiscence has implications for our understanding of the language change that is taking hold of the thematics of the city and its literary representation. One no longer speaks of the *city* but of the *urban* in the widest sense possible. The new discipline of urban studies not only provides us with terminology based on architectural history such as the Radi-

© 1993 by *Cultural Critique*. 0882-4371 (Winter 1992–93). All rights reserved.

ant City or the Garden City, but speaks in one breath, inspired by aesthetics, of megalopolis and futureoplis, of collage city and suburbia, of the global village, *ville panique,* or even necropolis.

There is no doubt as to what is being lost here or what is, nonrepresentationally, creating a new space for itself. The "organized complexity" of the modern city, as still claimed by Jane Jacobs (434), seems to have disintegrated without being able to establish a new "inherent nature" (428) of the urban. (Unless one takes the permanent state of construction in the cities and the rapid change in meaning in their nomenclature to be their new "actuality.")

Recognition that there are consequences associated with the problem of the narratability of the city in literature is hardly a recent development. Volker Klotz coined the apt term "the narrated city" for the nineteenth-century novel. The fate of this term in the literature of modernity is, however, questionable. At first glance, it would seem useful, like Klotz (in *Die erzählte Stadt*),[1] to analyze the thematics of the city as they relate to the form of the novel, in a certain respect as a fulfillment of the Hegelian dictum of the "prosaic character of relations" (Hegel 2: 4). What this immediately casts into doubt as far as the literature of modernity is concerned is, however, the epic ego, the "subject of epic form"; here neither the hero of the novel nor the narrator are able to introduce successfully a symbolic order into the domain of the city that could establish parameters for the course of the novel's narrative, regulating it and channeling it into a central meaning. Contrary to all the attempts of literary critics to impose this kind of order upon Alfred Döblin's montage novel, *Berlin Alexanderplatz,* which is the most prominent of its kind in Germany, and to rescue it as a *Bildungsroman,* Walter Benjamin reads Franz Biberkopf's story ironically as the "*Education sentimental* of a con" and views his ascension into the "heaven of novel characters" with skepticism (3: 236). From this point onward representation itself, the narration of the city in terms of traditional models of representation, is at issue. What I mean by traditional models of representation is meaning-filled *symbolization,* regulated *perception,* and interpretive "reading" of the "*text of the city.*"[2]

In the following analysis, the acts of demontage and modernization that are enacted upon the "edifice of the epic work" of the city (to use Döblin's formulation) will be investigated. In place of a subject-centered epic form, comprehensive delocalization, decentering, and decomposition of the city as a "locus of signs" become the ruling narrative principle in the literature of modernity. In Roland Barthes's text on Japan, *Empire of Signs,* this reflection is taken to the point of completely abandoning the western cultural realm, whose emphasis on the centrality of a rational truth he equates with the logocentric fixation of the city center. Japan's capital, Tokyo, with its "central emptiness," "pure contingence," and "visual experience" fascinates Barthes. He sees all of these factors as being stronger than any "manipulative" and identity-hungry inquiry into the domain of the city: "In this manner, we are told, the system of the imaginary is spread circularly, by detours and returns the length of an empty subject" (32).

It is precisely at this point, however—while reading Barthes's *Empire of Signs* or while marveling at Jean Baudrillard's aesthetic transfiguration of an "immaterial" New York[3]—that one must ask whether these texts are not indeed a resurrection under a different sign of a long-familiar urban visionaryism and exoticism. Although these images of the city avoid the moralizing symbolism that is common to representations of the city (where the city acts as the *negative* center of meaning for the subjective passions of vice, of the body, of power and possession: the city as whore, jungle, slaughterhouse, etc.), their purely aesthetic obsession with the signifier breeds a new mystification of urban complexity.

We must therefore ask whether the recurring question of the "narratability of the city" in modernity has been or can be addressed in a different way than by sidestepping to an "other" realm. That is, can the problem of narrating the city be solved in a way other than an aesthetic projection of the city as a play of signifiers? (This question has gained particular urgency, since it is now becoming obvious that a signifying surface that has been dispossessed of all social meaning is all the more effective in acting as the aesthetic locus of action or locus of play of individual desires.) It is hardly a recent phenomenon that a utopia that provides orientation or acts as a topographic ideal seems to have vanished on the horizon. Dream City as the locus of fantastic desire and Collage City as the manifestation of an elementary need for orientation must not preclude one another. In Michel

Foucault's work, for example, the impulses of the topographic and of the imaginary are not necessarily diametrically opposed to one another. What he calls "heterotopia" (24)—"space of illusion" that challenges the notion of the confinement of human life to "real space"—indeed affirms and supports social self-identification. "Other" spaces—the spaces that are off-limits, the bordello, the cemetery, all of the "colonies of the unconscious" and the points of conversion of unregulated fears and wishes—are understood by Foucault in terms of their compensatory function (27). The city is thus seen both as the site of the construction of social relationships and as the scene of imaginary interaction with these relationships.

Henri Lefèbvre speaks of a "differential space" (160) in his astonishing book *La révolution urbaine.* His focus is upon the "virtual object" (164) of the urban as based upon an underlying "logic of form" (169). Lefèbvre outlines a narrative of socio-logy of the city, in which he brings the realms of the homogeneous ("isotopies") and the realms of the other ("heterotopies") into association with one another. As a third dimension he maintains what he calls "u-topia," refraining from inscribing it with a specific meaning: its locus is "everywhere and nowhere" (171–74). Doesn't the labyrinth, one might ask, at least have straight lines and exact contours? Does the often-evoked feverishness and dynamism of the city induce nothing other than intoxication and hallucinations? Doesn't such a notion also rest on a desire—as in Brecht's *Lesebuch für Stadtebewohner*—to find life's necessities even in obscured traces: chances for survival that can be achieved only through discernibility, as a mode of self-identification for the city dweller? Of course the so-called "urban eccentrics" are the narrative terrain of the city that fascinates above all others: Balzac's powerful bankruptcies and his awe-inspiring fascination with money, Baudelaire's neurotic intensity with respect to the painful and the pleasurable in city life, and the orgiastic and apocalyptic urban experience of the German expressionists. However, there is another type of narrative of the city, found in these and other examples, that draws its conclusions from the notion of the loss of epic sovereignty and does so in such a way that the social conditions and the imaginary potential of the experience of the city work together to enact a structure upon the city.

The moment we are confronted with images of the city, we as a matter of course are dealing with aesthetic patterns. The narrative components of these images have a structuring function, where the specific mode of perception, the rhetoric of symbolic expression, and the "reading of signs" in the text of the city provide the contours. Seen in this way, some texts of the nineteenth century are *modern* in their "structural consciousness." Here I am speaking not only of Poe's "The Man of the Crowd" with its sociological scrutiny of the "tides of population" (135) or Heine's rhetorical evocation of an unmediated impression of the metropolis (see Brüggemann), but also of Friedrich Engels's description of London at the beginning of his study of "The Condition of the Working-Class in England." Before he begins to explain the "swarming" of the "big city" in terms of a class profile, Engels unfolds the following scene:

> A town, such as London, where a man may wander for hours together without reaching the beginning of the end, without meeting the slightest hint which could lead to the inference that there is open country within reach, is a strange thing. This colossal centralisation, this heaping together of two and a half millions of human beings at one point, has multiplied the power of this two and a half millions a hundredfold; has raised London to the commercial capital of the world, created the giant docks and assembled the thousand vessels that continually cover the Thames. I know nothing more imposing than the view which the Thames offers during the ascent from the sea to London Bridge. The masses of buildings, the wharves on both sides, especially from Woolrich upwards, the countless ships along both shores, crowding ever closer and closer together, until, at last, only a narrow passage remains in the middle of the river, a passage through which hundreds of steamers shoot by one another; all this is so vast, so impressive, that a man cannot collect himself, but is lost in the marvel of England's greatness before he sets foot on English soil. (4: 329)

At the basis of "sociology of space" (Georg Simmel) is the concept of a spatial immobility that is generated by the gaze of the viewer. In Engels's text, spatial immobility is generated *against* the (commercial) dynamics that are the focus of his analysis. His perceptual model still uses the fixed point of "colossal centralisation" as capitalism's symbolic mode of expression. Or, to quote Simmel, "one can define a sociological meaningfulness of a fixation in space by the symbolic expression of the 'pivotal point': the spatial fixedness of an object of interest gives rise to specific forms of relations that cluster around it" (256). Engels himself knows the whirlpool of perception that generates the "impressive" phenomena that are part of the city. In "The Condition of the Working-Class in England," the view of the city from afar and the distancing gaze associated with its perception act to construct a rational cartography. This cartography, in turn, shapes the transition to social conceptuality. But even this cognitive mapping is dominated by an aesthetic arrangement. The description of the masses of buildings, the shipping lines, and, soon to follow, of traffic gives rise to a "reflected" layout of the city that not only has the effect of leading the viewer toward a critical consciousness, but first awes him with the "marvel of England's greatness." What is "imposing" within the image of the city as Engels portrays it is not only a function of the text's reductionism in reference to the symbolic mode of expression. Nor does it depend upon the perception of the perceived objects or upon the cartographic sobriety of the text. Rather, it is produced through the *structural interplay* of these single elements within the aesthetic impression.

This interplay—which is in essence an integration of social condition and imaginary potential—is given new emphasis in the *fictional* portrayal of the "narrated city." The limitless surprises and "horrible happenings" in the city's bag of tricks, which the city novel (from Balzac, Dickens, and Sue, to Musil, Döblin, and Carlo Emilio Gadda) takes as its point of departure, determine the changes of meaning in the fictional pattern. The famous first paragraph of Robert Musil's *The Man Without Qualities* with its meteorological localization of Vienna ("The isotherms and isotheres were fulfilling their function") and its seemingly dispassionate city geography creates such a strong sense of order that the "horrible happening" of a traffic accident is immediately brought into the dimension of "an event within the proper framework of law and order" (6). Of course, Musil is beginning an account of a great passion. This, however, is subject to the modern flight from determinative qualities—away from "colossal centralisation" and unmistakable local meaningfulness:

> The excessive weight attached to the question of where one is goes back to nomadic times, when people had to be observant about feeding-grounds. It would be interesting to know why, in the matter of a red nose, for instance, one is content with the vague statement that it is red, never asking what particular shade of red it is, although this could be expressed in micro-millimeters, in terms of wave-lengths; whereas, in the case of something so infinitely more complicated, such as a town in which one happens to be, one always wants to know quite exactly what particular town it is. This distracts from more important things.
>
> So no special significance should be attached to the name of the city. Like all big cities, it consisted of irregularity, change, sliding forward, not keeping in step, collision of things and affairs, and fathomless points of silence in between, of paved ways and wilderness, of one great rhythmic throb and the perpetual discord and dislocation of all opposing rhythms, and as a whole resembled a seething, bubbling fluid in a vessel consisting of the solid material of buildings, laws, regulations, and historical traditions. (4)

Musil's structural (and in this way "impersonal") narrative mode is characterized by a precision of detail that is inspired by scientific thought. He responds to the loss of measurable meaningfulness (as concerns the "identity" of the city and the people who live in it) with an excessive exactitude. Musil's description of the city no longer addresses the overburdening of the city by endless streams of traffic, commodities, and information—by employing a symbolic reductiveness or amplification ("jungle," "Babylon"). Nor does he make use of an inflated mode of perception (the intoxication of speed; apocalyptic phantasies), but uses instead a paradigmatic, geometrically ordered perceptual mode. Out of points, lines, and intersections, rhythmic movements and countermovements, a principle of composition is developed—known in the film of the time as "Symphony of a City"[4]—that apprehends the "materiality" of the city discursively: as the "solid materials of buildings, laws, regulations and historical traditions" (Musil 4).

Under the influence of this narrative principle, social identification and aesthetic imagination enter into an impersonal "structural" relationship. Musil's novel shows that the transgression of the boundaries of the modern city, the loss of the once-secured terrain of the "narrated city" (Vienna: even in its name it is already a symbol and yet nameless) must not lead to the disappearance of the narrative act of social and aesthetic identification. On the contrary, the sense of orientation is heightened if the questions of "Where am I?" and "Why am I here?" are no longer answered solely according to the prescribed "feeding ground" of physical and mental nourishment.

Incidentally, there is no doubt that Musil's narrative demystification of the modern city can be read as partisanship for a type of novel that is seldom found in German literature, which generally thematized the country more often than the city and denounced metropolitan literature as "asphalt literature." Similar in this respect is the work of another Viennese, Karl Kraus. Kraus reads the riot act to today's and yesterday's "green" opponents of the city and to the advocates and protectors of a romanticized rural German lifestyle. In January of 1911 he wrote in the journal *Die Fackel:* "I expect from a city in which I am supposed to live, asphalt, street cleaning, house keys, hot-air heating and hot water pipes. Comfort I can provide for myself" (35).

Such a structural interplay of social condition and imaginary potential cannot, of course, be claimed for all city texts in modernity, nor can it be seen as a "unity." Is there an aesthetic symbolization, a mode of perception, and a modern mode of reading in the "text of the city" that can dispense with an underlying attempt to "rescue" the assumption of unity in the "narrated city"? Can the fiction of the city, as influenced by social modernization, still be seen to possess its own unique narrative mode? (By social modernization I mean the predominance of reproductive cultural technologies, our reorientation in time and space through new information technologies and the transmission of reality by media, where real experiences become unrecognizable.) Döblin's "factual phantasies," the solution that incorporates both social content and imaginary potential, must indeed be rethought. This is especially true if the problematics of representing or narrating the city is being subsumed by the self-representation of cities in architecture and advertisement, or is being suppressed by the self-production of the urban as *theatrum mundi,* where the social and the aesthetic seemingly converge unproblematically (in any case failing to question the basis for this newest postmodern urban illusion making) (see Sennett).

Although I do not see historical reconstruction as a panacea, it is helpful to conceive of the now-topical confusion of the urban, experienced both as pleasurable and deadly, in terms of a historical configuration. Maybe before arriving, we will be able to identify way stations on the road to Nowhere City, stopping-places in a narrative configuration that bring to light the problematics of *narrating the city.* I will illustrate this using several textual examples, where the three dimensions of the narrative of the city will be accented in terms of their historical sequence and in terms of a cross-comparison. What are the transformations that underlie the literary *symbolization* of the city, its *perception,* and its objectification as a system of signs in the "*text of the city*"?

The Symbolization of the City

It is, so it seems, a modern notion that the narrative of the city recedes behind the city that narrates itself—the "city as language, as ideology, as the conditioning factor of every thought and word and gesture" (Calvino 185). The arbitrariness of the urban topography cannot, however, be used as a basis for concluding that "imaginations" or symbolic values adhere to its localities. Rather, where the city narrates itself, we must assume that in the context of modernity's constant progression and rapid acceleration, the importance of the symbolic centering of the narrative of the city ("*Notre Dame de Paris,*" "*Der Roland von Berlin,*" "*Statione Termini*") is actually reduced. In the modern con-text, in the "web" of the city (Lefèbvre), the argument for a *moral* accountability of symbolic values in the city narrative (Berlin as the whore of Babylon, the frequent revival and condemnation of a Troy or Carthage, Sodom or Gomorrha) also loses its power to persuade.

Of course, this does not mean that the new functionalism of urban events (Brecht), its "functions in a void" (Ernst Bloch), can manage without totemic fixations. On the contrary, it is far more the case that the rationalization and differentiation of urban social and cultural realms awaken new needs for imaginary wanderings as well as symbolic certainty. In many ways, however, these new needs continue to be the old needs, as can be seen in the use of consistent, archetypal urban patterns. A "dematerialized" city[5] full of elementary symbolizations—the imagining of the city as female body, mother or whore, as apocalyptic inferno, etc.—is repeatedly invoked. Even the new variations upon this consistent mode of symbolization of the city lead back to the old (in German literature: Peter Weiss's early short story *Der Fremde,* Paul Nizon's *Canto,* Ginka Steinwachs's postsurrealistic *marilynparis*).

A different tendency can be observed in texts which insist that a constantly changing, self-renewing imaginary potential be identified with the social. Are such texts able to maintain this relationship of identification *under the conditions imposed by the new technologies of information, reproduction, and multi-media transmission,* which disrupt both unmediated perception and traditional symbolization? The signifying surface of the modern city is pervaded with inscriptions of all kinds, with aurally and visually engaging symbolizations, all demanding recognition. This profusion of signs absorbs and superimposes itself on elementary symbolizations. Ernst Cassirer identifies both the conditions for this change and its implications in his examination of the symbolic content of communication: "Physical reality seems to recede in proportion as man's symbolic activity advances. Instead of dealing with the things themselves man is in a sense constantly conversing with himself. He has so enveloped himself in linguistic forms, in artistic images, in mythical symbols or religious rites that he cannot see or know anything except by the interposition of this artificial medium" (25). In the modern city, the new artificiality of technical media is superimposed on the older forms of acculturation through the "artificial media" of myth, religion, and literature. What Cassirer identifies as symptoms of the withdrawal of a "physical reality" and of a dominant self-referentiality that acts to limit experiences thus becomes the precondition for the narrative of the city. In Döblin's *Berlin Alexanderplatz,* for example, information is dominant over narration. In other words, the "interposition" of "media," and the arsenal of symbols employed by the media, determines what is narrated and what is not. It determines what, as an individual history, is produced as narrative or what becomes dispersed in the montage text of the city. Here, even the "old media" of myth and religion are subjected to the prevailing lifestyle of the workers' district of northeast Berlin. And it is precisely out of what is in many ways a mocking desymbolization of the classical text that a new narrative potential is developed: Döblin arranges the narrative in such a way that Franz Biberkopf encounters himself, in the slums, as Orestes:

> Dimensions of this Franz Biberkopf. He is a match for old heroes. This Franz Biberkopf, formerly a cement-worker, then a furniture-mover, and so on, and now a news vendor, weighs around two hundred pounds. He is strong as a cobra and has again joined an athletic club/ He wears green putties, hobnail boots, and a leather jacket. As far as money is concerned, you won't find a great deal on him, his current income arrives always in small quantities, but just let anyone try to get near him. Is he hounded by things in his past, Ida, and so on, by conscientious scruples, nightmares, restless sleep, tortures, Furies from the days of our great-grandmothers? Nothing doing. Just consider the change in his situation. A criminal, an erstwhile God-accursed man (where did you get that, my child?), Orestes, killed at the altar Clytemnestra, hardly pronounceable that name, eh? Anyhow, she was his own mother. (Which altar do you really mean? Nowadays you could run around a long time looking for a church that's open at night.) I say, times are changed, up and at him, hey terrible brutes, trollops with snakes . . . the Furies dance . . . a mad frenzy, a delusion of the senses, a preparation for the booby hatch. But they don't hound Franz Biberkopf. Let's admit it, here's how . . . he drinks one mug after another at Henschke's or somewhere else. . . . Thus our furniture mover, news vendor, etc., Franz Biberkopf, of Berlin N.E., differs from the famous old Orestes in the end of 1927. Who would not rather be in whose skin? (121)

Döblin's hero makes his way through an endless number of symbolic values. These offer, however, little opportunity for identification. In *Berlin Alexanderplatz,* the old world of symbols becomes incorporated into what Döblin calls the conversation of the city. Not only do fictional characters take part in this conversation, but the narrator and reader become engaged in it as well. Döblin projects a complete iconography of the city and an imposed lifestyle of mobility and alienation upon the protagonist Franz Biberkopf, on his clothing, his gestures, his language. Since the metropolis, which is now only outwardly glamorous, no longer has a symbolic power of its own (glamour has, for one thing, never been of importance in the proletarian social milieu of the *Alexanderplatz*), the city novel can almost automatically cross, combine, and subvert the old and the new worlds of images. What is being constructed here is the city that is anti-illusion; it assembles its symbolic language anew out of diverse urban discourses.

Is it possible, using this particular narrative strategy, to construct an aesthetic opposition to the technocratic design of the city, the city as switchboard and information machine? Wolfgang Koeppen, who in terms of urban thematics is the only classical modern German writer since Döblin, attempts to create a text that resists this tendency. In his short prose piece "New York" (1976), the surplus meanings generated within the "organized complexity" of the most modern of cities seem to shift into what is almost unending resymbolization, inspired by the markets, stores, and night life, that shapes Koeppen's narrative orgy on the subject of Manhattan. The narrator remains the stranger, the voyeur—not mass man, but the man who observes the masses:

> I was not invited. I made do with being an onlooker. I fended for myself. Edgar Allan Poe's Man of the Crowd. Poor poet. They dragged their dragons, their eagles, their lions, griffins, snakes before them. St. Cecilia and St. Anthony swayed in their hands. They wore the Borsalino as a helmet . . . Isaac's sacrifice, strictly according to ritual, in kitchens that do justice to the family. The fun house of pornography and of psychotherapy. Powerful blacks returned to the totem pole, towered above everyone. Pubescent claw-footed frogs of Amazons climbed out of the warm shafts of the subway, secreting slime in the night, climbed up the facades. The image of the toad in the organ of procreation in the Dominican monastery in Colmar. Music from those damned boom boxes. The woods before Macbeth's castle. Only then the well-known skyline, stock market, Treasury, City Hall, St. Patrick's Cathedral, the cantankerous pigeons of Fifth Avenue, the night court, the dead

> of the Mayflower, the dead of the Hessian regiments, the children had become settled, Snow White's Lever House and all of the other skyscrapers among which in 1609 Henry Hudson vanished behind his small sails. Hudson had hardly a chance to tour the city. (250)

Koeppen, the occasional visitor to the US, masters the limitless city by means of a vast number of symbolizations. The metonymic concatenation of symbolizations that he links to the phenomena of the new world of the city is built upon the presupposition that because this marginalia from the history of Western culture has long since lost its power to symbolize, it can therefore be affixed at every turn to the phenomena of the new urban world in a chain of signifiers, from one event to the next. In this narrative strategy, the narrator is the flaneur and voyeur, but only (as he well knows) inasmuch as he is determined by *the conditions of high technology.* The passing impressions of the city are, often indiscriminately, taken from the street or received from the television screen, and are accompanied by an undercurrent of that "damned" stereo music; "Computers registered the woes of millionaires" (Koeppen 251). The primacy of high technology calls into question the city's narrative obligation to refer to the social. Musil, for example, was still able to wrest a social connection from his (nameless) Vienna, and Döblin could still reclaim it from the narrated city Berlin in the city "conversing with itself." The totemism that Koeppen evokes on the signifying surface of the city is, on the other hand, primarily a media spectacle. Koeppen's aesthetic opposition is thus radical indeed, but it leads nowhere. For this reason, the narrator's image as "poor poet" smacks of sentimentality or, closer to Koeppen's self-image, seems somewhat embarrassing.

Can the literary puzzle of demontage and the fascinating distortion of historical reminiscence out of previously guaranteed symbolic languages still give rise to a significant text of the city that possesses some sort of orientation? This question will hardly find an answer in the field of literature alone. Robert Venturi's postmodern city book *Learning from Las Vegas* has a stronger sense of reality than many other city texts. In the billboards of the famous "strip" and in the historicizing phantasy architecture of Las Vegas's motels and casinos, the "primacy of the symbolic" materializes as a commercial strategy. At present, German cities seem to be emulating this strategy in order that the standard clock does not remain the sole symbol on the faceless *Adenauerplatz*.[6]

The Perception of the City

Perception is, after symbolization, the second dimension of the narrative of the city that is at the disposition of writers in modernity. "Unmediated" perception, an "absolute" origin, and "identity" without alienation have for all practical purposes probably never existed (or, at best, existed only in a Rousseau-inspired political philosophy).[7] In nineteenth-century literature, long before the filtration of reality through new media and information systems, a consciousness of "re-perception" (see Fisher), a second or stereoscopic gaze, was common. Here the notion of "untouched reality" gives way to an aesthetic consciousness of a "second nature" and the first indications of an "aesthetics of the anorganic."[8] Nowhere does this consciousness of a broken or layered perception, a perception that is in any case *structurally active,* find as much to illustrate it as in the major city. And it is not only in the case of writers recognized as the literary star witnesses of a literary urban modernism, Baudelaire or Poe, that one finds this attention to and reflection on the "double gaze." This consciousness can sometimes be found in the bourgeois fictions of the German city novel (even acknowledging the comparative scarcity of this consciousness in a national literature hostile to the city). In Theodor Fontane's novel *Stine,* as later in Georg Hermann's *Jetten Gebert,* a window mirror, appropriately called the "spy glass," plays a special role as the optical mediator between the interior, petty-bourgeois realm of action, and the exterior, urban world of the street:

> Outside there was, however, an adjustable window mirror attached to the window. . . . Pauline Pittelkow would sit opposite the mirror, . . . not out of vanity (for she couldn't see herself), but out of simple curiosity and as a pastime. . . . Stine . . . put her hands over Pauline's eyes and said: "Surely you have had enough Pauline. By now you must know what the *Invalidenstrasse* looks like." "You're right, dear. But that's how

> people are; they always like and occupy themselves with the most ridiculous things, and when I look into the mirror and see all of those people and horses in there, then I think, yes, it really is different than to look with your eyes alone. And the street is a bit different too. It seems to me that the mirror makes things smaller, and making things smaller is almost as good as making them more beautiful." (174ff.)

The perception refracted in the window mirror in Fontane's Berlin novel is not yet acting as the foundation for an aesthetic phantasmagoria of a humanity going to ruin in the city. On the contrary, the optical instrument that is the mirror reinforces the jovial humanity of the novel by keeping the outside urban world at a distance. It integrates the outside world as a "picturesque" refraction of an image. Fontane's axiom, "Keep to the old ways as long as you can, and use the new only when you must (*Sämtliche Romane* 270), thus continues to hold for this phenomenon. This mode of perception, which departs from that of the "naked eye," differentiates and perspectivizes the visual material of the city. The implications of this differentiation can be, as in the case of Fontane's novels, a heightening of social characteristics and a strengthening of the sense of orientation. More frequently, however, under this mode of perception, aesthetic consciousness can abandon itself to the new appeal of a perception that focuses upon objects that are ever-mobile, ever-changing, and ever-diffuse. In any case, from now on, with a certain standard of technology becoming part of the equation, a change in reality will primarily be conceived of as a change in the perceptual apparatus. The term "modern" thus no longer means an understanding of the characteristics of the perceived. Instead, "modern" comes to signify a consciousness of the specific character of *production* of perception.

Walter Benjamin writes, for example, in his essay "A Small History of Photography," "The destruction of the aura is the mark of a perception whose sense of the sameness of things has grown to the point where even the singular, the unique, is divested of its uniqueness—by means of its reproduction" (*One-Way* 250). For Benjamin, the photographic medium brings out the fact that images of the city and the narrative fictions that support them are under the dictates of reproduction. This has a twofold consequence for approaches to the problematics of representation and narration; perception is reduced to a meaningful city in miniature or a second approach is taken, which is linked to the modern fact of reproducibility. Under this second option, reproducibility is used as the occasion for an interest in "other" aesthetic arrangements, where a new functionalism, opened up by new techniques of perception (from film to computer simulation), provides the framework.

As far as the images of the city of the 1920s are concerned, it seems as if Benjamin (and to a certain extent Siegfried Kracauer) follows the first scenario, and the artists of the *Bauhaus,* primarily the visually oriented László Moholy-Nagy, the second. Here my remarks on this development must, however, remain brief.[9] Benjamin's nostalgic affinity for flaneurs, from the Parisian Baudelaire to the Berliner Franz Hessel to the Surrealists, is well known, as is his melancholy reflection on the loss of the "aura." It is therefore not surprising that in "The Small History of Photography" he extols Eugène Atget's (hardly exceptional) photographs as precursors to surrealist photography. For Benjamin, Atget initiates the "emancipation of the object from the aura" by minimalizing the urban image and by focusing on detail, as in his reduction of the city to "a lamp-post with a life-buoy bearing the name of the town" (250). Atget liberates, in Benjamin's view, the isolated perceptions of "the missing and the displaced" as literary indicators of motifs: "they pump the aura out of reality like water from a sinking ship" (250). Benjamin knew, of course, that sedimentation is not a solution to the leveling pull of reproduced perception and that the representative sound of city names cannot be replaced by a reauthorization through a miniaturization of even the most basic images. He focused instead on the "unfamiliar gaze," and to an even greater extent upon the political gaze, which requires nothing other than the free signifying surface of the city in order to fill it with new meanings. Again, referring to Atget's photographs, Benjamin states: "The city in these pictures looks cleared out, like a lodging that has not yet found a new tenant" (251). In this statement, the imaginary view of Paris acts as the surface for the projection of liberal hopes. On the other hand, Benjamin theorizes the palpable reality of the city of Berlin, imagined as a great void, with the previously mentioned formula of Ernst Bloch—"Berlin: multiple functions in a void" (212).

While the futuristic cityscapes of the Italian artist Boccioni or Carrà could still freely endow their objects with imaginations from the world of technology, since their time the consciousness of the medial and functional refraction of perception has been formative in an altogether different way. Since the '20s, functional models of perception have been able to assert themselves successfully in texts of the city. In fact, there are cases where functional models of perception are used in connection with a social topography. This takes place in Döblin's *Berlin Alexanderplatz,* where neither the naked eye nor multiply fractured perception can adequately perceive what Bloch, as a theoretician of the urban, has proposed: a "homogeneous field" of an "unmediated" capitalism that defies understanding and is utterly effective by virtue of its *abstractness* (213). In most of the texts of the time, there are three dominant tendencies: a fascination with the new multiperspectivity, an interest in the undreamed-of possibilities of new ways of seeing under shifting media, and an interest in the new aesthetic arrangement of available materials, forms, and functions.

Already in the first half of the '20s, László Moholy-Nagy had developed a theory of reproduction where he examined the effects of "functional mechanisms" on the human sensory apparatus. He replaced the notion of an innovative, "unmediated" perception with the conviction that innovation could now be found only in "new relationships" created by joining together optical and acoustic "functional phenomena" as a "complex of effects" (30). Moholy-Nagy's 1924 film sketch, *Dynamic of the Metropolis* (122–37), conceives of an urban happening that is composed of an endless number of synchronically interconnected elements and images. This film script, which was never actually produced, dispenses with all of the "narrated city's" literary plot elements in favor of an aesthetic arrangement, created out of a collage of graphic, photographic, and mathematical signs, and out of words displaced of their original meaning. The script singles out the word *tempo* from a vanishing succession of letters; the symbols of a wheel and an arrow indicate the directions of motion and speed. The film was supposed to show a central traffic junction, where the traffic flow exiting the city could be reversed. Moholy-Nagy's camera movement is a vertical one: a fall from an aerial photograph's image of street intersections, downward to the top of a radio tower, and finally into the shafts of the subway and the sewers. Words removed from their contexts (given an importance equal to that of visual images) are arranged in grid squares that could stand for blocks of buildings. Numbers indicate the projected sequence of cuts in the film. The cinematic effect of the whole is supposed to proceed out of the associative perceptual activity of the viewer. Following the dictates of Bauhaus aesthetics, the "pure" functionalism that is exposed in the film should point to social reality. The cuts in this film script can no longer be interpreted, however, as "social" points of interference. Indeed, the pure logic of montage, as an aesthetic obsession, seems to have become overwhelming, as it later is in Walter Ruttmann's film *Berlin: Symphony of a City.*

Today, under the conditions of high technology, reproduction's twofold consequence for the perception of the city is making itself known in literature and film in a way that is still more radical than before. Again, by twofold consequence, I mean either an intensification of the perception of the city, reducing it to the miniature, or a technical association of impressions made concrete in information systems and media. The difference between these two approaches to the problematics of narrating the city could not be greater. One example of a deliberate repatriation by a physically and sensually active perceiving ego of perceptive functions that have become increasingly influenced by technology is Günter Kunert's *Fahrt mit der S-Bahn* [a ride on the S-Bahn]:

> But one evening between two train stations, it just so happens that I look, full force, into a lighted window. The window seems to have been cut after the fact into a fire wall as dark as a raven's feathers, and it glows out of the face of the wall as its only interruption, as I am passing by on this evening between two stations. . . . Several figures had gathered in the room, and I try to identify them from the fleeting impression upon my retina as the train begins to slow and comes to rest in one of those stations that are emblems, hardly worth mentioning, of our situation [i.e., postwar Berlin—KS]. I hurry over the surface of trampled-down concrete, of crushed remains of cigarettes, scraps of paper, dirt, enduring since the construc-

> tion of the station and preserved for the hour of archaeologists who have yet to be born. (59ff.)

Here again Kunert revives the city, "emptied" of emblems [*Wahr*zeichen][10] and leveled to a gray signifying surface. The passing view into the apartment's interior (the "house in cross section" being a topos common since Expressionism) is far removed from a direct "virginal" gaze upon a reality that is as yet untouched by the technologies of perception; the "identification" of the passing events takes place on the surface of the retina! In addition, it is obvious that the spectator's aesthetic understanding of the object has long since etched a "second nature" of the objects of perception into the aesthetic consciousness. Were this not the case, Kunert's *S-Bahn* story would be a violation of all the signs of his time. The distance between the German *S-Bahn* poet and the never "immaterial" information systems and communication systems[11] as portrayed with great refinement in many American city narratives are immense. Compared to Paul Virilio's aesthetics of disappearance and aesthetics of speed,[12] where the fictional innocence of a direct gaze has long been rejected as a narrative impossibility, Kunert's perception at the speed of the *S-Bahn* is irritatingly slow.

The irrevocable secondary naturalization of the real (Bälke 41–43) brought the mode of perception of the '20s, with its partial engagement in montage, toward the new technology of special effects. A comparison between Ruttmann's *Berlin: Symphony of a City* and Godfrey Reggio's American city film *Koyaanisquatsi* (1983) immediately brings this to light.[13] Reggio's urban aesthetic, built on time-lapse photography, shifts the focus of the narrative entirely to the level of the *organization* of sensual perception. His (continually accelerating) modifications of objects of perception in *Koyaanisquatsi* are nothing other than technical manipulations of perceptions. Produced in this way, the hyper-reality of the city cannot be ascribed to an idea or to an ideal image of the city. Even more astounding (but also insightful in a certain way) is the fact that the absolute acceleration of reality produced in Reggio's film ultimately dissolves into the ancient myth of the apocalypse.[14] Is it in this way, by taking new paths to an old, long-known destination, that we have reached the most modern of cities, Nowhere City?

The Semiotics of the City

The decline of the symbolic appeal of the city [*Wahr*zeichen] and the technologization and functionalization of perception have also had an effect on the time-honored metaphor of reading the city "like an open book" (Ludwig Börne). Under the conditions of high technology, the pleasure experienced in deciphering the "secrets of Paris" or the activities of the flâneur cannot be easily continued as a specific type of reading in the text of the city *en miniature.* This must not mean, however, that the loss of the potential for narrating the city is the only thing still worth discussing. This is especially important in light of what is repeatedly claimed to be a socially critical fatalism that is inherent to urban thematics. If anything, the conflict between the reality of the city and its meanings has not been diminished, but has been intensified by an all-encompassing urban functionalism. In fact, there is no end in sight to this conflict. Nor has a viable resolution emerged. Rather, what was once a literal urban symbolism and unambiguous strategy of perception are now being rearranged into a semiotic notion of the text of the city.

Victor Hugo, known as the semiotic forefather of the metaphor "reading the city," set the precedent for this development. In the third and fourth books of *Notre-Dame of Paris,* Hugo deals with the city as a "book of stone." For Hugo, architecture, as an art displaying consistent, discernible characteristics, is destroyed by the new art of book printing. The city's "chronicle of human life" (198) is thus no longer a "chronicle in stone" (148) but can be written indiscriminately: "Present-day Paris, therefore, has no overall physiognomy. It is a collection of specimens from several centuries" (149). Here, modern urban semiotics has stripped Hugo's image of the city as a "book of stone" of its metaphoricity and has rethought it "structurally" as an analogy between language and city. The semiotics of architecture of the 1970s, in fact, made direct use of this model to claim that the city is structured like language.[15] The basis of this structural analogy in the philosophy of language is indebted less to Wittgenstein than it is to Saussure (while Wittgenstein described the city as a language, he did so in terms of the architect's drawing of an "ancient city" [245]). In the *Course in General Linguistics,* Saussure establishes the "identity of language" in difference and uses the example of a street. The street undergoes multiple (material) reconstructions without in the process losing its (immaterial) dimensions (108). Or as Jürgen Trabant states: "The positional value of the street, its relationship to other streets, its location in the network of the city, is for Ferdinand de Saussure the identity of the street" (82–83).

Approaching the city in terms of difference has made it possible to take the "language of the city" beyond the "purely metaphorical stage" to where it can be given a "real meaning" in the urban world of "signifiers and correlations" (Barthes, "Semiotik" 40). Barthes's readings of the city take on a new aesthetic fascination. Barthes goes beyond the (old) position of a privileged center, opening up new realms of free play that are composed of metonymic chains of meaning, erotic energies, etc. He espouses a new pleasure in the text of the city with the stipulation that the city be "emptied" of the old symbolic fixations and of semantically fixed perception. In other words, for Barthes, the principally "empty structure" of the city should not become reinvested with "material" narrative elements and consequently be undermined.

Compared to Barthes's neo-hedonistic reading of the city, Max Bense's aestheticization of the same phenomenon verges on the puritanical. In Barthes's play of meaning, the "cities of signs" or "cities of words" no longer have to be associated with a functional reality or a social reality of the city. Bense, on the other hand, conceives of the semiotic system of the city as a communicative world of signs that provides orientation, as in traffic or in the domestic realm. Bense's claim is that this urban system, which can be determined, mitigates the "labyrinthine character of cities" (101). His understanding of the city as text (as a body of text with subtexts) adheres to both the notion of centralization and to the boundaries and demarcations that delimit the city. Like Barthes, however, he sees centralization and delimitation *solely* as structuring principles. Furthermore, he is similar to Barthes in his conception of the structuring principle at work in the city as a purely functional mechanism. He consequently does not draw associations between the increasing "aestheticization of the world and its connection to the semiotic" (103). Instead, Bense's interpretation is goal-oriented: "the physical and technical signaling elements of objects" (103) are transformed into a sign system that can be reflected upon and directed toward an end point within the experience of continuous movement and change. The emphasis is thus not upon the enjoyment of the pleasure of the texts, but upon the successful completion of the cognitive mapping of the urban, or what might be called a course in urban orienteering.

Under such conditions, what direction is the narrative fiction of the city now taking? The older narrative voice that creates and imposes metaphors ("the city as . . .") has not died. Moreover, it has proven itself impossible to eradicate. (And why should it be eradicated?) Recent questions and answers concerning the problem of narrating the city are, however, leading away from metaphors and toward a *description* of meanings. Ultramodern communication systems and information systems that mold the city are now determining the structure of what can be narrated. The modern world is quite simply a structured world. But it is also, as Benjamin insisted, a world ruled by phantasmagoria. The most recent literature takes a variety of approaches in shaping the narrative text of the city and does so in one or the other of these two dimensions: structure and phantasy. In this way, the logic of structures and phantasms of meaning can enter into a productive relationship. While the American postmodern has at best used the classical modern metaphors of "switchboard" and "information machine" as the occasion for fantastic descriptions of wild or subversive structures (in the works of Thomas Pynchon or Donald Barthelme, for example) (see Ickstadt), it appears that German authors have yet to deal extensively with this newest refinement of urban aesthetics. In German city poetry, which is once more taking its inspiration from the community of the urban neighborhood (the new "green spaces" in the prosaic character of relations), the old traffic in experience still dominates. Both emotional affect and "genuine" feelings are again being gleaned from the urban experience of the Berlin counterculture's "scene."[16] But what has seemed to be the most effective is a satirical intervention in the text of the city where the scope of the city is simply reduced, and thus made narratable, again by sealing it off on the imaginary city map.[17] The fact that it is possible to reinscribe this play of meaning onto the reality of the text of the city can be seen in the events of the summer of 1987 in West Berlin. During the visit of the American president, the district

Kreuzberg was sealed off for purposes of internal security. A literary examination of this chapter in the text of the city would indeed find it difficult to distinguish between fiction and reality!

It appears that the more accomplished of the new German narrators of the city are keeping to the legacy of linguistics. Their challenge has been to find a "structural" solution to the city's overdetermination by an infinite, unquantifiable stream of commodities, information, and communication. In the text "*Berlin Stadtbahn (veraltet)*" [Berlin Metropolitan Railroad (antiquated)], Uwe Johnson considers the (old and new) difficulty of representing the city. His task is complicated by the fact that representation must now mediate between meanings that are no longer semantically fixed and a concept of the city that is anchored in its real localities:

> Allow me to use this title to report on some of the difficulties that hindered me in the description of an urban train station in Berlin. One person among many steps out of the train that has just arrived, crosses the platform and leaves the station, heading toward the street. No matter how often it takes place, this event remains the same. . . . It will not allow itself to be adapted to a long sentence or to four short sentences of the desired dimensions, and thus I exchanged it for another event which had the same effect. After a while, however, it became irritating that this simple train station scene would not allow itself to stand for the name Berlin, so I tried to write a story with the train station alone: a description for it alone. But there were problems with this.
>
> It seemed as if the name Berlin could be used as a model for a major city. Several million people are continuously in residence in an area that can be defined territorially or politically. . . . The city produces and trades in daily necessities, services, news and cultural attractions for a differentiated scale of needs. . . . Compared to these dimensions, the stratum of social relationships is complex. . . . But to look at it, the city does not seem to be complex. Put into the right words, it should be easily comprehensible for anyone who has command of perception or experience related to the concept of the city. But this act of delimitation collapses the concept of the city. Delimitation cannot be assumed to be common knowledge. (77ff.)

Johnson's narrative *report* doesn't find its way back to narration. Since it is impossible to produce a representation of the "narrated city" (and this impossibility also applies to the miniaturized signifying surface of the *single* event of the train station), the only appropriate course of action is an "inversion" of the narrative problematic. In this inversion, perception and concept are no longer engaged in a familiar relationship of opposition. Moreover, it is necessary that the "name" of the city be written out of the complex narrative text. One could call the narrative that can still be narrated, that still remains possible "research work" in the sense that it acts to structure urban complexity. The narrator of the city thus becomes, like scholars of the urban, engaged in the structural mastery of urban complexity. If this structural approach is successful, perhaps there will again be free spaces opened up for this or that narrative phantasm of the city. Of course, these would be located in the corners or even at the grid intersections of the urban map. Johnson believed he had found these places of potential in no other place than in New York, in the information world of his novel *Anniversaries: From the Life of Gesine Cresspahl.*

But does the most modern urban literature have the function of relieving or unburdening the city; does it have a compensatory function? Helmut Heißenbuttel's inscription of historical recollections upon a list of urban localities in the poem "*Westberlinlandschaftsgelegenheitsgedicht*" would seem to answer this question in the affirmative. Heißenbuttel ultimately, however, dismisses this memory work as falling for the deception of the "black box" called Berlin: "[N]othing is really a given, everything real is completely depleted" (95). Hans Joachim Schädlich's textual collage "*Ostwestberlin*" also appears to work against a compensatory function in urban literature. Schädlich's text no longer possesses its own meaning. Its dis-possession of meaning is endlessly reduplicated, reconstructed, and worked through linguistically in the actions of the always already complete texts of advertisements, information systems, and media, and the urban discourse that revolves around them (163–80).

There has yet to be an author who has actually set out on a trip to Nowhere City. Rather, they have all used their own imaginary texts, whether painful or pleasurable, as foundations for texts of the city as they "really" know it. The hope for a successful resistance to "structural emptiness," for an integration of a topographic sense of orientation and a fantastic play of meaning, has not been abandoned. The readers of the city, so it seems, are all watching and waiting, each in an individual borough or district, for relationships of meaning. Is this just a more modern or even postmodern version of Döblin's "factual phantasies"? Evidently, these phantasies are needed, and not only for pleasure or as ornamentation.

Translated by Lisa Roetzel

Notes

This article first appeared in German in *Die Unwirklichkeit der Städte,* ed. Klaus Scherpe, Reinbek: Rowohlt, 1988.

1. For a further exploration of this subject, see Scherpe, "Ausdruck, Funktion, Medium."
2. On the literary history of the city from the triple point of view of dramatization, subject centeredness, and symbolization, see Scherpe, "The City as Narrator."
3. On the subject of New York, see Brüggemann, "*Aber schickt keinen Poeten nach London!*"
4. This refers to Walter Ruttmann's film *Berlin: Symphony of a City* (1927). For further information on the film, see Kracauer, *From Caligari to Hitler* 182–88.
5. As in Hassan, "Cities of the Mind, Urban Worlds."
6. The passage I refer to here translates as follows: "*Adenauerplatz,* as the locals said, neither offered a monument to look at, nor a bench to sit on. The trees had long since been torn out of the earth, the bushes in the middle of the traffic circle had been removed. . . . The square was ugly, nothing further. The standard clock, as the only thing that wasn't for sale or that didn't urge one to buy, shone out over one of the entrances to the subway. Among the compressed asphalt streets and the ornamented buildings, the simple face and the uncorruptable fact of its hand seemed almost like a piece of nature" (*Berlin Alexanderplatz* 24).
7. I suspect that, for example, a promising guide to this subject like Axthelm's *Sinnesarbeit* ultimately reproduces this idealistic norm. On the question of the perception of the city in literature, see Brüggemann, and Silvio Vietta, "Großstadtwahrnehmung und ihre literarische Darstellung."
8. Voss is working on an "aesthetics of the inorganic." See his "Die Rückseite der Flanerie."
9. Here I am profiting from a masters thesis by Till Bartels on Benjamin's statements concerning photography in the context of historical source material.
10. Here I draw attention to Kunert's use of the word *Wahrzeichen* (translated as "emblems"). My italicization of the word *wahr* [true] emphasizes the fact that *Wahrzeichen* implies an understanding of the sign as possessive of symbolic truth (LR).
11. See Ickstadt, "Kommunikationsmüll und Sprachcollage."

12. See his *Ästhetik des Verschwindens, Krieg und Kino: Logistik der Wahrnehmung,* and *Panik Stadt.*

13. On the development of the film, see Ron Gold, "Untold Tales of Koyaanisquati."

14. See Wolfgang Sofsky, "Der Untergang der Städte."

15. See the three volumes edited by Carlini and Schneider: *Architektur als Zeichensystem, Die Stadt als Text, Stadtbild.*

16. Works of this type include the poetry anthology *Stadtansichten,* edited by Peter Gerlinghoff, and Bodo Morhäuser's novel *Die Berliner Simulation.*

17. One such tale of the city that deals with the urban matter of Munich is Paul Wühr's *Das false Buch.*

Works Cited

Axthelm, Dieter Hoffmann. *Sinnesarbeit. Nachdenken über Wahrnehmung.* Frankfurt: Campus, 1984.

Bälke, Friedrich. "Elemente einer Ästhetik des Kriegs-und Kinokultur." *KultuR-Revolution* 15 (July 1987): 41–43.

Barthes, Roland. *Empire of Signs.* Trans. Richard Howard. New York: Hill and Wang, 1982.

———. "Semiotik und Urbanismus." Carlini and Schneider, eds., *Die Stadt als Text,* 13–42.

Baudrillard, Jean. *America.* Trans. Chris Turner. London: Verso, 1988.

Benjamin, Walter. "Krisi des Romans: Zu Döblins *Berlin Alexanderplatz.*" *Gesammelte Schriften.* 8th ed. Vol. 3. Frankfurt: Suhrkamp, 1980. 7 vols.

———. *One-Way Street and Other Writings.* Trans. Edmund Jephcott and Kingsley Shorter. London: NLB, 1979.

Bense, Max. "Urbanismus und Semiotik." Carlini and Schneider, eds., *Architektur als Zeichensystem* 101–18.

Bloch, Ernst. *Erbschaft dieser Zeit.* Frankfurt: Suhrkamp, 1973.

Börne, Ludwig. *Briefe aus Paris.* Hamburg: Hoffmann und Campe, 1832.

Brüggemann, Heinz. *"Aber schickt keinen Poeten nach London!" Großstadt und literarische Wahrnehmung im 18. und 19. Jahrhundert.* Reinbeck: Rowohlt, 1985.

Calvino, Italo. *The Literature Machine: Essays.* Trans. Patrick Creagh. London: Secker and Warburg, 1987.

Carlini, Alessandro, and Bernhard Schneider, eds. *Architektur als Zeichensystem.* Tübingen: Wasmuth, 1976.

———. *Die Stadt als Text.* Tübingen: Wasmuth, 1976.

———. *Stadtbild.* Tübingen: Wasmuth, 1976.

Cassirer, Ernst. *An Essay on Man: An Introduction to a Philosophy of Human Culture.* New Haven: Yale UP, 1944.

Delius, Friedrich Christian. *Adenauerplatz: Roman.* Reinbek: Rowohlt, 1984.

Döblin, Alfred. *Berlin Alexanderplatz.* Trans. Eugene Jolas. New York: Frederick Unger, 1961.

Durth, Werner. *Die Inzenierung der Alltagswelt: Zur Kritik der Stadtgestaltung.* Braunschweig: Vieweg, 1977.

Engels, Frederick. "The Condition of the Working-Class in England." *Karl Marx, Frederick Engels: Collected Works.* Trans. Florence Kelley Wischnewetzky. Vol. 4. New York: International, 1975. 8 vols.

Fisher, Philip. "City Matters, City Minds." *The Worlds of Victorian Fiction.* Ed. Jerome H. Buckley. Cambridge: Harvard UP, 1975.

Fontane, Theodor. *Sämtliche Romane.* Frankfurt: Ullstein, 1976.

———. *Stine.* Munich: Hanser, 1969.

Foucault, Michel. "Of Other Spaces." Trans. Jay Miskowiev. *Diacritics* (Spring 1986): 24–32.

Gerlinghoff, Peter, ed. *Stadtansichten: Gedichte Westberliner Autoren.* Berlin: Herrmann, 1977.

Gold, Ron. "Untold Tales of Koyaanisquatsi." *American Cinematographer* (March 1984): 63–73.

Hassan, Ihab. "Cities of the Mind, Urban Worlds: The Dematerialization of Metropolis in Contemporary American Fiction." *Literature and the Urban Experience: Essays on the City and Literature.* Ed. Michael C. Jaye and Ann Chalmers Watts. New Brunswick, NJ: Rutgers UP, 1981.

Hegel, G. W. F. *Lectures on the Philosophy of Religion Together with a Work on the Proofs of the Existence of God.* Trans. E. B. Speirs. Vol. 2. New York: Humanities, 1968. 3 vols.

Heißenbuttel, Heinz. *Ödipuskomplex made in Germany: Gelegenheitsgedichte, Totentage, Landschaften 1965–1980.* Stuttgart: Kett-Cotta, 1981.

Hugo, Victor. *Notre-Dame of Paris.* Trans. John Sturrock. New York: Viking, 1978.

Ickstadt, Heinz. "Kommunikationsmüll und Sprachcollage: Die Stadt in der amerikanischen Fiktion der Postmoderne." Scherpe, ed., *Die Unwirklichkeit der Stadte* 197–224.

Jacobs, Jane. *The Death and Life of Great American Cities.* New York: Random House, 1961.

Johnson, Uwe. *Anniversaries: From the Life of Gesine Cresspahl.* Trans. Leila Vennewitz. New York: Harcourt, 1975.

———. *Berliner Sachen.* Frankfurt: Suhrkamp, 1975.

Koeppen, Walter. "New York." *Gesammelte Werke in sechs Banden.* Vol. 3. Frankfurt: Suhrkamp, 1986. 6 vols.

Koltz, Volker. *Die Erzählte Stadt. Ein Sujet als Herausforderung des Romans von Lesage bis Döblin.* Munich: Hanser, 1989.

Kracauer, Siegfried. *From Caligari to Hitler: A Psychological History of the German Film.* Princeton: Princeton UP, 1947.

Kraus, Karl. *Die Fackel* no. 415/416 (January 1911): 35.

Kunert, Günter. *Drei Berliner Geschichten.* Berlin: Aufbau, 1979.

Lefèbvre, Henri. *La révolution urbaine.* Paris: Gallimard, 1970.

Moholoy-Nagy, Lászl6. *Painting, Photography, Film.* Trans. Janet Seligman. Cambridge: MIT P, 1967.

Morshäuser, Bodo. *Die Berliner Simulation.* Frankfurt: Suhrkamp, 1983.

Musil, Robert. *The Man Without Qualities.* Vol. 1. Trans. Eithne Wilkins and Ernst Kaiser. London: Secker and Warburg, 1953. 3 vols.

Nizon, Paul. *Canto.* Frankfurt: Suhrkamp, 1972.

Poe, Edgar Allan. *The Complete Works of Edgar Allan Poe.* Vol. 3. Ed. James A. Harrison. New York: AMS P, 1965. 17 vols.

Saussure, Ferdinand de. *Course in General Linguistics.* Trans. Wade Baskin. New York: McGraw, 1959.

Schadlich, Hans Joachim. *Ostwestberlin.* Reinbek: Rowohlt, 1987.

Scherpe, Klaus R. "Ausdruck, Funktion, Medium. Transformation der

Großstadterzählung in der deutschen Literature der Moderne." *Literatur in einer industriellen Kultur.* Ed. Gotz Grossklaus and Eberhard Lämmert. Stuttgart: Cotta, 1989. 139–61.

———. "The City as Narrator: The Modern Text in Döblin's *Berlin Alexanderplatz.*" *Modernity and the Text, Revisions of German Modernism.* Ed. David Bathrick and Andreas Huyssen. New York: Columbia UP, 1989.

———, ed. *Die Unwirklichkeit der Städte: Großstadtdarstellungen zwischen Moderne und Postmoderne.* Reinbek: Rowohlt, 1988.

Sennett, Richard. *The Fall of Public Man.* New York: Knopf, 1977.

Simmel, Georg. "Soziologie des Raumes." *Georg Simmel: Schriften der Soziologie.* Ed. Heinz-Jürgen Dahme and Otthein Rammstedt. Frankfurt: Suhrkamp, 1986.

Sofsky, Wolfgang. "Der Untergang der Städte." *Frankfurter Hefte* 6 (1983): 57–64.

Steinwachs, Ginka. *marilynparis.* Basel: Stroemfeld, 1979.

Trabant, Jürgen. "Die Stadt und die Sprache: Eine Saussresche Analogie." Carlini and Schneider, eds., *Die Stadt als Text* 82–96.

Venturi, Robert, Denise Scott Brown, and Steven Izenour. *Learning from Las Vegas.* Cambridge: MIT P, 1972.

Vietta, Silvio. "Großstadtwahrnehmung und ihre literarische Darstellung." *Deutsche Vierteljahresschrift* 48 (1974): 354–73.

Virilio, Paul. *Ästhetik des Verschwindens.* Trans. Gustav Rossler and Marianne Karbe. Berlin: 1986.

———. *Krieg und Kino: Logistik der Wahrnehmung.* Trans. Frieda Grafe and Emmo Patalas. Munich: Hanser, 1986.

———. *Panik Stadt.* Trans. Ulrich Raulf. Berlin: Vieweg, 1979.

Voss, Dietmar. "Die Ruckseite der Flanerie." Scherpe, ed., *Die Unwirklichkeit der Stadte* 37–60.

Weiss, Peter. *Der Fremde: Erzählungen.* Frankfurt: Suhrkamp, 1980.

Wittgenstein, Ludwig. *Philosophische Untersuchungen.* Vol. 1. Frankfurt: Suhrkamp, 1984. 9 vols.

Wühr, Paul. *Das false Buch.* Frankfurt: Fischer, 1985.

Under the Sign of Orientalism: The West vs. Islam

Mahmut Mutman

In the last ten years, a rapidly growing mass movement has erupted into the world political scene: an Islamic fundamentalism challenging Western economic, political, and cultural hegemony in its totality. In many Muslim countries today, from the Middle East to Southeast Asia, a new radical-popular nationalism is being articulated by a revival of Islamic religious tradition, principles, and rituals. By rewriting modernity as a fake and corrupted world and modernization as a false historical narrative, Islamic fundamentalism has brought to the surface a historically sedimented antagonism, the one between the West and Islam. This antagonism has many different layers and is overdetermined by a series of binary oppositions: reason vs. dogma, democracy vs. despotism, civilization vs. medievalism, modernity vs. tradition, and so on. Our aim here is *to locate it historically.* The antagonism between the West and Islam is not the expression of an eternal conflict between two separate and irreconcilable worlds. This historical location is quite recent and specific. Whatever the literal content or political tendency of Islamism, its very presence signi-

© 1993 by *Cultural Critique.* 0882-4371 (Winter 1992–93). All rights reserved.

fies something about its peculiar relationship to modernity/the West: it can well be seen as something that happened *after* the onset of Western intrusion, modernity, and modernization. If the "death of God" is inscribed in the modern project, Islamic fundamentalism appears to be one good instance of Nietzsche's ironic remark about the multiple reversals of such an inscription: "the return of gods." Thus it may help us to question one important dimension of the way in which Western hegemony has been constructed: the evolution of Western reason/modernity by a process of what Johannes Fabian calls in the context of anthropology "pushing the other back in time."[1] "Other" cultures thus enter into the process of *hegemonic* construction of Western Self, Order, and Reason. As Edward W. Said, speaking of the image of Islam in the Western media, warns us in *Covering Islam:*

> [T]hese enormous generalizations have behind them a whole history, enabling and disabling at the same time. . . . [W]e must immediately note that it is always the West, and not Christianity, that seems pitted against Islam. Why? Because the assumption is that whereas "the West" is greater than and has surpassed the stage of Christianity, its principal religion, the world of Islam—its varied societies, histories, and languages notwithstanding—is still mired in religion, primitivity and backwardness. (10)

This is why it is always a *limited* approach to put Islamic fundamentalism on the same line with other, equivalent religious fundamentalisms in Western societies. Islamic and Christian fundamentalisms might have some similar "causes" or similar religious aims, but they do not have the same kind of relationship to hegemonic order. Carrying a different temporality, Islamic fundamentalism should be seen as part and consequence of a specific history. But if this history and temporality should be distinguished and specified, such specification is not for the simple aim of knowing Islam better. Rather, from the site of such specificity, my aim is to interrogate the way history (as we know it) has been constructed.

The layer of history that I want to bring up here has been articulated in the last decade or so. In his pioneering work *Ori-*

entalism, Said studied Western discourse on the Orient, and especially the Islamic Orient as it has developed over the last two centuries. In a later work, *Covering Islam,* he focused on the representation of Islam in the contemporary Western media. In the first part of this essay, I will try to identify certain issues and will develop certain concepts through a critical dialogue with Said's work. This consists of criticizing and abandoning certain themes and arguments in his work, and following certain others in a stronger way than Said himself has done. It is important to emphasize in the beginning that I take Said's work as "paradigm-constitutive." In other words, everything that I am going to say about it is possible only in the *horizon* that Said has opened for us. In the second part, I will look at the more specific issue of Islam/Islamism in the light of these critical elaborations of selected themes in Said's work.[2]

Said defines Orientalism at three different levels: an academic discipline, a style of thought, and a corporate institution. By drawing our attention to the way in which the knowledge of Oriental societies and cultures is historically and institutionally linked with imperial and colonial powers, such an initial approach helps him to pose the question of Orientalism (or Orientalism as a question) beyond a naive positivist epistemological criticism. Following Foucault, he constructs Orientalist formation as an apparatus of power/knowledge. If Orientalist knowledge is linked with colonial/imperial economic and political powers, this is because they cannot be the powers they are without the knowledge of the Orient and the Oriental, while, at the same time, the production of this knowledge is unthinkable without the support and the context that the network of power provides.

However, both power and knowledge in the Orientalist formation seem to be broken, multiple, dispersed: latent as well as manifest knowledge; ideological imagery as well as scientific truth; academic authority as well as colonial domination; economic exploitation and brute repression as well as subtle hegemony and the power of austere disciplinary knowledges. In this hegemonic formation that is composed of heterogenous elements (institutional, scientific, literary, political, geographical, imaginary, disciplinary, etc.), there should nevertheless be some kind of *center* which defines its unity by bringing these different elements together under the specific force of its concept. How can one say that a textual fragment or discursive statement is "Orientalist"? When Said refers to Orientalism as a "style of thought" that can accommodate authors as diverse as Hugo, Dante, and Marx, he refers to this center whose strange force is characterized by an imperceptible, unbounded, and silent dissemination of its sign: "an ontological and epistemological distinction made between the Orient and the Occident" (2–3).[3]

In his approach to language, Saussure argues that language is not the expression of prelinguistic ideas with phonetic means. It is the differential activity of signs that makes clear and distinct "ideas" by segmenting the vague, shapeless mass of thought (110). It is not a coincidence that, when Said treats Orientalism as a *discursive* object, he has to point to a formal dimension, that is, an Orientalist *style* of thought which is characterized, like language, by division or distinction. The "Orient" as a clear, distinct, and identifiable entity appears through the segmentation or differentiation of a shapeless mass of impressions and fusions.

How should we interpret this central, constitutive principle that characterizes Orientalist formation? Apparently, this center does not look like a center: in the place of a full and clear identity that can exist in and by itself, we have a difference, a distinction. But, as Said's choice of the word "distinction" (signifying power and status hierarchy rather than a mere difference) already implies, this does not make Orientalism a "decentered structure"—or, certainly not, if we understand by "decentered" a center-less structure. By being placed under the sign of difference, the center/concept of Orientalism comes into being through an act or operation of *centering*, which is indispensable to the most typical feature of Orientalist discourse: totalization.[4] As the production of a chain of equivalences, such a totalization is a metaphorical operation that cuts across the different modes of Orientalist discourse; for instance, the homogenization of so many different societies under "abstract essences" such as the Orient or Islam, which Said frequently points out. This "other" place, the "Orient," is thus a Western invention, a product of Orientalist inscription. But such homogenization does not inscribe the Orient or Islam only; the inscription of this homogenization of several different places under the sign "Oriental" *positions* the West as the privileged or dominant pole of a distinction or opposition. This is exactly how Orientalist discourse is related to Western *hegemonic investment* and the colonial/imperial *apparatus of power* that embodies it: Orientalism is not what it presents itself to be; this appearance of a "discourse on the Orient," whether it is spoken by the expert, the politician, the governor, the sociologist, or the poet, is indeed the lure that characterizes Orientalism, the illusion that is proper to it. Orientalism is a hegemonic operation, a *centering*, an operation of distinguishing the West from an Oriental space signified as its other by a complicated strategic move that is multiplied in different modes of discourse (literary, scientific, journalistic, political) and which is articulated in and by different institutional instances of power (colonial, economic, academic, moral). What is important is that there is a "discourse" on the Orient; that is, the Orient is marked as different and thus requires a special area of expertise. We learn from Said's text that Orientalism is one of those discursive instances where the Foucauldian question of "who speaks" is answered on the level of discourse itself, where the materiality of a hegemonic location is inscribed.[5] By inviting us to turn away from the innocence of a neutral, uninscribed knowledge of Oriental cultures, Said enables us to see the force of a desire, an investment of power in the discourse which produces knowledge and truth: the production of the sovereign Western subject who establishes his sovereignty by marking the other and by other-ing the different. Orientalism is the "way" or discourse in which the Western imperial subject hides itself. It is Western power which *marks* this difference that can be marked only in and by language, so as to give way to language by erasing its face and letting its other rise in discourse in order to secure a space for itself where it alone is sovereign without even appearing, or appearing victorious only afterwards, once that space is guaranteed as neutral, blank. This marking transforms the possibility of a difference between the West and East into an absolute necessity and gives it a direction: the Orient is where one is orient-ed. Would the West be the *hegemonic* power that it is without this act/writing? In one and the same gesture, which is both central and dispersed in time and space, the East/Orient is marked as the "other" and the object of both knowledge and intervention—a gesture which not only produces the West as a position of power and center, but, by being embedded in language, produces such power as the universal position of knowledge. It is sufficient to bring only the most heterogeneous fragments (from journalism to science to literature) together under the sign of this unique principle of distinction in order to see how this most widespread and most natural marking actually takes place.[6]

However, the relations among the three instances of Orientalism are not always clearly articulated by Said. Either such relations are empirically described or we are reminded of the network of economic interests or power constraints behind Orientalist works. In other words, the relations between knowledge and power are conceived *externally*. This leads to the emergence in Said's text of a tendency toward a sociology of knowledge that cannot go further than placing ideas in their social contexts. It is precisely this which prevents us from seeing the *constitutive* aspect of discourse. This is a tendency that becomes more explicit in *Covering Islam*.

It might be useful to return at this point to Said's original critical, antipositivist argument. For Said, the Orient "is not merely there, but a man-made idea that has a history and tradition of thought, imagery and vocabulary that have given it reality and presence in and for the West" (5). (In the light of our above elaboration of Orientalism's operation of centering, we should also say that it is an "idea" that made "Man.") However, Said makes a number of important *qualifications* that should be the starting point of any further elaboration, for these qualifications are made with the purpose of showing that the man-made idea is not just an idea, nor is it produced by purely ideational conditions. If the "Orient" is a man-made or a constructed idea in the sense of not being a natural given, Said wants to show which nonideational conditions determine this idea and make it the particular idea that it is.

First of all, the Orient is of course not essentially an idea or "a creation with no corresponding reality"; it has its own "brute reality greater than Western discourse." Yet Said is interested "not in the correspondence between Orientalism and Orient, but in the internal consistency of Orientalism and its ideas about the Orient" (5). Although Said rightly insists that the internal consistency of

Orientalism is more important than any correspondence between it and the Orient, his way of formulating this problem makes it difficult to think of the *relationship* between the two, insofar as the Orient is also the *reference* of Orientalism. In other words, Orientalist discourse and the Orient are not just separate things—there is a relationship between them. However, by "tacitly" acknowledging that "the cultures and nations whose location is in the East . . . have a brute reality obviously greater than anything that could be said about them in the West" (5), Said makes it difficult to formulate the relationship between the internal consistency of discourse (Orientalism) and its referent (Orient). This relationship is never innocent or blank, but always inscribed or marked. It is a citational activity, an activity of *referring* to something that is "already there" and "different" or "other." Since there is a split or division rather than a full meaning in the beginning or center of Orientalism, the production of the Orient is always a result or an effect of drawing a line, of referring to an "other."[7] The Orient is thus born out of a shift or delay; it is *both* constructed and displaced. It is, at the same time, an object of knowledge and is characterized by a resistance to knowledge (for instance, an essential mystery in the Orientalist language).[8] In other words, Said's acknowledgement of the brute reality of cultures in the East as greater than Western discourse does *not necessarily or naturally* guarantee a site of non-Orientalist knowledge located in the identity (or identities) of the Orient itself, for as he himself writes, "Orientalism is based upon exteriority" whose "principal product" is *representation* (*Orientalism* 20–21). Such a knowledge is always produced through a *struggle* that is *never outside* representation. (And this is the *real* difficulty: the "outside" of Orientalism is not outside of language and representation.)[9]

Second, according to Said, ideas cannot be understood without their configurations of power; the Orient is not a mere creation of imagination:

> Ideas, cultures, and histories can not seriously be understood or studied without their force, or more precisely their configurations of power, also being studied. To believe that Orient was created—or, as I call it, 'Orientalized'—and to believe that such things happen simply as a necessity of the imagina-

> tion is to be disingenuous. The relationship between Occident and Orient is a relationship of power, of domination, of varying degrees of a complex hegemony. . . . The Orient was orientalized not only because it was discovered to be Oriental in all those ways considered commonplace by an average nineteenth century European, but also because it could be—that is, submitted to being—made Oriental. (5–6)

The explanation of this submission under which one is made Oriental requires the insertion of power into the middle of discourse and knowledge. However, it is often Said's rather easy acceptance of a simple contextualism, or a simplistic denial of idealism (for instance, idealism as a mere disingenuousness), that deprives him of the means of achieving this essential aim. Can we explain, not just submission, but "submission to being made Oriental," unless power is placed not only outside as a merely external context but also *inside* of discourse? This does not mean that power is discursive in the sense of being purely linguistic or ideational, for power shall remain in some sense outside a discourse as the context of it. The truth of a discursive exchange is *never entirely present* within that exchange.[10] But this context of power as a difference from discourse is also *expected* or *demanded* by discourse. It is also internal to it, for there must be something in discourse which establishes precisely this relationship to the outside context and through which discourse makes itself in constant movement and change. It is only when power is also internal to discourse in this sense that the internal consistency (which Said proposed as a first qualification as opposed to empirical correspondence) would be more than a logical one: it would be a *coherence* of dispersed and opposing forces, contradictory and equivalent statements, etc. In other words, the internal consistency of Orientalism could then be seen as a coherence of multiple and contradictory elements that is produced and sustained through a *desire* for the Orient as Other, that is, through the *pressing force* of the central/centering operation of drawing an epistemological and ontological line between the West and East.

Finally, according to Said, the structure of Orientalism should not be understood as "a structure of lies or of myths which, once the truth about them were told, would simply blow away" (*Orientalism* 6). This last qualification is of great significance, and it is directly related to the notion of discourse in Said's work. The question that we should pose is, exactly in what way would the structure of Orientalism be "a structure of lies or of myths which, once the truth about them were told, would simply blow away"? It is important to see that here Said refers to a *mental* operation, or rather to the limits of the mental, rational operation as such. If such a discursive structure would not blow away once its truth were known, then it must be related to an economic interest or to a power structure. In other words, the totality in question, Orientalism, should not be seen as being mental or ideational. It should not have a modality that would be blown away by the mental act of knowing it, having a consciousness of it, and so on. But this is the strategic moment in the text: how do we conceive of the discursive totality of Orientalism?

Ernesto Laclau and Chantal Mouffe develop a useful approach to the concept of discourse by arguing that the discursive construction of objects is not a mere mental event, but the material properties of objects are part of discourses which make them meaningful within the actual contexts they have articulated. They call "discourse" not the linguistic action as such, but the totality that it constitutes with nonlinguistic action. What is important from our perspective is their general argument that every such totality, that is, every discursive construction, is at the same time a *hegemonic* construction.[11] In this sense, an Orientalist statement ("They are weak, corrupt and sentimental; they cannot rule themselves") and a Western imperialist or colonialist action (military operation, colonization) construct a totality, or they mutually implicate each other. Orientalism should therefore be seen as the command/order, or the discipline of the epistemological and ontological distinction between the West and East.[12]

In order to develop the concept of hegemony in the context of Orientalism, we shall have to refer to another site of the historical articulation of Orientalism—the colonial site. Indeed, Homi Bhabha's analysis of "colonial discourse" develops through a critical dialogue with Said's approach to Orientalism. According to Bhabha, although Said rightly refuses to conceptualize Orientalism within the limits of a theory of false consciousness and introduces the concept of discourse, he is reluctant to break with an instrumentalist concept of power.[13] As a result, Orientalist discourse becomes a merely *ideological* injustice that the dominant subject does to the dominated. As Bhabha has succinctly argued, this is *strategically* problematical:

> [I]t is difficult to conceive of the process of subjectification as a placing *within* Orientalist or colonial discourse for the dominated subject without the dominant being strategically placed within it too. There is always, in Said, the suggestion that colonial power and discourse is possessed entirely by the coloniser, which is a historical and theoretical simplification. The terms in which Said's orientalism is unified—the intentionality and unidirectionality of colonial power—also unify the subject of colonial enunciation. (24–25)[14]

Said's tendency to construct "colonial power and discourse [as] possessed entirely by the coloniser" implies that colonial enunciation is identical to what its enunciator speaks. This prevents us from understanding the colonial relationship as *discourse,* that is to say, as a *relationship* which inscribes both dominant and dominated subjects, and not a relationship between two simple identities external to each other. Colonial relationship is not just "between" the colonizer and the colonized, but also "outside" them constituting one as colonizer and the other as colonized. When we have found a difference, a split in the middle of Orientalism as the defining characteristic of this discourse, we have defined Orientalism as an operation of centering. By doing so, we have subjected Orientalism itself to a diacritical operation of difference. This diacritical operation, which signifies a space that is "before" or "outside" of Orientalism, is also a bind. In the very act of centering, the center binds itself to margins that are thus bound to it and that have become its margins without which it could not be a center.

This colonial/Orientalist inscription, that is, the production of Western hegemony, should be seen as a question of difference that is constituted and deconstituted at the same time, an "absorption," as Gramsci would call it. The notion of absorption implies that the West establishes not only a hierarchy (such as the evolutionary hierarchies which fix time by distributing it in space) but also a *comparative grid of differences* that is almost invisible but always at work and in which the West effaces its own name in order to make it hegemonic; that is, it empties a space (of truth) to be marked as universal. "Difference" is then compared not just against the West, but against a *central* position that the West simply fulfills (science, democracy, progress, reason, etc.). This position or location is not only impossible to deny, but it also might be strangely empowering—though not unproblematic, for it is not just empty but also always already filled by the West in the very split that produces it. Orientalism as discourse, as an embodiment of power in the problematic of language, is therefore the *hegemonic* moment of Western imperialism. The Orient, or the Other of the West, is always compared to something other than the West, which the West is simply supposed to occupy. The distinction between the West and East is the marking of the *East.* This is why whenever we attempt simply to reverse the conceptualizations of Eastern societies, to rewrite their histories, their modes of production, their political structures, we confront immense difficulties. The reason is that what is historically given to us is an already hegemonized difference. What is attempted to be written in many cases is not the history of the East, but a reverse history of the West, or a duplication of it in the East. For from the point of view of Orientalist discourse, the West constitutes its own history, its time and itself, among other things, through its *difference* from the East by characterizing the latter as *lacking* history, civil society, urban structures, individuality, and so on.[15]

But there is perhaps another history to be written. Can we write the history of this very constitution, of this play of absence and presence, of the bifurcation that "worlds the world" in Spivak's words? Such history would not be a history of the past, of the things passed, but a history of the present, as Foucault would have it; that is to say, a history that reveals not the past but the status of the very division which distinguishes present from the past, which thus projects a future and constructs a temporality.[16]

We will now look at a more specific site of Orientalism: the articulation of the antagonism "West vs. Islam." Clearly enough, it is impossible to make sense of this antagonism unless it is placed within the economy of Orientalist discourse. Indeed, what is today called "Islam" is produced *within* such a discursive economy. This production of Islam by Orientalism is the consequence of a material, historical process characterized by an *interruption.* What we have to show is not only that the West is wrong or has false ideas and images about other cultures, but that what is today called Islamism is part and consequence of a history in which the West established its hegemony over the world.

We have already pointed out the structural complicity between Orientalism and colonialism (though colonialism is obviously not limited to Orientalism). Quite clearly, the processes of Westernization and/or modernization in the Third World are also meaningful in the *background* of Orientalism as an operation of centering.[17] There is, of course, a significant difference between colonial and post-colonial regimes. But the "post-colonial" national(istic) modernization (the development of large-scale bureaucracies, education, industrial production, etc.) also required a certain articulation of Orientalism.[18] This does not mean that a Westernization process led by a national petit bourgeois elite is the same as modernization under colonial domination. On the contrary, colonial *presence* shows the irreducibility of cultural difference. But, since Orientalism is tied to *imperialism,* a general condition has continued to exert its force in the opening or incision that is characteristic of Orientalism, even after colonialism. Indeed, if our concept of Orientalism is not limited with Orientalist books, it is necessary to see that other differences and splits (such as modern/traditional or elite/people as they operate in the Third World) are meaningful only on the basis of the forgetting of a *prior* Orientalist "worlding" or "distinction" that opened them up, a forgetting or repression whose material supports are power and capital. This has been particularly visible in the case of the Muslim Third World where *religious* difference played the chief role in the articulation of cultural difference.[19]

Westernization/modernization can be seen as an operation which divides a Third World society into two different sections, such as *modern* and *traditional,* or *civilized* and *backward,* and which, generally speaking, constitutes Third World subjects as objects and targets of a transformative practice along the lines of Western/modern hegemonic reason and order.[20] (Indeed, at the moment we say Third World, we are entirely within the general problematic that informs such a division.) As an operation of power, hegemonic operation too is characterized by a repression or reduction; but a hegemonic power is the one that is determined by a problematic of language or an irreducibility of difference. It is thus a regulative ordering that constitutes its subjects in particular ways by distinguishing them from each other, by creating functional hierarchies among them, by putting each in its "place" in relation to the other. The necessity that underlies this formation of power is not a full and clear identity, but a necessity of difference. Since centering, demarcating, and ordering are acts that are *possible only* by comparison with others and by a calculation or an account of differences, otherness *never* leaves the hegemonic order. That is to say, the notion of hegemony refers to a *strategic* field of moves and countermoves through which the identity of subjects is constantly articulated rather than simply being fixed once and for all. Hegemonic space is radically different from a purely functional space. Precisely because it is a discursive, relational, and strategic field, the space of hegemony is never identical to what the hegemonic force is capable of constructing, imposing, articulating, dominating, and so on. In other words, the concept of hegemony implies a certain corruption of the fullness and sovereignty of the sovereign power.

It is precisely for this reason that Derrida's notion of spacing is useful in understanding this hegemonic operation. I am of course using the notion of spacing in Derrida's sense, "in a different field, articulated differently." He defines it as follows:

> (1) . . . [S]pacing is the impossibility for an identity to be closed on itself, on the inside of its proper interior, or on its coincidence with itself. The irreducibility of spacing is the irreducibility of the other. (2) . . . [S]pacing designates not only an interval, but a 'productive,' 'genetic,' 'practical' movement, an 'operation.' (94)[21]

Following Derrida, we can understand the Orientalist distinction or Westernism/modernism's bifurcation as spacing, that is to say, as an act which generates its subject in the irreducibility of its otherness. What the West encounters, in the act of colonization, is not just an identity, not just a difference in the sense of an identifiable "different" culture, but the irreducibility of the other. Therefore, spacing signifies not an act of dividing an identity that is already there—not a simple division, but an act that generates identities, meanings, or differences. It is in this sense that what is constructed as Islam or the Orient or Third World constructs at the same time the West. Therefore, although such an operation constitutes the Western/modern identity as civilized, true, and desirable, the desire that is invested is much more complicated: *the act of Westernizing/modernizing is bound to Orientalize as well as Westernize, and traditionalize as well as modernize its subjects.* It is not a question of repressing an identity that is there, nor is it a question of constituting a full identity simply by repressing another. Since the other is irreducible, identity is never full. Identities themselves are constructed and marked as hierarchical, spatially and temporally ordered differences in relation to each other. Since spacing is not a simple division, but a productive one characterized by otherness and difference, the interval that gives it its name is never closed. In other terms, spacing opens up a hegemonic field in which identity (or difference) is never fixed once and for all but should be seen as being constantly articulated.

Insofar as the Muslim Third World is concerned, this bifurcation has led to the emergence of two narratives: a modernist/Westernist narrative and an Islamist one. The relationship between these two narratives is not linear, although their presentation has to be so. Rather, they constitute a certain discursive economy specific to the Muslim Third World. This discursive economy has developed in very different ways in different contexts. It is impossible to mention all these contexts here. What follows is no more than a rough outline of the development of this narrative economy. The initial Islamic resistance to colonial occupation was articulated around the question of territory. The question was "Can we live under a Christian (or infidel) government and still be devout Muslims?" Colonization thus produced a religious and cultural anxiety about space and boundaries, and consequently a dialectic of deterritorialization and reterritorialization within Islamic discourses and communities, especially in India and North Africa. The distinction between "territory of Islam" and "territory of war" (the territory where the infidels live) became the most important problem. The earliest anticolonial resistance movements were inseparable from Muslim communities' displacements and migrations.[22] However, although early colonization introduced the conditions of a new "worlding" of the Muslim world, the "Christian vs. Muslim" antagonism that characterized these movements was, in a sense, still premodern.

With the development and consolidation of colonialism and the increasing hegemony of Western Europe over the Muslim world, it is possible to observe, starting from the late nineteenth and early twentieth centuries, the slow and persistent evolution of a different antagonism, one between the *West* and Islam. Colonialism cultivated Islam everywhere in the Muslim world in several different ways. First, in many colonized places, the perception of Islam from within the Christian conceptions of religious hierarchy and bureaucratic organization separated prior social connections between religion and custom, and made the Islamic organization much more rigidly bureaucratic. (This is partly why the transition from the so-called "Asiatic-despotic" to a "rational-bureaucratic" governmental apparatus was not necessarily a transition to a more "flexible" and "functional" form of government, but indeed the production of an authoritarian governmental apparatus.) Second, generally speaking, colonialism cultivated Islam as an antagonistic construction. We may take the Algerian national liberation war as a paradigmatic case of Islamic anticolonial resistance. Bourdieu describes how "the observance of the Moslem religion . . . has taken on the function of a symbol in the colonial context" (*The Algerians* 156): the increasing number of mosques in Kabylia after the French conquest, women's articulation of the veil as a symbol of affirmation of national identity and heritage (and we should add as a rejection of colonial penetration). The *veil* gained an entirely new meaning in the colonial context: whereas earlier it was a natural, internal moment of traditional Islamic discourse, with the increasing disarticulation of the latter in the face of a violent foreign presence and the new relations that it introduced, the veil turned out to be a symbolic, metaphorical element that signified resistance to the foreign order.[23] The predominant element in the Algerian case, however, was national identity. In other words, what was important was not the Muslim-ness of such practices of resistance. A Muslim religious-popular element functioned insofar as it articulated a national identity. This is why it cannot be characterized as properly fundamentalist. Of course, this does not mean that the religious element was not important; it only means that it was articulated in a nationalist rather than a religious-universalist direction.

If we return to the earlier instances of radical nationalist discourses against colonial domination in the Muslim world, it is possible to observe that these nationalist discourses too had to cultivate an Islamic element in a complex ideological move that was characterized by a criticism of the existing situation in the Islamic world. Such criticisms and arguments could have been developed only from within a petit bourgeois bureaucratic class habitus. They could not have been developed without a depository of discursive genres and cultural capital, such as educational, literary discourses and bureaucratic power/knowledge, which were the monopoly of this particular social group. Typical examples of this position can be found in the *Kaum Muda* movement in Malaysia, the journal *Al-Manar* in Egypt, or the Young Ottoman movement in the Ottoman Empire. (Although the Ottoman Empire was not colonized, it was becoming increasingly dominated by Western Europe.)[24] These movements had common themes: the criticism of existing Islam (especially its impurities and contamination, which were believed to be caused by local customs and forgetting of principles as well as by a mindless imitation of Western culture); the compatibility of the original, genuine Islam with reason, progress, and development, or even republican forms of government; and, as a consequence of all these criticisms, a call for a return to an original, authentic Islam. The early anticolonial resistance (the question "How can we liberate ourselves from the Western/Christian rule?") was now tied to the type of questions that were very different from the mere territorial anxiety of the initial response to colonial occupation: "How can we become independent, sovereign nation-states?" (or in the Ottoman Empire: "How can we save the State?"); "Is Islam compatible with Reason, Science, and Progress?"; "How can we keep up with the Western development?", and so on. The question of Islam's compatibility with Reason and Progress (which was answered in the affirmative in these early movements) is of course the hegemonic moment of such discourses, for it is the very sign of an attempt to first void and then occupy the space of truth as power in a double gesture (a gesture which effaces its own mark). By the same token, as the incorporation of a comparative grid, it is the emergence of a strange paradox that makes such discourses powerful and weak at the same time.

These typically hegemonic arguments that characterized the early petit bourgeois radical-nationalist movements were accompanied by a criticism of both religious establishments and colonial or corrupt native governments, and established the grounds for national liberation movements. However, they were also marked by the production of a separate, authentic Islamic element. On the one hand, the establishment of a new identity, which they seemed to require, depended on a strong critique not only of clergy and colonial government, but also of local customs and thus contributed to the process of the separation of religion from custom, and its increasing purification as an idea; on the other hand, the need to show Islam's compatibility with modern reason led the radical-nationalist movements to an argument for a return to original Islam on a programmatic level.[25] These two dimensions, separation from customs and return to origins, led to the emergence of a distinctly "Islamic" element that marked the character of the public and popular field of argumentation and contestation in Muslim countries. It is the historical cultivation of this element of Islam that we should perceive as an event correlative with Orientalism in Muslim social and political space. This correlation is what might be called the inscription of Islam in general.[26]

In the post-colonial period, the difference between the Western and Islamic elements became even more clear and led to the production of two radically opposing narratives, especially in the last two decades. Despite the fact that in many places not only institutional but also social life was secularized, Islam could not be completely and successfully absorbed as a secular moment by indigenous nationalist discourses and has continued to form an antagonistic element. This fact has generally been supported by the imperialistic relationship between the West and the Muslim world. The oil crisis in 1973 has particularly contributed to this increasingly antagonistic relationship.[27]

The first narrative, which is a progressive and positivist national one, emerged out of an evolution of the early Muslim reformism referred to above. It constructed the State as lacking (or possessing) necessary institutions for progress and society as a space of intervention, reformation, and correction along the lines of a modern Western civilized state apparatus. The difference between the native society and the West was narrated as a gap or interval that should and could be closed. In this Westernist/modernist narrative, (Islamic) religious discourse was increasingly constructed as the space of dogmatism, zealousness, backwardness, and so on.

The second narrative emerged as a response to the first: the rapid development of capitalist commodity relations, rapid urbanization, and the bureaucratic modernization of the State and dominant institutions were not isolated from the articulation of peripheral Muslim countries to the Western capitalist centers. Since these developments seemed to be represented by the first, hegemonic Westernist/modernist discourse, the religious discourse was increasingly disarticulated from hegemonic institutions and shifted toward the *popular field* formulating another, "oppositional" narrative: an Islamic discourse constructed Westernist/modernist acts, interventions, and reforms by the State as the *symbol* of a loss of faith and authenticity, an act of betrayal, collaboration, snobbism, pretentiousness, mindless imitation, and so on. In this narrative, the questions that characterized the earlier radical nationalist arguments were reproduced in a strongly moral and critical tone, and were given a specifically anti-Western dimension. Modernist/Westernist reform was increasingly transformed into an agent of Western imperialism, for everything modern, new, different came to signify the West. This Islamic narrative was also constituted as a reversal of the hierarchical temporalizing of Western hegemonic inscription: since everything that was modern/Western came to stand for a denial of religious (Muslim) identity as backward, this evolutionary temporality itself was denied as a response. Western progress was considered as representing a false narrative, a fake and corrupt world from which one could cleanse oneself only by a return to authentic religious origins. Religious narrative constituted a framework by which several social groups (urban working masses, rural petit commodity producers, the middle and small merchants of the metropolitan areas, the small business of the interior or hinterland areas) could articulate their stories vis-à-vis the state capitalist elite, liberal industrialist or comprador upper classes. (In Iran, clergy, bazaar capital, and shanty town semiproletariat came together under this narrative that operated in the mosque, where these three groups came into everyday contact.)

An "Islamic" element in political culture became much stronger than it could have been in any religiously organized society. In the long run, the Western intrusion first disarticulated the Islamic element from its traditional context, and then sent it back to its origins. It led Islam to relate to itself in terms of its distinct origins and foundations. I am referring here of course, *not* to fundamentalism as such, *but* to an Islamic narrative element as a sort of floating signifier that was hooked on all those terms and conditions which demanded it.

In other words, what is in question here is not a simple action-reaction schema, but rather the *dissemination* of a signifying force in the general field of power. For instance, in Muslim countries where Westernization/modernization was realized through an authoritarian state capitalism (Turkey, Egypt, Iran), this popular-religious, "Islamic" element came to be sedimented in the political culture through its *articulated* and *deferred* presence in several different discourses, and in different combinations. Therefore, if these two narratives (Westernist and Islamist) constructed *antagonistic positions,* their negotiation was also constantly attempted in several ways, in several different political discourses (populist, liberal, nationalist, social democrat, socialist, fascist). Each of these different discourses had to construct its content as an identity. But the interior of each of these narrative elements (West and Islam) was already inhabited by its exterior as the very condition of spacing, thus preventing each from ever relating only to itself.[28] Modernist discourses can never be constructed by a simple rejection of Islam, as is clear from the secular reorganization of religious practices by modernist hegemonies. Nor can the Islamic discourses be characterized by a simple rejection of the West/modernity, as increasingly became clear to many fundamentalists in populist-religious movements, especially during the twentieth century. (Insofar as scientific rationality is concerned, many fundamentalists have developed discourses which articulate the meaning of God with Western scientific reason, an articulation that did not stop them from being fundamentalist.) In many places, through the double process of cultural modernization and commodification of social life, secularization achieved the transformation of religious practice. But, because of the very displacement and dissemination of the Islamic element, there remained an irreducible interval and a space of tension between the modernist and Islamist narratives, despite all hybridizations. Thus, a possibility of fundamentalist Islamism was inscribed in this discursive economy.

From this point of view, perhaps the most interesting part of a text such as *Covering Islam* is Said's discussion of what he aptly calls a "double bind." According to him, the immense image-making power of the capitalist American media makes Americans see Islam only reductively, coercively, and oppositionally: as an atavism, a threat to democracy, and a return to the Middle Ages. In turn, in Muslims' eyes, Islam becomes "a reactive counterresponse to this first image of Islam as threat," and they resort to an apologetic form of discourse, which sometimes elicits the attempt to equate Islam with the immediate situation of one or another Muslim country. Said argues that "all these relative, reductive meanings of Islam depend on one another and are equally to be rejected for perpetuating the double bind" (51–52). He then writes:

> How dire the consequences of this double bind are can be seen when we consider that United States support for the Shah's modernization came to be regarded by Iranians as a rallying cry for opposing him, which was translated into a political interpretation of the monarchy as an affront to Islam; the Islamic revolution set itself in part the goal of resisting United States imperialism, which in turn appeared to resist the Islamic revolution by reinstating the Shah symbolically in New York. Thereafter the drama has unfolded as if according to an Orientalist program: the so-called Orientals acting the part decreed for them by what so-called Westerners expect; Westerners confirming their status in Oriental eyes as devils. (52)

Here Said describes a *real* political process: a series of different meanings (US, Shah, modernization, West, imperialism, Christianity) are translated into each other, are made equivalent; and this new connotative unity symbolizes a *denial* of Islam. That is to say, we have a particular situation in which all these terms make sense only as a denial of Islamic belief and identity. As Laclau and Mouffe argue in their explanation of the construction of social antagonisms:

> [I]f all the differential features of an object have become equivalent, it is impossible to express anything *positive* concerning that object; this can only imply that through the equivalence something is expressed which the object *is not.* Thus a relation of equivalence absorbing *all* the positive differential positions between the two, simply because it dissolves all positivity: the colonizer is discursively constructed as the anti-colonized. (*Hegemony* 128)[29]

How do we read, then, Said's words, "support," "opposition," "translation," "turn," "reinstating," "symbol," "unfolding," which describe the double bind? These words cannot simply refer to a false idea, to an "imprecise and ideologically loaded label," or, as we were already warned in *Orientalism,* to "a structure of lies or of myths which, once the truth about them were told, would simply blow away." This "dramatic unfolding of the Orientalist program" is a real process. If, in Said's words, the United States "in turn appeared to resist the Islamic revolution by reinstating the Shah *symbolically* in New York" (emphasis added), this was not a merely "symbolic" supplement, but such a symbolic *supplement* should be read as a political-discursive necessity. If there is a double bind, then this "turn" or symbol is at the very origin of the Orientalist drama: precisely because the Shah had *always* been *there* symbolically, it was necessary to put him there *really.* To put it another way, these translations, symbols, turns, metaphors are neither just mental nor simply linguistic relations; they are *real social relations* between subjects. Not just the way they "perceive" each other, but the very relationship between an American and an Iranian is metaphorical. The "Orientalist text" is not merely an image or idea in our minds, but *inscribes* its players in and through a history which made them present.

Let us first look at the difference between this articulation of Islam and the earlier radical nationalist or anticolonial discourses. To be sure, present Islamic discourse is nationalist in the sense that the religious element symbolizes a national space against

Western imperialism. But whereas in the case of Algeria, Western imperialism was identified more with the immediate threat, which was French colonialism, in the case of today's Iranian fundamentalism, the enemy force is identified as a civilizational form: Western civilization itself, represented by the US. Since the immediate antagonistic force was actually an indigenous authoritarian *Westernist* and *modernist* regime rather than a particular foreign military-administrative force, such an indigenous regime represented what might be called a "civilizational form" in its entirety. In Iran, the more the Shah's regime increased its repressive measures, the more Islam appeared not only as a symbol of national heritage, but also as a "civilizational" alternative against the West. In this case, we have the *extreme* form of Westernist/modernist antagonistic construction (or Orientalist program). Islamic religious discourse played a very significant role by articulating a popular will which desired a different civilization, a different world. "Fundamentalism" is also the signification of this crisis of nationalism as a question of globality and universality, as a question of "civilization." Foucault's description of the Iranian revolution as "the spirit of a world without spirit" can be read in this sense ("Iran" 221–24).

Taken together, both Algerian and Iranian Islamic discourses share a common feature. They signify what Laclau and Mouffe call a "*popular subject position* that is constituted on the basis of dividing the political space into two antagonistic camps" (*Hegemony* 129). Sami Zubaida also shows by a close reading of Khomeini's discourse that the fundamentalist argument depends on a typically modern, revolutionary discourse which articulates power as a pole antagonistic to people (1–37). The popular subject position emerged in Iran as the overdetermined totality of several different popular demands. The fundamentalist Islamic narrative provided people with a popular and powerful idiom with which to fight the repressive Shah regime. But as it brought people together and created a collective will, the antagonistic Orientalist economy on which it had to depend forced it to function as a violent suppression of other possibilities. As a result, Iranian Islamic narrative could signify and construct itself in a political and ideological form of representation that is typically Western/modern: totalitarian. It is not difficult to find in the present fundamentalist regime the most typical characteristics of the totalitarian form as described by Claude Lefort: the denial of internal division, the affirmation of an opposition between the people-as-one and an Other regarded as enemy, and the affirmation of a power-as-one (an omnipotent and benevolent Other, embodied by the militant) which sustains the people-as-one as a homogenous social body (292–306). The fundamentalist regime appears as a denial of the hegemonic dimension of modern/Western power: the hegemonic position of truth is filled by a full and sovereign subject who is *not corrupt*, and whose presence is identical to truth rather than articulating truth as/at the site of discourse.[30]

However, these totalitarian characteristics do not make it the same as other totalitarian regimes such as Nazism or Stalinism, for not only is the fundamentalist regime positioned differently vis-à-vis the Western democracies and thus articulated to a different set of questions, but also the political condition out of which it emerged was the condition of an extremely repressive police state rather than a Western bourgeois democracy. These two related characteristics imply a most important question: why are the political struggles in the Third World characterized by extreme forms of antagonism? Why and how, in the contemporary "international order," do the most antagonistic political conditions and violence become the province of the Third World? The instance of fundamentalism is only one among the many that must nevertheless enable us to question the conditions, context, and meaning of a *hegemonic global order* in which the essentially peaceful and democratic nature of political processes in the West has constantly been contrasted with violence in the Third World.[31]

I have tried to show here that if today's fundamentalism often functions as a demonstration of typical Orientalist statements and images, this is *not only* because of the selectivity, ethnocentric bias, or distortions of the Western media, *but also* because (as a result of an emergent model of reading [or writing] Islamic religious discourse in terms of its authentic origins and foundations) the historical development of Muslim societies in the last two centuries has been characterized by an increasing *fundamentalization* of Islam.[32] This model of reading is not simply typical of Orientalist texts in a narrow sense, but is also rendered necessary by the power of Western hegemonic inscriptions. The Orientalist incision, "the distinction between the West and East," has thus unfolded a past that has slowly emerged from the future. In the last two centuries of the Orientalization of the Orient, Islam itself has increasingly become a Western command.[33]

Given that such a command is not explicit, fundamentalism is only one among many other interpretations and articulations of Islamic discourse. In many Muslim countries today, Islamic movements or parties occupy metonymic, "democratic" positions as well.[34] Indeed, the presence of fundamentalism is the sign of the possibility of a certain closure, hence the possibility of another opening. The questions that we need to ask at this juncture are perhaps more important than a simple criticism of the fundamentalist result: for instance, to ask a question like "*What is Islam?*" is to accept that there is a distinct object called "Islam" which exists in the proper form that such a rationalistic question will answer. Indeed the answer is already given: "Islam is. . . ." That is to say, Islam exists in the form of the statement "It is. . . ." All I have argued here, by simply following Said's argument, is the complicity, complexity, and metaphoricity, or the *social bond* of this Orientalist question/answer "what is Islam?" Such a question will have to be answered, whether analytically or apologetically, yet always identically. For exactly the same reason, we should be careful in our strategic inversion of this question by opposing an empirical multiplicity of Islams to an (Orientalist) view of a homogenous Islam. Or at least, this inversion should *not* come *before* accounting for the way this concept/reality ("Islam") was made—within one and the same economy with the West. The making of Islam finds its correlate in the making of the Muslim subject. The question that will keep the multiplicity of the ways of this "making" open while accounting for the way in which an antagonistic and duplicitous economy is always at work is precisely the question of *how,* under what pressures, by what powers and desires, one is *made* a Muslim. For it is only this question of "how" which reveals the position of enunciation that is erased in the question of what Islam is and which can bring the complexity of the social bond back into the analysis. How can we pose a question that accounts for the plurality and otherness of the terms and conditions of the metaphor "Islam" without remaining blind to the antagonistic economy which produces it as metaphor? How can we account for the multiplicity of libidinal and political economies that cut across

Orientalism's antagonistic construction by producing positions and effects for subjects, by making them unable to speak, resist, or articulate, in one or another direction?

This argument has proceeded through a critical dialogue with Said's work by rejecting certain questions, transforming some, and formulating yet others. But my correction and elaboration of the concept of Orientalism cannot simply make it better than it was earlier. Like every writing, this one too cannot be determined outside interpretation, not simply because there are different minds with different frameworks, but because, in the "first" place, this argument too has been written as it writes itself. This, however, does not mean that we cannot know or control such discourses and practices. On the contrary, it means never giving up the *questioning* in the face of the political imperative and implies the *necessity* of a space and means to deal with the questions that need to be asked anew: what makes a statement or act Orientalist or imperialist? what desires and powers are invested or articulated in a specific discourse? what positions for speaking and acting are made available and unavailable, and what is negotiable and not negotiable as a result of these investments and articulations?

From this point of view, fundamentalism is not simply a political mistake or an unfortunate religious dogmatism specific to Oriental species, but the parody of a more general and global instance: a discursive mode that depends on a denial of its own conditions and terms, and a mode of cultural politics according to which culture has no other. If this mode finds the comfort of a final answer in the identity and authenticity of its question, we should confront it, from our intellectual site, with a radical discomfort that produces questions which aim to articulate the very space that it shuts off, silences, and makes invisible behind its mask of authenticity. *This space is other than fundamentalism's other, and is other than the fundamental(ist) complicity of/with the Reason of Enlightenment.* It shall have to be named as the space of the *people in struggle in the Third World.* The experience and time of this daily struggle that has no guarantees is other than what we experience, and it is continuously masked by the appearances, the pleasurable and profitable binaries of our civility supported by prevailing global antagonisms. Let me finish then with the most controversial instance of this (in)visibility, which I seemed to avoid so far: the "Rushdie Affair." Many talked about the rights of man and of literature, others about the rights of Muslims, their cultural autonomy, their injured feelings or political position vis-à-vis the West. It is not a coincidence that as a text of literature, Salman Rushdie's text overdetermines the most important values that we have on "both sides," and thus signifies *the* text of civility and democracy, the space of hegemony, the measure of measures. In taking this universal measure, however, in speaking and writing, let us *not forget* that since, according to the law of spacing, it is always the other which makes the measure or the value universal, we remain *in debt*. . . . This text, already written, shall have been written, *there*.

Notes

Earlier versions of this paper were presented at the "Rethinking the Political" conference at the University of California, Santa Cruz, the Strategies of Critique Conference at York University, and at the Annual Meeting of Marxist Literary Group's Institute on Culture and Society at the University of Oregon. I would like to thank Stephen Heath, Ernesto Laclau, Fred Dallmayr, and Meyda Yegenoglu for their suggestive criticisms and comments on these earlier versions. My special thanks go to Christoph Cox and Geoffrey Batchen for taking the additional burden of careful editing.

1. See his criticism of mainstream anthropology and social science in his *Time and the Other*. Despite its sophisticated discussion of the problematic of time (and of anthropological uses of time) as it has developed historically in the West, Fabian's account cannot explicitly articulate this "pushing back of the other in time" as *the way in which the Western Self has been produced*. Conceiving what is actually a structure of marking in terms of a subjective denial of coevalness (or of subjectivity), such an account dangerously leaves (the constitution of) the Western subject out of the picture. When the *dependence* of the anthropological discourse on its other is thus made invisible, one wonders how Fabian's phenomenological intersubjectivity, that is, the "we" of coevalness, would not be another hegemonic mask of the Western subject.

2. I will look at two texts only: *Orientalism* and *Covering Islam: How the Media and the Experts Determine How We See the Rest of the World*. I shall not include Said's writing on Palestine, for my purpose here is to deal with more general theoretical issues. Indeed, I do not make a comprehensive and detailed reading of these two texts either; rather, I aim to reorganize the *concept* of Orientalism.

3. In his reconsideration of his work, Said also called this difference, "the line separating Occident from Orient," "the common denominator between three different aspects of Orientalism" ("Orientalism Reconsidered" 90).

4. I suggest that the originality and value of Said's work is his way of posing

the "difference or distinction between the West and East" *before* "totalization of different societies under the sign of Oriental." As my text unfolds, I think it will be clear to the reader that I am suggesting here something that seems to run counter to Said's own intention, but which nevertheless I draw from his text. Gayatri C. Spivak's explanation of her understanding of the notion of text comes close to my reading of Said's reading of Orientalism:

> [T]he notion of textuality should be related to the worlding of a world on a supposedly uninscribed territory. When I say this I am thinking basically about the imperialist project which had to assume that the world it territorialised was in fact previously uninscribed. So then a world, on a simple level of cartography, inscribed what was presumed to be uninscribed. Now this worlding actually is also a texting, textualizing, a making into art, a making into an object to be understood. (*The Post-Colonial Critic* 1)

5. The notion of hegemonic location here is close to what Said means by "strategic location": "the author's position in a text with regard to the Oriental material he writes about" (*Orientalism* 20). Said distinguishes this from the "strategic formation," which he describes as "a way of analyzing the relationship between texts and the way in which groups of texts, types of texts, even textual genres acquire mass, density and referential power among themselves and thereafter in the culture at large" (20). The Orientalist formation itself could be seen as a strategic formation, a vast citational network that sustains its unity by the *repetition* of a difference, a continuous and dispersed centering.

6. It seems that this gathering of different discursive pieces could not be achieved by anyone. The "personal dimension" that appears at the end of the introduction to *Orientalism* (25–28), namely, Said's reference to his own inscription as an Oriental, should not be seen as simply external to his text, but indeed a layer of the text itself. A layer that does not appear as such in the text (except in the introduction) but still inside the text, it carries a *force* producing the text as text in its very movement, in its analyses, in its stops and hesitations, in its margins and frames. If Said's text is one that is made up of so many sufferings, passions, interests, questions, and challenges, it is this layer of power that makes it a politics, a life as text. As his attempt "to compile an inventory of the traces upon himself as an Oriental," *Orientalism* can be regarded as Said's *autobiographical* work, but a strange autobiography that is both singular and multiple, written and writing in space where the author is produced as a concrete synthesis, as an effect of a contingency that is necessary. No doubt Said felt this necessity; *he could but write.* Critical analysis of the hegemonic inscription of Orientalism could only be produced from within the *embodied position* such a victorious hegemony could but inscribe. The questions of the specific date (and place) of this turn of power and of the historical genesis of this embodiment have not yet been addressed. Must these questions not have something to do with the post-colonial situation? And what other things we wish to call post- . . .?

7. Of course Said refers to this citational activity, and he calls it "the restorative citation of antecedent authority" (*Orientalism* 176–77). However, he sees this citational activity as a systematic exclusion of the actualities of the modern Orient, in which "the narrative consciousness is given a very large role to play" (177). The point, however, is not just the excess of narrative consciousness. But more importantly, if we take the assumption of the *making* of the Orient seriously, there should be a historically deep connection between the restoration of

authority in citational, that is, discursive, activity and that *imaginary* "cumulative picture" produced by an "arrangement of textual fragments" (177).

8. This fantasmic dimension of Orientalism cannot be isolated from its epistemological dimension. As the dimension of desire, and with the structural misrecognition inherent to it, it is a *condition* of Orientalist knowledge and truth.

9. It seems important to point out that my position differs from James Clifford's on this point. He finds a contradiction in Said between an argument of distortion or misrecognition (of a real Orient) and an argument of pure textual construction (of an idea of Orient) (260). But given that this contradiction is self-evident in his text, why, one needs to ask, does Said make this "mistake"? Should we not see the very economy of discourse here? Since the Orient is produced only insofar as it is displaced, Orientalism is also the production of the very difference between the real Orient and its concept, image, etc. There would be no Orient without this difference. Clifford's criticism misses this crucial point, for he locates contradiction outside meaning. Contrary to what Clifford suggests, we should read in Said's tautological expression "Orientalizing the Orient" not his but Orientalism's tautology: indeed, why would one want to say that the Orient is Oriental? My emphasis here is different: the actual Orient is not a natural guarantee of a non- or anti-Orientalist knowledge, for, as the site of a struggle, it is always already contaminated by representation. This knowledge can only be a knowledge of struggle, which should be *produced* by a calculation and arrangement in each *specific* instance.

10. See, for instance, Bourdieu, "The Economics," 650.

11. For their approach to the discursive construction of objects, see Ernesto Laclau and Chantal Mouffe, "Post-Marxism Without Apologies," 82, and *Hegemony and Socialist Strategy: Towards a Radical Democratic Politics,* 180. For the argument on hegemony, see esp. chaps. 1 and 2 of *Hegemony.*

12. Here I am directly referring to the school as a hegemonic apparatus and the instructor's discourse as command, which is how Gilles Deleuze and Felix Guattari approach language in *A Thousand Plateaus:* "[T]he compulsory education machine does not communicate information; it imposes upon the child semiotic coordinates possessing all the dual foundations of grammar (masculine-feminine, singular-plural, noun-verb, subject of the statement-subject of enunciation, etc.). The elementary unit of language—the statement—is the order-word" (75–76). We can add to their list the learning of directions (orders and routes) as part of the grammar of the (Western) subject.

13. In "The Other Question," Bhabha contends that "this is a result of Said's inadequate attention to representation as a concept that articulates the historical and fantasy" (25). For instance, when Said refers to Chomsky's work as showing the *instrumental* relationship between the Vietnam War and the notion of objective scholarship, he writes: "Now because Britain, France and recently the United States are imperial powers, their political societies impart to their civil societies a sense of urgency, a direct political infusion as it were, where and whenever matters pertaining to their imperial interests abroad are concerned" (*Orientalism* 11). But if we want to locate the instrumental relationship within the context of hegemony, we have to see that such an imparting, or direct political infusion from political to civil society, could not be successful at all, if it did not find some place in the Orientalist *memory* of Western *civil society.* This memory is a layer of inscription that marks the Western subject as a citizen of its national-popular culture, "identifying 'us' Europeans as against all 'those' non-

Europeans," as Said himself has brilliantly remarked a few pages back (*Orientalism* 7).

14. Abdul R. JanMohamed criticizes Bhabha for assuming, without any demonstration, the unity of the colonial subject. See "The Economy of the Manichean Allegory: the Function of Racial Difference in Colonialist Literature." It seems to me, however, that this is precisely what Bhabha criticizes as the main weakness of Said's conceptual apparatus. By producing a concept of colonial subject as split, Bhabha aims to reveal a strategic space of "articulation," a space of "racial or sexual . . . modes of differentiation, realised as multiple, cross-cutting determinations, polymorphous and perverse, always demanding a specific and strategic calculation of their effects" (19).

15. I am referring here to the "social scientific" domain of comparative history, comparative study of revolutions and social changes, etc, which is Weberian-positivist in orientation.

16. I am referring to a writing of history in Michel Foucault's sense in *Discipline and Punish:* not "a history of the past in terms of the present," but "the history of the present" (31).

17. Depending on the particular distribution of forces and elements in a particular situation, one might like to distinguish between modernization and Westernization. But I believe that such a distinction cannot be made in general. Contrary to the claims of Third World nationalist bourgeoisies, modernization necessarily involves Westernization.

18. I am not simply referring to collaborative bourgeoisies here. Indeed, such Orientalism was rendered necessary by the unequal and combined development of capitalism in the age of imperialism, and includes nationalist bourgeoisies too.

19. Orientalism is differently articulated for different parts of the Orient. This issue of specificity is also touched upon by Lata Mani and Ruth Frankenberg, who see it as a weakness of Said's work: "Equally confusing, Said fails to adequately qualify that he is not here constructing a general theory of Orientalism but a theory of Orientalism as it developed in relation to West Asia. . . . [I]t would appear from Said's investigation that the production and elaboration of Orientalism was entirely a European enterprise and that Orientals or natives are involved only as objects of scrutiny" (176). However, Said *does* construct a theory of Orientalist discourse by linking it to the *general* context of imperial/colonial *Western power* and by defining its common denominator as the *distinction between the West and East,* as these critics themselves also emphasize (178). I tend to read Said's text as a theoretical beginning rather than a comprehensive description. As "imposing" and "monolithic" as they are, theories are also usually contaminated by specific sites. The fact that Said is *Middle Eastern,* or more specifically *Palestinian,* further demonstrates the force of contamination in producing theory. Mani and Frankenberg's rewriting of the Middle East as "West Asia" amounts to an erasure of Said's context. Generally, their criticism needs to be further clarified. For, given that they want to emphasize the role of imperialism, it is even more confusing when they identify "specificity" with "native involvement" and reach the conclusion that Orientalism is therefore "an essentially dialogical process" (178). "Specificity" should mean that Orientalism is always inscribed, complex, different, that is, always changing according to the nature and limits of the forces involved in it, rather than simply dialogical.

20. "Modernity" has been a status marker, a distinction in the Third World. Jean Baudrillard makes a similar argument in relation to the material inscription

of the sign "European" in several European countries in his *For A Critique of the Political Economy of the Sign* (57–61). Despite his sophisticated analysis of sign and value, interestingly (or indeed typically) Baudrillard does not think this sign outside Europe.

21. See also Gasche, 198–202.

22. The question "Can we live under a Christian government and still be proper Muslims?" was differently resolved. As it led to migrations and social movements, it also unavoidably led to practical or in some cases (e.g., India) doctrinal distinctions between living space and religious space. See Peters.

23. The main reference to the veil is of course Franz Fanon's early analysis in the first chapter of *A Dying Colonialism.* For an analysis of the place of the veiled Muslim woman in French colonial discourse, see Malek Alloula, *Colonial Harem.* For a more complex account which also includes a criticism of Said from a feminist-psychoanalytic perspective, see Meyda Yegenoglu, "Veiled Fantasies: Cultural and Sexual Difference in the Discourse of Orientalism."

24. See, for Malaysia, William Roff, *The Origins of Malay Nationalism;* for Turkey, Caglar Keyder, *State and Class in Turkey* (although the Ottoman Empire was not colonized, from the point of view of the global political, economic, and ideological pressures that we discuss here, the group in question acted through the same ideological parameters); for Egypt, Jacques Berque: *Egypt: Imperialism and Revolution.*

25. While these radical-nationalist arguments were made from within an urban petit bourgeois class habitus, many peasant uprisings made from within a different, subaltern location were characterized by different kinds of articulations. See Ranajit Guha and Gayatri C. Spivak, *Subaltern Studies;* and Shaharil Talib, *After Its Own Image: the Trengganu Experience, 1881–1941.* Both the authors of *Subaltern Studies* and Talib show, in different ways, that these peasant uprisings were developed in the context of emerging colonial practices of power/knowledge.

26. Clifford Geertz talks about "ideologization" of Islam in reference to similar developments in his *Islam Observed.* However, the notion of ideologization assumes a nonideological, religious Islam.

27. For how the oil crisis introduced a purposefully negative image of Islam into the Western media, see Said's *Covering Islam,* esp. 33–40.

28. For a theoretical specification of this self-effacing dimension of the "infrastructure of spacing," see Gasche, 190–191.

29. Is it a coincidence that Laclau and Mouffe refer to *colonialism* as an illustration of their *theory* of the construction of antagonisms?

30. Since I am not making a full-blown analysis of the Iranian revolution here, I ignored some specific dimensions, such as the Shiite discourse. Obviously, none of the dimensions that I look at here (including fundamentalism) has any inherent or necessary relationship with Shiism. Although the Shiite notion of the martyr might have contributed to the formation of a popular revolutionary discourse, the relationship between the two is not necessary. For the Iranian Revolution, see Abrahamian.

31. In their analysis of political space, Laclau and Mouffe draw our attention to an important difference between "a logic of difference" and "a logic of equivalence." According to them, these two different social logics roughly correspond to the struggles in the West and the Third World, respectively. Whereas the political space in the West is characterized by a "proliferation of antagonisms and

multiplicity of democratic struggles which does not form a people and does not divide the political space into two antagonistic camps," in the Third World, "imperialist forms of exploitation and brutal and centralized forms of domination endow the struggles with a center, and a clearly defined enemy." The first logic corresponds to a delimited antagonism and a democratic subject position, the second to a popular antagonism/subject position (*Hegemony* 130–31). Laclau and Mouffe emphasize that they make no more than an observation of tendencies. Nevertheless, their important distinction could have benefited from a closer examination of the difference between the ways the metropolitan and peripheral national political spaces are formed in relation to each other. Such a difference signifies a global "order of things," that is, an analysis of the discourses of imperialism.

32. There is no doubt that the media is biased and distorts grossly. But is the media solely responsible for this? I am following Said here: "[T]hese enormous generalizations have behind them a whole history, enabling and disabling at the same time" (*Covering Islam* 9). Interestingly, when Said questions the Islamic apologists by giving the example of Khomeini's announcement that "the enemies of revolution will be destroyed," his reference is a report by *Reuters* news agency (*Covering Islam* 52). By this insistence on the *historical* dimension, I am again trying to understand the double bind as put forward by Said.

33. Of course, I am referring back to note 12. The "authentic" Islam proposed by fundamentalism can also be seen as a simulation in a sense close to Baudrillard's: the simulator is the one who produces his own symptoms (*Simulations* 5). However, since Baudrillard believes that, with the death of the Enlightenment utopia, the problematic of representation has no relevance whatsoever either, he sees only what is microscopically convenient for his all-sweeping view: the simulations in the museum (*Simulations* 13–23). Ironically, in a recent interview, he finds the West "weak and vulnerable in the face of the certitudes of radical Islam," which is the only "exception" standing as a challenge to postmodernity's "radical indifference" ("After Utopia" 54). Baudrillard points out that Khomeini's question should be taken as "our question" ("what happens after the great orgy of freedom that has left us all indifferent?"). But this "us" has already been positioned vis-à-vis "them." Baudrillard's easy acknowledgement is symptomatic of his equally easy, wholesale abolishment of difference. It seems, however, that the Baudrillardian idea of *radical* indifference assumes a radical or absolute difference—that can nevertheless be absorbed, or even made useful.

34. I am using this concept of a metonymic position in the sense suggested by Laclau and Mouffe (*Hegemony* 130–31).

Works Cited

Abrahamian, Ervand. *Iran Between Two Revolutions.* Princeton: Princeton UP, 1982.

Alloula, Malek. *The Colonial Harem.* Minneapolis: U of Minnesota P, 1986.

Baudrillard, Jean. "After Utopia: the Primitive Society of the Future." *New Perspectives Quarterly* 6.2 (1989): 52–54.

———. *For A Critique of the Political Economy of the Sign.* Trans. Charles Levin. St. Louis: Telos, 1981.

———. *Simulations.* Trans. Paul Foss, Paul Patton, and Philip Beitchman. New York: Semiotext(e), 1983.
Berque, Jacques. *Egypt: Imperialism and Revolution.* London: Faber, 1972.
Bhabha, Homi K. "The Other Question." *Screen* 24.6 (1983): 18–36.
Bourdieu, Pierre. *The Algerians.* Trans. Alan C. M. Ross. Boston: Beacon, 1962.
———. "The Economics of Linguistic Exchanges." *Social Science Information* 16.6 (1977): 645–68.
Clifford, James. *The Predicament of Culture: Twentieth-Century Ethnography, Literature and Art.* Cambridge: Harvard UP, 1988.
de Saussure, Ferdinand. *Course in General Linguistics.* Ed. Charles Bally and Albert Sechehaye. Trans. Roy Harris. La Salle: Open Court, 1989.
Deleuze, Gilles, and Félix Guattari. *A Thousand Plateaus.* Trans. Brian Massumi. Minneapolis: U of Minnesota P, 1988.
Derrida, Jacques. *Positions.* Trans. Alan Bass. Chicago: U of Chicago P, 1982.
Fabian, Johannes. *Time and the Other: How Anthropology Makes Its Object.* New York: Columbia UP, 1983.
Fanon, Franz. *A Dying Colonialism.* Trans. Haakon Chevalier. New York: Grove Weidenfield, 1967.
Foucault, Michel. *Discipline and Punish: The Birth of the Prison.* Trans. Alan Sheridan. New York: Vintage, 1977.
———. "Iran: Spirit of a World Without Spirit." *Politics Philosophy Culture: Interviews and Other Writings 1977–1984.* Trans. Alan Sheridan. Ed. Lawrence D. Kritzman. New York: Routledge, 1990. 211–224.
Gasché, Rodolph. *The Tain of the Mirror: Derrida and the Philosophy of Reflection.* Cambridge: Harvard UP, 1986.
Geertz, Clifford. *Islam Observed: Religious Development in Morocco and Indonesia.* Chicago: U of Chicago P, 1971.
Guha, Ranajit, and Gayatri C. Spivak. *Subaltern Studies.* New York: Oxford UP, 1988.
JanMohamed, Abdul R. "The Economy of the Manichean Allegory: the Function of Racial Difference in Colonialist Literature." *"Race," Writing and Difference.* Ed. Henry Louis Gates, Jr. Chicago: U of Chicago P, 1986. 78–106.
Keyder, Caglar. *State and Class in Turkey.* London: Verso, 1989.
Laclau, Ernesto, and Chantal Mouffe. *Hegemony and Socialist Strategy: Towards a Radical Democratic Politics.* Trans. Winston Moore and Paul Commack. London: Verso, 1985.
———. "Post-Marxism Without Apologies." *New Left Review* 166 (Nov.-Dec. 1987): 79–106.
Lefort, Claude. *The Political Forms of Modern Society: Bureaucracy, Democracy, Totalitarianism.* Trans. John B. Thompson. Cambridge: MIT P, 1986.
Mani, Lata, and Ruth Frankenberg. "The Challenge of *Orientalism.*" *Economy and Society* 14.2 (1985): 174–92.
Peters, Rudolph. *Islam and Colonialism: The Doctrine of Jihad in Modern History.* Paris and New York: Mouton, 1979.
Roff, William. *The Origins of Malay Nationalism.* New Haven: Yale UP, 1967.
Said, Edward W. *Covering Islam: How the Media and the Experts Determine How We See the Rest of the World.* New York: Pantheon, 1981.
———. *Orientalism.* Harmondsworth: Penguin, 1978.
———. "Orientalism Reconsidered." *Cultural Critique* 1 (1985): 89–107.
Spivak, Gayatri C. *The Post-Colonial Critic: Interviews, Strategies, Dialogues.* Ed. Sarah Harasym. New York: Routledge, 1990.

Talib, Shaharil. *After Its Own Image: The Trengganu Experience, 1881–1941*. Singapore: Oxford UP, 1984.

Yegenoglu, Meyda. "Veiled Fantasies: Cultural and Sexual Difference in the Discourse of Orientalism." *Cultural Studies,* forthcoming.

Zubaida, Sami. *Islam, the People and the State: Essays on Political Ideas and Movements in the Middle East.* London and New York: Routledge, 1989.

THESIS ELEVEN

Interpreting Modernity

Thesis Eleven is an international and interdisciplinary journal of European social thought that is committed to a pluralism of approaches, and to making previously untranslated texts by leading European theorists available to English readers.

Located in Melbourne, Australia, ***Thesis Eleven*** has established a large international network of authors including Castoriadis, Habermas, Heller, Luhmann, Touraine, and Wallerstein.

Thesis Eleven is published three times a year—in March, July, and November—by MIT Press Journals. ISSN 0725-5136

Yearly Rates:
Individual *$25*
Institution *$55*

Ouside U.S.A., add $14.00 postage and handling. Canadians add additional 7% GST. Prepayment is required. Send check drawn against a U.S. bank in U.S. funds, MasterCard or VISA number to:

MIT Press Journals
55 Hayward Street
Cambridge, MA 02142-1399 USA
TEL (617) 253-2889
FAX (617) 258-6779

Editors:
Johann P. Arnason
Peter Beilharz
Michael Crozier
Kevin McDonald
Peter Murphy
David Roberts
Gillian Robinson
Philipa Rothfield
John Rundell

Editorial Advisory Board:
Michele Barrett, London
Zygmunt Bauman, Leeds
Teresa Brennan, Cambridge
Cornelius Castoriadis, Paris
Jean Cohen, New York
David Ames Curtis, Paris
Ferenc Fehér, New York
Rita Felski, Perth
Agnes Heller, New York
Barry Hindess, Canberra
Axel Honneth, Frankfurt
Dick Howard, Stonybrook
Martin Jay, Berkeley
Joel Kahn, Melbourne
Niklas Luhmann, Bielefield
György Márkus, Sydney
Maria Márkus, Sydney
Thomas McCarthy, Boston
Stephen Mennell, Melbourne
Andrew Milner, Melbourne
Carole Pateman, Los Angeles
Barry Smart, Auckland
Gareth Stedman Jones, Cambridge
Alain Touraine, Paris
Julian Triado, Melbourne
Immanuel Wallerstein, Binghamton/Paris
Anna Yeatman, Aukland

"A Jumble of Foreignness": The Sublime Musayums of Nineteenth-Century Fairs and Expositions

Meg Armstrong

Writing of the Midway at the World's Columbian Exposition in Chicago in 1893, contemporary observer Julian Ralph declared: "It will be a jumble of foreignness . . . a bit of Fez and Nuremberg, of Sahara and Dahomey and Holland, Japan and Rome and Coney Island. It will be gorgeous with color, pulsating with excitement, riotous with the strivings of a battalion of bands, and peculiar to the last degree" (qtd. in Hinsley 351).[1]

What sort of aesthetic governs "a bit of Fez and Nuremberg . . . Rome and Coney Island"? What is meant by the combination of the adjectives *gorgeous, pulsating, riotous,* and *peculiar*? Why the desire to have these sensations stirred by fragments of the exotic and familiar? Thackeray's Mr. Molony expresses sensations similar to Ralph's when viewing the "sublime musayum" of London's Great Exhibition of 1851:

© 1993 by *Cultural Critique*. 0882-4371 (Winter 1992–93). All rights reserved.

Amazed I pass
From glass to glass
Deloighted I survey'em
Fresh wondthers grows
Before me nose
In this sublime Musayum!

Look here's a fan
From far Japan
A sabre from Damasco;
There's shawls ye get
From far Thibet
And cotton prints from Glasgow! (191–92)

Mr. Molony parodies the pretense to sublimity at the Great Exhibition: he gives us a (potentially) confusing whirl of products and people contained in the Crystal Palace.[2] In other measures of his verse, Molony provides wry commentary on the seeming *hysteria* that motivates the collection of the odd trappings of "civilization," progress, and colonialism. Molony's "deloight" is provoked by the odd conjunction of seemingly disjunct objects: Japanese fans, Tibetan shawls, German flutes, teapots, "Injians and Canajians," and steam engines.

In his parody of the fair, Thackeray is also ridiculing the subliming of the exotic, as he had earlier in *Eastern Sketches*. There, Thackeray satirizes Alexander Kinglake's attempt to play the poet in his travel book *Eothen* (1844) and mercilessly compares it to Byron's wish to sublime the Orient in such works as *The Giaour* and *The Corsair*. The subliming of the exotic and oriental had, by the time of the Crystal Palace, begun to seem commonplace; by the end of the century, it appears as a requisite of the commercialization and commodification of exotic others in fairs and expositions. The mnemonic devices of the fair—photographic souvenirs chief among them—capture both the reification of this exotic sublimity and its containment in the stereotypes of difference born on the midways of the world.[3]

The hysterical jumble of non-European "cities," objects, and peoples in the context of fairs—spectacles meant to promote the hegemony of European or American "civilization" in all things[4]—provokes thought about the role of the exotic in such magnificent public displays of power. It is well known that ethnological displays of exotic peoples at many world fairs were designed to promote a hierarchy of races that maintained the dominance of white Europeans and Americans.[5] The evolutionary ideology that governed ethnological displays was, however, complemented at such fairs as the Columbian Exposition of 1893 by strips or arcades of exotic villages that were thrown together in a space designated for more popular amusements. In Chicago in 1893 this strip was the Midway Plaisance; at the St. Louis fair (1904) it was the Pike; at Seattle's fair (1909), the Pay Streak; and at Portland's exposition (1905), the Trail. On the midways, a competing (though oddly complementary) aesthetic ideology is at work: the exotic is a chaos, a jumble, a sublimely grotesque and bawdy array of colors, sights, scents, and sounds. While the ethnological museums show the steady and orderly progress of the races toward the pinnacle of technological achievements among the white races, the midways are a parodic counterdisplay of the exotic as a grotesque chaos, distinguishing it from the monumental architecture and technology of European and American displays of industrial prowess. Whereas the ethnological exhibits "order" the chaos of the foreign, the midways exhibit the other in a state *prior to* the ordering processes of European powers. Both forms of exhibition are, of course, framed by the European planner's gaze; what is important to note is that they complement and reinforce each other, despite the disparity between their modes of presentation.

On the midways, in exotic arcades, the "exotic" is seen and understood as a "jumble of foreignness." This jumble may tell us a great deal about the ways in which "exotic" objects and people are circulated, the fashion in which they are incorporated in a more general exoticizing aesthetic alive in public spectacles of the last century. In this essay, I will discuss aspects of this exoticizing process and suggest ways in which the collected fragments of the "sublime musayum" helped to form exotically sublime and stereotypical others in nineteenth-century Europe and America—and thereby as well to shape, as it enacted, a modern cosmopolitan sensibility. The sublimity of the spectacle affected all viewers and contributed to the impact of the perceived differences among nations. For example, in his study of the display of Islamic architecture in nineteenth-century fairs, Zeynip Çelik emphasizes the astonished reaction of visitors from the Near and Middle East upon viewing displays of European technological power (electricity and the Eiffel Tower). The Turkish novelist Halid Ziya remarked upon the sublimity of one such vista: "The Eiffel Tower was a wonder of the time. One night in an unexpected moment, when this iron tower three hundred meters tall was suddenly painted in red flames by an electric current, the thousands of people gathered beneath it unconsciously cried from their hearts in a startled, fearful voice" (qtd. in Çelik 48).

How does the fair-goer approach the spectacle? Perhaps thinking of Baudelaire, Curtis Hinsley has suggested that the Columbian Exposition, like other expositions, encouraged the spectator to adopt the attitude of the *flâneur,* to take on the "walkabout" sensibility of the one who, as Benjamin phrased it, "goes botanizing on the asphalt"—but this time through created "cities" and "villages" of exotics on the Midway. Hinsley mentions H. H. Bancroft's *Book of the Fair* (1894) to reinforce the idea of the fair as a "jumble" of foreignness available to the cosmopolitan *flâneur.*[6] Other contemporary observers were struck by the "vivacious cosmopolitan medley" of the Midway Plaisance, and the fair in general (*Chicago Tribune* 30 Apr. 1893). The author of the Chicago Record Co.'s *History of the World's Fair* (1894) noted the merits of Columbia Avenue (the main aisle of the Manufactures building):

> A man walked the length of the street. It was a good day for aimless promenading. The wooden pavement was damp and cool underfoot. Refreshing breaths of lake wind caught him at each corner. He saw first, high tiers of graceful statuary ranged under velvet canopies and guarded by swarthy Italian marines. He saw men from Switzerland leading visitors through a fairyland of carvings and jewels. He saw men from Norway and Denmark standing at the street doorways of their pavilions. Russians in solemn black coats, buttoned up to their heavy beards, lounged among the kiosks. He saw Belgium's heavy arches and France's magnificent doorways. Through them he caught glimpses of silks, bronzes, porcelains, golden ware. He leaned on plush ropes and looked into the most luxurious apartments known to England. He saw Germany's minarets, the riotous show of rich colors and foliate decora-

> tion, the dripping fountains and the tangled grill-work. . . . The peaked roof and sheltering eaves of Japan's airy castle invited him to a ramble among the fireflies and dragons. He saw many more things through the glass stalls or wide doorways of the miniature palaces, yet the best thing he saw was the street itself. (81)

The Chicago Record's advice for amateur "kodakers" shows us just how close the different "worlds" and "villages" were to one another:

> The operator who does not find enough character for his purposes in ordinary park flora will perhaps be able to do something with the following buildings from the various points of view indicated: The fisheries and government, from behind a thin screen of willow and bamboo near the middle one of the three north bridges; the Japanese bridge and building, as seen over a large mass of arrowhead leaves on the shore near the west pavilion of the fisheries; the Brazil building, seen through the maze of tropical foliage at the east entrance of the Illinois building . . . and the Japanese tea garden, looked down upon from the road that crosses the old iron bridge. The island may also be taken, in a somewhat general fashion, from behind the mounted Indian that stands in front of the transportation building. . . . These views, however, will be found more curious than complete. (118–19)

The fair-going *flâneur* (somewhat like the avid kodaker) is confronted with successive images of miniature palaces of Columbia Avenue or "native" life in Germany, Hungary, Africa, and other countries of the Midway (see maps, Figs. 1 and 2). While the kodaker is busy with individual frozen prints, the ritual process of walking through the fair creates a particular relationship between the fair-going *flâneur* and the spectacle: the fair-goer is the passive gaze that is constituted *as* the one upon whom the collage of exotica is thrust or projected. The agency of the fair-goer arises in his activities as a rag-picker, a bricoleur of foreign objects (or "events") on his visual plane that will contribute to his own museum of exotica and to which he will give an aesthetic order. The fair-goer is the one who, in walking through the fair, collects and

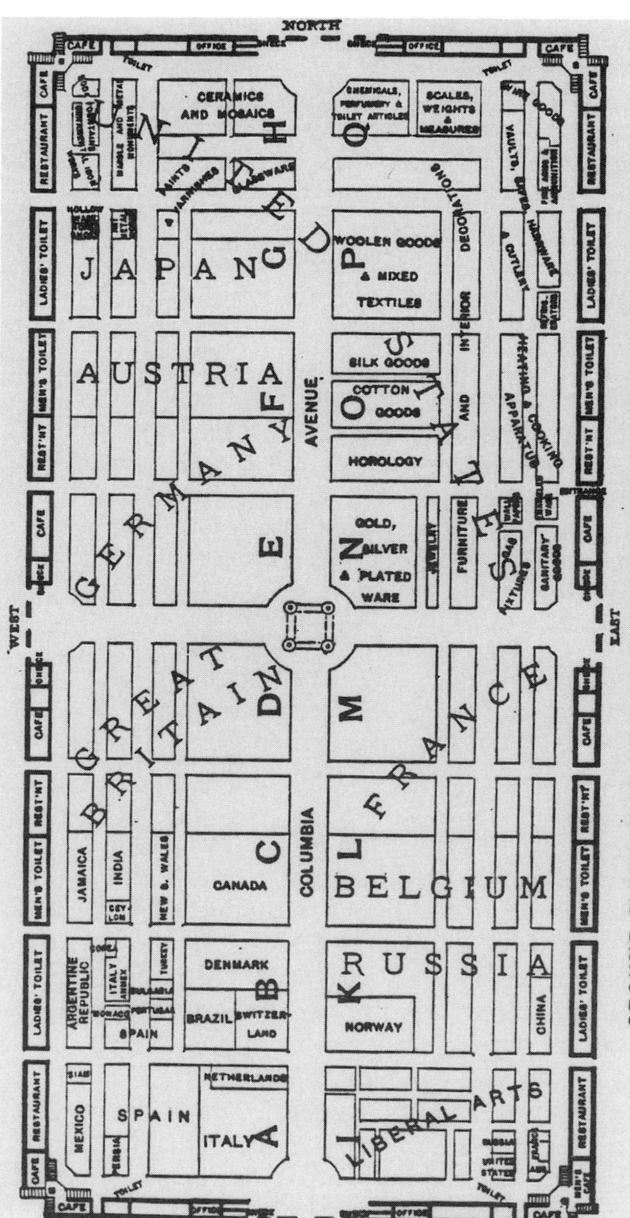

Fig. 1. Columbia Avenue from *The Economizer*.

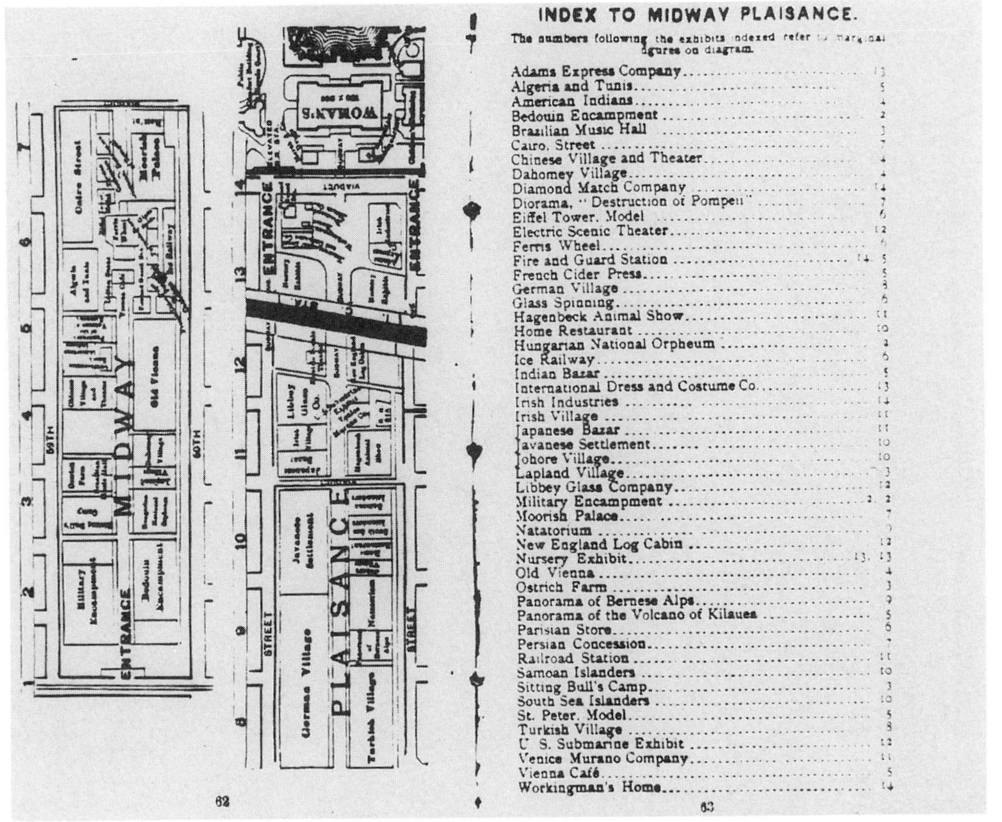

INDEX TO MIDWAY PLAISANCE.

The numbers following the exhibits indexed refer to marginal figures on diagram.

Adams Express Company 13
Algeria and Tunis 5
American Indians 4
Bedouin Encampment 2
Brazilian Music Hall 3
Cairo, Street 7
Chinese Village and Theater 4
Dahomey Village 4
Diamond Match Company 14
Diorama, "Destruction of Pompeii" 7
Eiffel Tower, Model 6
Electric Scenic Theater 12
Ferris Wheel 6
Fire and Guard Station 14, 5
French Cider Press 5
German Village 8
Glass Spinning 6
Hagenbeck Animal Show 11
Home Restaurant 10
Hungarian National Orpheum 2
Ice Railway 6
Indian Bazar 5
International Dress and Costume Co. 13
Irish Industries 14
Irish Village 11
Japanese Bazar 11
Javanese Settlement 10
Johore Village 10
Lapland Village 3
Libbey Glass Company 12
Military Encampment 2, 2
Moorish Palace 7
Natatorium .... [illegible]
New England Log Cabin 12
Nursery Exhibit 13, 13
Old Vienna 4
Ostrich Farm 3
Panorama of Bernese Alps 9
Panorama of the Volcano of Kilauea 5
Parisian Store 6
Persian Concession 7
Railroad Station 11
Samoan Islanders 10
Sitting Bull's Camp 3
South Sea Islanders 10
St. Peter, Model 5
Turkish Village 8
U. S. Submarine Exhibit 12
Venice Murano Company 11
Vienna Café 5
Workingman's Home 14

Fig. 2a. Midway Plaisance. From *The Economizer*.

Midway Plaisance.

BARRE SLIDING RAILWAY — A novel means of transportation; runs 100 miles per hour. Fare 10 cents.

MILITARY ENCAMPMENT of National Guards from the different States.

BEDOUIN WARRIORS — Giving sham battles, dances, and camel races. Admission 10 cents.

SITTING BULL'S LOG CABIN — A typical American Indian camp. Admission 10 cents.

HUNGARIAN ORPHEUM — Music by native Hungarian orchestra. Café in connection. Admission 25 cents.

CALIFORNIA OSTRICH FARM — Many large birds, and collection of eggs and feathers. Admission 10 cents.

BRAZILIAN CONCERT HALL — Native singers and orchestra. Admission 25 cents.

LAPLAND VILLAGE — Composed of thirty-seven natives and twenty-five reindeer. Admission 25 cents.

DAHOMEY VILLAGE — Nearly 100 native Africans and amazons, giving barbaric dances, etc. Admission 25 cents.

MEXICAN CONCERT HALL — Formerly the Captive Balloon Park. Instrumental music free.

CHINESE VILLAGE — Consisting of joss-house, theater, and restaurant. Admission 10 cents.

OLD VIENNA — As it appeared in the sixteenth century; very realistic. Admission 25 cents.

AMERICAN INDIAN VILLAGE — Composed of tribes from the Northwest. Admission 10 cents.

PANORAMA OF VOLCANO OF KILAUEA — A magnificent painting covering 22,248 square feet of canvas. Admission 25 cents.

EAST INDIAN BAZAAR — Offering for sale unique jewelry, etc.

ALGERIAN AND TUNISIAN VILLAGE — Showing a street in Algeria, with theater. Admission 25 cents.

VIENNA CAFE — A cool resort, serving lunch and refreshments. Moderate prices.

FRENCH CIDER PRESS — Making cider after the manner of French peasantry.

MODEL ST. PETER'S CHURCH — Required ten years to construct; one-sixtieth the size of original. Admission 25 cents.

ICE RAILWAY — Furnishing a real toboggan slide on ice. One ride 10 cents.

FERRIS WHEEL — 266 feet high and 264 feet in diameter; carries 2,160 persons. Two trips 50 cents.

PERSIAN GLASS SPINNING — An interesting exhibition. Admission 10 cents.

MODEL EIFFEL TOWER — One-fifth the size of original in Paris. Admission 25 cents.

MOORISH PALACE — Very interesting collection of wax figures. Admission 25 cents.

64

Midway Plaisance, continued.

PERSIAN PALACE — With theater and dancing-girls. Admission 50 cents.

POMPEIIAN HOUSE — Showing style of architecture previous to eruption of Vesuvius. Admission 25 cents.

EGYPTIAN TEMPLE — A characteristic reproduction, with mummies and obelisks. Admission 25 cents.

STREET IN CAIRO — Over 300 natives, with camels and donkeys. Admission 10 cents; theater 25 cents.

TURKISH VILLAGE — Consisting of mosque, theater, and bazaars. Admission 25 cents.

GERMAN VILLAGE — Representing the Germany of old days. Free concerts in garden. Admission to museum 25 cents.

PANORAMA BERNESE ALPS — Magnificent painting, 560 feet long and 65 feet high. Admission 50 cents.

VIENNA CAFE — Seating capacity, 4,000 persons.

JAVANESE VILLAGE — Comprising 125 natives, 36 of whom are females. Admission 10 cents.

JOHORE VILLAGE — An interesting feature of the Plaisance. Admission 25 cents.

SOUTH SEA ISLANDERS — In bamboo huts; dancers, medicine men, and acrobats. Admission 25 cents.

JAPANESE BAZAAR — Articles on exhibition are for sale.

HAGENBECK'S ANIMAL SHOW and ethnographical collection of weapons, household implements, etc. Admission 25 cents to $1.

IRISH VILLAGE — Reproduction of Donegal Castle and Drogheda Gate. Admission 25 cents.

VENICE MURANO EXHIBIT — Thirty Venetian glass-blowers at work. Admission 25 cents.

LIBBEY GLASS WORKS, showing the process of glass manufacture. Admission 10 cents.

SUB-MARINE DIVING — Exhibitions of diving in regulation diving-bell. Admission 10 cents.

NEW ENGLAND LOG CABIN, furnished in "old tyme" style. Admission 10 cents; dinners 50 cents.

ELECTRIC SCENIC THEATER — Alpine scenery made gorgeous by electricity. Admission 25 cents.

COLORADO GOLD MINE, showing method of mining in the mountains. Admission 10 cents.

NURSERY EXHIBIT — Displays by France and California.

INTERNATIONAL BEAUTY SHOW of forty-five handsome women in native costume. Admission 25 cents.

PHILADELPHIA WORKINGMAN'S HOME; contains seven rooms, including bath.

ADAMS EXPRESS OFFICE, where money or packages can be forwarded or received.

IRISH INDUSTRIES — Reproduction of Blarney Castle. Admission 25 cents.

DIAMOND MATCH BUILDING, containing World's Fair offices of the company.

65

Fig. 2b. Midway Plaisance. From *The Economizer*.

pieces together the "sublime musayum" of disarticulated and displaced fragments and ruins of exotic others. In making this jumble his own, he is also painting a portrait (albeit a somewhat ironic one) of himself as a true cosmopolitan: he has been everywhere, *at once.*

Influenced more by Peter Berger and Thomas Luckmann than by Charles Baudelaire, Robert W. Rydell has argued that the world fair, at least in America in the late nineteenth and early twentieth centuries, can be understood as a "symbolic universe," a structure of legitimation providing meaning for social experience. "These events," Rydell says of the expositions, "were triumphs of hegemony as well as symbolic edifices" (2). As symbolic universes, the fairs legitimate the "world order" they create. For Rydell, this symbolic universe, represented in ethnological exhibits, was the product of a union between "Darwinian theories about racial development and utopian dreams about America's material and national progress" (235). In the exhibits the fair-goer could walk from white civilization to dark barbarity (Rydell 64–65). On the midways, however, a competing symbolic universe is at work. In the case of these entertaining arcades, we must acknowledge a "symbolic order" that consists of a narcotic jumble of images of all that is "exotic": a hallucination of voyage, an illusion of different "lives" readily entertaining or "purchasable" in the form of foods, beverages, and photographs. This competing universe is the chaotic or grotesquely sublime exotic affirmed on the midways; it complements the scientific realism of evolutionary hierarchies of race, providing an illustration of an irrational babel of backwardness in contrast with the future-oriented rationales of progress evident in the exhibits of the industrialized white nations.[7]

Exhibitions of colonial power, of colonial peoples and "exotic objects" of various realms, certainly did serve to create and reinforce the sensibility of empire. The act of exhibiting a particular collection of objects and others, whether at fairs, museums, or galleries, is definitive: the exotic other is constituted *for* European and American audiences through such displays. But why the *jumble* on the midways? Why the seeming hysteria in presentation? The novelty does not lie in the display of people in a "Gallery of Nations" style, for this phenomenon is at least as old as the sixteenth century (see Kirschenblatt-Gimblett 339). In the case of nineteenth-century world fairs, the foreign is often as much of a "jumble" as it was in earlier displays of curiosities except that the incredible *magnitude* of the great expositions combines vastly different forms of the foreign in the "Small World" atmosphere of a gallery of nations.[8] Exhibitions of villages and countries were not far from each other—or from the more obvious amusements of the exposition. A contemporary tells us that "the Persian Palace of Eros" was "so near the Ferris wheel that you could skip a cracker from the yard of the wheel to the roof of the incongruous building with its *olla-podrida* architecture."[9] For instance, Çelik argues that at the Universal Exposition of 1878 in Paris, "the idea was to provide an architectural collage, with each nation represented according to its own taste and tradition." Each nation was given a pavilion five meters wide, and some nations—England and the United States among them—were allowed more width (68). The facades were not necessarily designed by each nation, however, and at this exposition, the ensemble of facades to represent Morocco, Tunisia, and Persia was designed by a French architect. In some cases, as well, the colonial bond between nations was inscribed in the architectural planning: in the 1878 exposition, the colonial relationship between Algeria, Tunisia, Morocco, Egypt, and France was symbolically represented in the Trocadero (Çelik 69).

The contiguity and quantity of "worlds" increases the magnitude of the *effect of the foreign* at the same time that it diminishes or miniaturizes their singularity and difference from each other as well as the particularities of their differences from Europe. Here the gigantic alternates with the miniature, the sublime with the hopelessly mundane or ridiculous. This dialectic of contrary tendencies, however, indicates not so much an indecision or a simple confusion as a deep anxiety concerning the status of the exotic, different, or culturally other in the nineteenth century. The vertigo of these hysterical jumbles is balanced with an attempt to control, type, and thereby minimize the anxieties pertaining to race and gender in an increasingly cosmopolitan world, as well as the anxieties concerning the fall of empires. The aesthetic of the fairs mediates these crises and resolves them at a controllable—albeit abstract and aesthetic—level. And yet from this aesthetic resolution come far-reaching implications for the culturally and historically generated perceptions Europe came to have of "the Rest," and reflexively of the West as well. Expositions of the exotic and stereotypically foreign help to form what Sander Gilman calls our "myth-making" capacities. "Stereotypes," he says, "can assume a life of their own, rooted not in reality but in the myth-making made necessary by our need to control our world" (12).

The Chicago exposition of 1893 provides some curious examples of this cultural bricolage of the sublime and mundane, the gigantic and the miniature. On the Midway, villages of exotic peoples included a Bedouin camp, a Persian palace, an Algerian and Tunisian village, a Japanese bazaar, a Chinese market, and villages from Samoa, Java, Dahomey, and Turkey in addition to exhibits of "white" countries such as Ireland and Germany (Benedict 58). These exhibits, in addition to being "educational," as the planners hoped, were amusements: they were sensational spectacles, included shows of dances and the performance of daily tasks, and, in cases like Little Egypt's (Chicago, 1893), also offered the exotic as an object of sexual desire, packaged to the tune of the "hootchy-cootchy" dance.[10]

In 1894, the American Engraving Company of Chicago published *Midway Types: A Book of Illustrated Lessons About the People of the Midway Plaisance World's Fair 1893*. This volume of "lessons" is composed of captioned photographic "souvenirs" of all the cultural and physically distinct types of the Columbian Exposition; we might think of it as a not-so-distant relative of the "physiologies" popular in Europe in the middle of the nineteenth century (see Benjamin 35–36). The captions assert repeatedly that those who strolled the Midway "will never forget" these faces, the dances and practices of the Samoans, the Javanese, the Egyptians. The "souvenir" album expresses the desire that we remember in a certain fashion, that our memory suggest to us general impressions of the phototypically foreign. The physiologies served to alleviate anxieties about class differences and other frictions of society, to convince the Parisian that really these other types were merely "harmless oddballs." *Midway Types* tries as well to promote a genial attitude toward the foreign, to help us to appreciate the "sweet little Javanese" and to show us the humor in the "savage tigresses" of Dahomey. The contradictions and differences among the exotic types *and* between the exotics and the Europeans and Americans, however, greatly interfere with this aspiration.

Perhaps one of the reasons for this lies in the contradictions inherent in the simultaneous display of the "progress of civilization" and peoples who were, in the late nineteenth century, regarded by many as evidence of barbarism, if not retrogression. In his speech at the inaugural ceremonies for the Columbian Exposition on 1 May 1892, Director-General Davis expressed the hope of the organizers "that this great Exposition may inaugurate a new era of moral and material progress, and our fervent aspiration that the associations of the nations here may secure not only warmer and stronger friendships, but lasting peace throughout the world" (Chicago Record 37). Davis was followed by President Cleveland, who gave another goal to the fair that, ironically, expresses a view which became somewhat contrary to the "friendship" spoken of by Davis. Cleveland felt that the fair was "to illustrate the growth and progress of human endeavor in the direction of a higher civilization" (38). The illustrations in *Midway Types* hover on the edge of these aspirations and tend to support the illustrational purposes to which Cleveland obliquely refers: to establish that the *direction* toward higher civilization implies the *degenerate* and backward nature of many non-European cultures. Thus, the genial aspect of the physiological project of *Midway Types* is often subverted by the aesthetic standards with which it begins, the list of "harmless oddballs" transforming itself into an elaborate stereotyping system or *guide* to a bewildering proliferation of racial characteristics and categories of gender.

One might even say "gender mistakes." A number of the Midway Types present stumbling blocks for the caption writers, particularly in the area of gender, as if the pageant of exotics were specimens of the "What is She?" variety of Barnum and Bailey curiosity shows. For example, the caption for "Between the Acts" (Fig. 3) "puzzles the physiognomist":

> Form and feature are manlike, but there is a womanish expression in the eyes and around the mouth. It is as much of a revelation of sex as one has a right to expect from an Egyptian actress, with whom vivacity would be a penalty for living,

Fig. 3. "Between the Acts." From *Midway Types.*

and energy the precursor of extinction. Solaced by her narghileh, this type of the modern dancing woman from an ancient city cared but little for the judgment of her audience, and left the Exposition with a feeling of contempt for people who wanted fire and not cinders. (*Midway Types*)

In this passage we sense the struggle to define the Oriental female apparent in other captions which, in the name of liberating her from the stifling vices of her Asiatic oppressors, define what sort of vibrance and sexual appeal she *should* have. Her beauty, as this and other captions present it, is defaced by the harsh conditions under which she lives—she comes alive on the Midway, only to return to the drugged and listless state of the "manlike" actress discussed here. Achieving distinction as a "female" is in this manner linked to racial or national attributes (it is an *Egyptian* actress who does not reveal her sex), which in turn determine behavior *as* a "woman." It is suggested that the cause of characteristics deemed aberrant to her sex, such as "manlike" features, is found in her oppression by Oriental males. She remains "The Hidden Woman," as one caption reads, until freed from her "tyrannical seclusion." The Hidden Woman is a type of all the women who were kept indoors during most of the exposition, and who, when outdoors, were heavily veiled. Her features are revealed in the photograph; they are marked by a "masculinity" which, we may surmise, has been provoked by the oppressive practices of her Algerian captors: "Masculine and heavy of feature, devoid of sentiment, barren of education, yet the woman had the softer feelings, the yearnings, the hunger for companionship, that are the ever-pleading accompaniments of her sex." Her femininity, defined as her yearning hunger and desire for a companion, is left unrequited by Algerian men.

This unhappy view of the Egyptian is well illustrated by the caption to "The Egyptian Musician," a portrait of an Egyptian woman. The caption claims that "[o]ne versed in Egyptian history can readily comprehend why the faces of its women wear such a sombre, gloomy look":

> Intellectually they are ciphers in the mathematics of a civilization that, born in Egypt, has indented the world with material evidences of its power. Socially, they have a place with their beasts of burden and are slaves to men as ignorant as the women. Their religion has been of a gloomy character from the time Egypt's history began to be written, and their music is like their religion. The sound maker in this Luxor temple, beating her drum into weird music, had the imperturbable face of the Sphynx. If her dreamy eyes grew bright under any

> hidden fire it was from fever of homesickness which parched the lives of all these women from the Nile.

The reference to the "Sphynx" links the woman not only to a creature that was thought to be half-woman, half-beast, but to an ancient, and therefore timeless, monument.[11] Her face will never change; she will disappear back into the bondage to which she was born. Linking Egyptians to their monuments is not an accidental feature of this caption. Of the woman "Born to Drudgery" (Fig. 4), the caption writer tells us: "The type above is a fellah woman. The social and intellectual conditions of this class have undergone scarcely any change during centuries of misrule. If they are no longer subjects to the hazards of the highest bidder, they are still the sad, living symbols of a system of drudgery older than the Pyramids." Similarly, modern Egyptian women are invariably linked to Cleopatra, reinforcing the perception of them as unchanging, timeless, and, somewhat tangentially, bestial. Of "A Dancer in Street Costume" they write, "the woman from the Nile [in contrast to women of the New World] dons the same sort of drapery, only a little more of it, perhaps, as that which Cleopatra wore more than a thousand years ago." These women, like their Bedouin sisters whose faces "show the brand of as hopeless a bondage as women can bear," are caught in conditions of ignorance and oppression which have not changed in centuries. "[I]t would require centuries of education," the caption for "Bedouin Women" (Fig. 5) tells us, "to cause them to mutiny against their condition and struggle for a refinement and a freedom of which they have only the faintest, if any, conception." The Columbian Exposition brings them something new, an alternative to Mecca: "while not a journey to Mecca," it brought "a world more full of wonders than any contained in the Arabian Nights stories."

In these remarks, it is quite clear that the linking of the modern Egyptian woman with ancient monuments and thousand-year-old Cleopatras imprisons her in a timeless vessel: her clothing, her expression, are seen as part of her bondage at the same time that the stereotypical statements of the captions serve only to seal her in the past. She becomes less individual, more mythic—and oddly also more "masculine" in some cases—as her powerlessness is unveiled.

Fig. 4. "Born to Drudgery." From *Midway Types*.

Fig. 5. "Bedouin Women." From *Midway Types.*

Miles Orvell argues that what mattered in most nineteenth-century photography was that the photographic subject be viewed "as a general representation of reality, *a type*":

> By type . . . we must understand not the scientist's general summation of a class; rather, the typology of nineteenth-century photography is—to borrow a word from poetic terminology—metonymic, whereby the pictured subject, with all its concrete particularity, *stands for* a more general class of like subjects. The individuality of the subject is thus presented on its own terms while it simultaneously serves the larger purpose of representing a general category. . . . with varying degrees of sophistication, the photographic community did accept a typological concept of the photographic representation, whereby the image was viewed as both a mimetic and an artificial construction, both specific and general. (88)

Photographic captions in *Midway Types* create as they repeat stereotypes of race and national culture, suggesting more the anonymity and general representativeness than the individuality of each of the "Midway types." We are often assured of the "likeness" of the photograph to the "original" type; of "Esquimau Mother and Child," we are assured they bear "good likeness" to the real people: these are "authentic" exotic others at the same time that they are "like" them, imitations by virtue of their use as "representatives of" a cultural reality which cannot be "real" at the fair but must always be fake or counterfeit. Other statements contradict the importance of the individuality of the "types." Of "Peter, the Sentinel at 'Old Vienna,'" the caption says, "a figure which was often mistaken for an imitation man."

Most obviously, the titles of the photographs themselves assert the typical rather than the sentimental and individual aspects of the portraits. They are also used to establish in memory the general characteristics of each class of human being and to establish preferences among exotic peoples on the basis of custom, aesthetics, and physical traits observed at the fair. What is characteristic is, in part, established by the posing of the subject obvious in most of the photographs. Underneath the photographs we read "Chinese Beauty" (Fig. 6), "A Bulgarian," "The Hindoo Jugglers," "Samoan Belles" (about whom it is said, "They are excellent types of the South Sea Islanders"), "Three Little Vagabonds from Cairo," "A Typical Turk," or "Cairo Street Dudes" (Fig. 7). In some accounts, the typicality of each is set *against* the eccentricity and individuality of the American. Thus, in the Chicago Record's *History of the World's Fair,* it is remarked that exotics from countries such as China, Japan, Egypt, or Turkey each exhibit a uniform type of national costume which allows us to "tell the difference between a Turk and a Javanese at a quarter of a mile," whereas Americans dress according to individual tastes. "The Americans," the writer states, "give the greatest costume exhibit at the Exposition. You may pick out a larger assortment of hats worn by them than you could find in a week's search through the plaisance villages" (75).

The statements about the types not only discount the individuality of those portrayed but also offer stereotypical generalizations and replicate the framing of the photographer's gaze as well as the relationship of power it implies (see Alloula 14). An

Fig. 6. "Chinese Beauty." From *Midway Types.*

Fig. 7. “Cairo Street Dudes.” From *Midway Types*.

Fig. 8. "A Group of Soudanese." From *Midway Types.*

example is found in "A Group of Soudanese" (Fig. 8). Having reminded us of the contemporary conflict between an insatiable Great Britain and the people of the Sudan, the caption describes the scene. "The picture shows men and women, their costumes and their musical instruments, all of which are worthy of close study. In the foreground was a cunning little shaver in royal robes, whose chief attraction, beyond his color and size, was his ability to dance his way into the hearts of the public; *for a picaninny is a favorite whether from the Africa of South Carolina or that of the coast of Guinea*" (emphasis added).

This supposed favoritism—which refers to the "Africa" of American slavery and implies a "favored slave"—is established pictorially by the insertion of the listless male observer on the right. The African was not, however, a favorite of the publishers, who preferred the politely industrious Japanese[12] and "little" Javanese to the threatening Soudanese, Dahomeyans, and Amazons. This is made clear by the facetious tone of many captions given to photographs of these people, and by "aesthetic judgments" which disparage the lack of beauty in their physiognomy.

The savagery of a group of "Black Continentals in their Scarce Regimentals," the caption suggests, redeems the (more beautiful) American Indian:

> Now that the Dahomey village is far away it may be remarked with safety that its inhabitants were just the sort of people the managers of the Exposition did not banquet or surfeit with receptions. The group pictured shows a regretful absence of tailor-made clothes, and a leaning toward a plethora of black skins. In the occasional parades these gentle reminders of Africa never allowed themselves to be overlooked. Their Amazons, feather decked and sword girded, bearing the scars of hasty carvings, and savage as tigresses, were the belles of the occasion. None of them seemed to know the meaning of fear. Once when a fire broke out in the village a few of the people trampled upon the flames with their bare feet and others tore at the burning shingles with their teeth. There were sixty men and forty women in the village and they amused the public by giving war dances, songs and specimens of savage amusements that made our native Indian seem "a thing of beauty and a joy forever."

In addition to the unappealing sight of the "savage tigresses" of the Midway, Dahomeyan women are depicted as entirely "uncouth" (a favored phrase for dreary forms of exotics) and lacking in the beauty ascribed to favored races. "In True Dahomeyan Style" ridicules an "Amazon" for carelessly dangling her legs over the edge of the hammock in which she is being carried along the Midway:

> Behold an Amazon warrior, a belle of the village of duskiness, carried in state down the highway of nations. . . . The beauty reposes in state. Her hands are raised to smooth down her frizzes, for woman's vanities are inherent and universal peculiarities of her sex. This vanity seems to have extended to the Amazon's legs, which dangle carelessly over the edge of the hammock and display all the fine points of anatomy incident to those extremities. Cleopatra never journeyed in happier state than rode this dusky beauty on the bright summer day that gave to the Midway a procession combining African savagery with the civilization of the Exposition.

Obviously, the caption writers find the Amazon comic for her vanity, their ironic illusion to Cleopatra invoking a popular "type" of Oriental beauty to reinforce, by contrast, the savagery of the Amazon. Cleopatra and the Amazon[13] are aligned in their vanity, the merits of which in each case are decided by the caption writer. The aesthetic concerns of "beauty" or, as in the case of the Dahomeyan, "dusky beauty" and "savagery," are common to many of the portraits in *Midway Types*. This may be, in part, because of a preoccupation with the Congress of Beauties of Forty Nations, which is a recurrent theme of the book. Beauty, on the Midway, is an extension of perceived cultural or "personal" traits, and is also the common measure of civilization at the exposition. The "Chinese Beauty" receives no commentary; the "Javanese Beauty" is of a "people who were favorite types of study for all who visited them, their small stature, gentle ways and marked air of contentment winning the liking of all who saw them." Categories of race and the feminine are set apart *as* bases on which the photographer and the fair-goer pass aesthetic judgment, and are linked as things to be judged in this way.[14] The importance of the female types is established largely by the relative aesthetic value of their beauty; their beauty is established by the (cultural and personal) preferences the viewer holds for particular forms of "the feminine," "the Oriental," or "the Irish." From these preferences, the status of nations as savage or civilized is determined. Although some captions refer to recent political conflict between the British and the Sudanese or the American government and "Indians," the animosity generated by this conflict is substantiated by the perception of savagery in the "type": its physiognomy, mannerisms, and performances.

The caption for "A Daughter of Arabia" provides such a judgment that the exotic is hardly beautiful because she is wild and rugged, and therefore has no permanence or endurance:

> Every well informed reader can recall those phrases about "Araby's Daughter," "Araby the Blest." But poetry is too often but a masquerading costume for poverty stricken facts; and lean, attenuated truth sometimes puts on the robe of purple. The picture above, of the Midway Arab girl, disillusionizes one of many rosy ideas. Poetry would make an houri out of this subject, but the stern unpitying eye of practical men and

> women saw only a type of human nature as wild, as untutored, as corrugated in spirit as the nomadic creatures of a great city's streets. There were barbaric accessories of costumes and of manner in favor of the daughter of the desert; *but the heaviness and coarseness of the face, even if approaching to a sort of rugged beauty, was not likely to last long, and this belle of today will probably be, in a couple of years, a wrinkled and rugged old woman.* (my emphasis)[15]

This aesthetic judgment of the exotic is both disapproving of her "corrugated spirit" and titillated by her "barbaric accessories of costumes." The inference from this judgment to the supposition of aesthetic tastes (or lack thereof) of the exotics themselves also displays this ambivalent attraction and repulsion, and the added resolution of ambivalence in the wish to "erase" the exotic and to assert, through typification, that it will not endure in its wild state. "An Egyptian Interior" is meant to illustrate the "voluptuary" tendencies of Egyptians:

> The Egyptian is a voluptuary. His form, habit, and home show it. In this interior view of a little parlor in a building on Cairo Street, art gives a finish to the personal characteristics of the occupant. His tendencies are as readable as if the room were an open, printed book. The hangings are of rich materials and the colors strikingly strong. Gay colors are the binding threads of the life of an Oriental. The screen is rich in fine carving and dainty inlaying. The tables and stands show skillful handicraft. The most fragile and artistic of chinaware is like moulded air, yet it is handled as nimbly as if of ordinary porcelain. Each article is, in itself, painting and sculpture, and so the walls become barren of the triumphs of the easel. The chandelier, cumbrous in form and crude in design, intensifies by the light filtered through its rude glasses, the laziness of life it illumines. The fadism of the day is to make this old and far away evidence of comfort, the standard of taste, omitting, however, the fateful symbol of the Turk in the doorway, a symbol that is in fact, the human hyphen that weds ancient voluptuousness to modern energy.

"Gay colors are the binding threads of the life of an Oriental": with rich materials, strong colors, every article is "artistic" in itself—there is no "art" on the walls. Every object in the room is a cipher for what a Turk is (and he is not a creating artist) *because* he is described *as* his objects: "His tendencies are as readable as if the room were an open, printed book." Art merely "gives a finish to the personal characteristics of the occupant." He is as voluptuous in his taste for strong and gay colors as he is ethereal; like the chinaware, he is "moulded air." He is composed as well of light filtered through the rude glass of a crude and cumbrous chandelier. He is a hyphen (of laziness) between his objects and the modern taste which desires them. He is more than "finished": his completion by art and the spectator's taste have all but erased him; indeed, he seems present here only to vanish in the numerous reproductions of his objects in American homes.

The voluptuary and crude tastes of the Egyptian are also ascribed to his humor. In "A Street Entertainment," we have "an opportunity to study the *mummery* of the Orientals, and to learn *how little of the grotesque* was necessary in order to put them into good humor and produce a laugh" (my emphasis). The judgment that the exotic or Oriental is wed to or finds kinship in the grotesque applies to religion as well. Describing "The Joss House," the caption writers explain: "Here prayed to their gods the almoneyed [sic] subjects of the Flowery Kingdom, and the grotesque ceremonials of the strange religion of hundreds of millions of people was sheathed from modern civilization only by the thinnest of walls, and the respect of a liberal minded people. . . . [The Midway was] the abiding place of the incongruous in everything."

Given the opportunity, it seems, the fair-goers' exotic could become, if not a simple parody of a way of life, a grotesque curiosity. It is difficult to define the effect of the "lessons" learned from such observations and souvenirs. The ephemeral nature of the fair suggests, however, that its lessons in international cooperation and the appreciation of cultural differences will not last, and analysis of the captions in *Midway Types* suggests a willful erasure or diminution of the (perceived) wild and grotesque sublimity of the exotic. *Midway Types* embodies the contradictory nature of the fair as educative and yet also somewhat of a curiosity show. The spectacle appears to have promoted appreciation of the "little" Javanese or the stately Greek, and to have stimulated some sort of creature-feeling of fair-goers for people of many nations. It was also, however, conducive to odd comparisons between and among exotics; even a favored race was described in ludicrous terms. "Where's Java?" asks a caption. "Put head, arms and legs on a huge coffee berry that was aesthetically roasted and a Java pigmy would be suggested. . . . [The Javanese] represented pages of history of which every one read something and remembered a great deal. . . . They disappeared like figures dry rubbed from a slate." Another caption queries: "Isn't She [a Javanese] Sweet? . . . Would a glass envelope be out of place in exhibiting this toy-like native?" The breathtaking curiosities of the Midway world tour serve more as a symbolic gesture of incorporating and controlling, through the judgments of type and aesthetic as well as parody, entire worlds within the fairground or Midway. The peculiar forms beheld in the carnivalesque atmosphere of the Midway are linked to insanity. Under a photograph of a vendor entitled "Ice Cream *a la* Turk" (Fig. 9), the pathology attributed to the image is clear: "Ten years ago the man would have been declared insane who prophesied that not only would the Turk still be a thorn in Europe, but that he would sell ice cream in Jackson Park."

From the Midway, the Hindoo Jugglers and the Chinese beauty are transferred to the souvenir book where they become, like the sweet Javanese toy native, fit for display in glass envelopes. In aesthetic terms, Ralph Julian's "jumble of foreignness" is hysterically sublime[16]—in "unmapping" the familiar, everyday world, the Midway is remade in the mold of existing prejudices and power relations. The souvenir book of types lives on to commemorate the acts of fantasy and classification alive on the highway of nations. The types have become "Skeletons"; the fair is ephemeral, leaving only the ghostly outlines of buildings and portrait types. The much-loved Javanese village is long gone: "The hives of the brown bees have no honey; the flowers of the Exposition are dead; everywhere there is going on the process of oblivion."[17] From this process of oblivion we have *Midway Types,* which rises from the ashes of lived realities of power and race prejudice to assert new beings, the racial and cultural stereotypes of late-nineteenth-century American culture. The jumble of foreignness magically erases as it builds, obscures as it highlights.

Fig. 9. "Ice Cream *a la* Turk." From *Midway Types.*

The Tea Box Voyage

The "hysterical sublime" is part of fairs in other ways. The *sublimity* of such spectacles is first created in their much-remarked monumentality. Not only are they gigantic in terms of the range and quantity of things they display—appliances, peoples, rides, and so on—but also in their architecture. In early world fairs, this monumentality is symbolized in the main buildings. One analyst of the fairs conceives of these structures as "collective representations" of the fair itself: "Often of fantastic and extravagant design, such as the Crystal Palace in London in 1851 and the Palace of Industry in Paris in 1855, such buildings encompassed the whole of the fair, but they also symbolized it. They were collective representations in a literal sense, for they collected everything within them" (Benedict 13). Later fairs, such as the Centennial Exposition in Philadelphia in 1876, added other buildings to the main hall, but the symbolic center of the fair was always a monumental building or structure. For example, the Porte Monumentale in the Place de la Concorde at the 1900 Paris Exposition Universelle was so vast that each hour the fair was open, 60,000 people were able to make their way through its turnstiles. Burton Benedict draws attention to the fact that in many fairs the main buildings "dwarfed the spectators": "The Crystal Palace was 1,848 feet long with a transept 108 feet high. The arches supporting the 450-foot Tower of Jewels at the Panama Pacific International Exposition of 1915 were higher than the Arc de Triomphe in Paris" (16).

In addition to buildings, exhibits of food and other goods emphasized the monumental. This is a good term for the state of Iowa's "River of Corn" at the 1915 San Francisco Panama Pacific International Exposition and for Santa Clara County's armored knight and horse made of prunes at the California Midwinter Exposition held in San Francisco in 1894.[18] Rivers of corn and horses of prunes, while highly peculiar, are not "exotic," as I have been using the term to mean having to do with the non-European. What makes them strange is their *size:* they are significant because of their quantity, which gives them an awesome quality. Further, they are made from highly bizarre materials, mixing categories—of prunes and men—according to a logic similar to that which describes a Javanese as an aesthetically roasted coffee berry with legs. The difference is the size: the knight of prunes is monstrous, the Javanese coffee berry diminutive. Exotic objects and others, once disconnected from their "original" context, are displayed in fairs which are *monumental,* and it is by their association with the monumental and fantastic atmosphere of the fair—as in the River of Corn—that we can attribute to them a hysterically sublime character: they are fragments, ruins on a sublime vista.[19] But the vista itself, in many fairs, was created by architecture that itself was a hodge-podge of European and "Oriental" characteristics. In "Sailing to Byzantium: The Architecture of the Fair," Gray Brechin gathers remarks and plans of architects and critics of the San Francisco fair of 1915, and shows ways in which its architecture strove not only to be *older* than other architecture in San Francisco but also more Spanish, more Italian, more Greek, and more *Oriental.* Very much the Coleridgean "pleasure dome" invoked by Brechin, many fairs, such as the 1915 San Francisco Panama Pacific International Exposition, produced a fantasy atmosphere with domes and minarets, elaborate arches, towers of jewels, and light displays:

> More surprising is the vaguely located "Orientalism" of the walled city. One guidebook describes the Palace of Horticulture as "Byzantine in its architecture, suggesting the Mosque of Ahmed I, at Constantinople, its Gallic decorations have made it essentially French in spirit." The color, the travertine walls with their immense portals, the green and golden domes, the vaguely minaret-like towers and the fountains in the courtyards all conjured an Arabian Nights fantasy whether seen from within, from the Bay or from the backing ridge of Pacific Heights. "[The Exposition]," wrote journalist Ben Macomber, "reflects in its plan the walled cities of the Orient of the Mediterranean, where fountains play in the courts of palaces, in public squares and niches in the walls; and pools lie by the mosques, and in the gardens." (Brechin 103)

The sublime aspects of the architecture are clear from Brechin's description: in its color, immensity, and fantastic aspects, the Orient in San Francisco is an exotic mixture of exciting elements from distant lands. Conveying a great deal of the mystery of this false city, Brechin describes what a spectator would see on approaching San Francisco from the bay in 1915:

> At one point on the western edge of North America, the long wall of the Coast Range funnels inward to a precipitous cleft. A passenger on a steamship in the summer of 1915 entering The Narrows would have beheld an enchanted spectacle, for ranges of golden hills, like the wings of a vast stageset, opened around the bay and receded into the California hinterland. Just ahead and to starboard, an iridescent walled city rose from the water, an orderly array of domes and minarets backed by a long ridge of closely-packed mansions. Had it been twilight, a colossal tower rising from the center of the city would have been enveloped in an ambient film of light, the ancient walls would have been lambent with color and moving auroras would have filled the sky overhead. (94–95)

Fairs, like the Panama Pacific exhibition, were ephemeral—pieces of them were torn down, some sold, and others either destroyed or exported to the foreign lands that they had represented at the exposition (see Greenhalgh). In 1939, the Panama Pacific exhibition was recreated as a "treasure island" encrusted with the exotic and fantastic. "Blending Mayan, Incan, Malayan and Cambodian architecture, the walls of the Magic City arose on the newly created Treasure Island" (James and Weller 25). The architectural commission for the exhibition studied both the traditional orientation of the Panama Pacific exhibition of 1915 and the modern emphasis of the Chicago Columbian Exposition, combining features of both within the dominantly Oriental, Cambodian, and Mayan styles. There are two primary reasons for combining these styles. The first is that the Exposition was to be a "Pageant of the Pacific" and therefore "it was natural that the architects should select a structural style set by a race that ran a course and died, leaving remains of a forgotten people whose noble temples suggest a high civilization" (James and Weller 26). The second is that the fair's covert motif was Pacific peace and unity. This motif is illustrated in *The Peacemakers,* a mural in the Court of Pacifica whose central figures are a Buddha and an Occidental woman. Similarly, a fountain in this court was decorated with sculptures of different cultural groups: "Sargent Johnson's happy Inca Indians playing the Pipes of Pan; Carl George's American Indian and Modern Woman; . . . a South American group by Cecilia Graham of a Primitive Woman Making Farina, A South American Fisherman, and a Young Native Riding an Alligator; and a group of Chinese Musicians by Helen Phillips" (35).[20]

Seemingly more central to the exhibition, however, were the light shows:

> Casting its sheen of gay and lambent light upon the placid waters of San Francisco Bay, the brilliant aureole of Treasure Island pierced the sky with scintillating fingers and cast a myriad of radiant paths across the reaches of land and sea. . . .
>
> A battery of 10,000 flood-lights, new in design and rivaling the rays of the sun, bathed the magic isle in brilliant beams. Cylindrical lanterns, eighty-six feet high, cast a soft exotic glow along the pathways and through the courts. (James and Weller 41)

Nineteen colors governed the choice of lighting for the buildings as well as the flowers for their courts. These were assigned according to the official "palette of color," which was "drawn from the coloring of Pacific shores": "Exposition ivory, Sun of the Dawn yellow, Pagoda yellow, California ecru, Old Mission fawn, Santa Barbara taupe, Polynesian brown, Santa Clara apricot, Pebble Beach coral, Imperial Dragon red, Death Valley mauve, Evening Star blue, Pacific blue, Southern Cross blue, Del Monte blue, China Clipper blue, Hawaiian emerald green, Ming jade green (light and dark), and Treasure Island gold" (42).

Within the sublimely lit and monumental context of the fairs, there is, as critic Henri Loyrette has insisted, a diversity of architectural forms:

> Expositions and the literature which it instigates with the same linguistic lip-smacking of a Julien Gracq reading Huysmans, frequently butting up against a word, ceaselessly obliged to open his dictionary. And how else would it be? Enumerating only the constructions of the Champ de Mars in 1867 which we never meet with in any city—bridge, palace,

> green-house, aquarium, ruins, trophies, house, farm, school, cottage, tomb, lighthouse, monument, gallery, camp, temple, stable, okel, catacombs, windmill, chalet, theater, creche, fountain, caves, factory, dairy, cafe, church, Isba, mosque, turkish bath, chapel, station, tent, street, boutique, how would it obtain a discourse more literary, more "melange" so as not to succumb to the temptation of seducing hypotyposes? Similarly, the veritable obstacle when one speaks of the Architecture of the Universal Expositions is to avoid the kaleidoscopic effect which results from a description more or less attentive to these diverse constructions.

For example, in Paris in 1878 *La rue des nations* exhibited adjacent facades of Luxembourg, St. Marin, Morocco, and Siam (see Loyrette 221). The grande facade of the Exposition at Anvers in 1885 was billed as a "Palais des 'Mille et une Nuits'" which, in gigantic proportions, depicted the many strange architectural attractions of the fair.[21] Exhibits like the "Façades des pavilions étrangers" of the Exposition of 1900 were popular at Paris fairs: a steet in Cairo (1889), in Portugal (1878), a Finnish pavilion (1900), and one of Norway (1889). Speaking of the 1867 exposition in Paris, François Ducuing remarks: "Under the same sky, separated only by the leaves of a few trees, the massive palaces of old Egypt, Swiss chalets, Chinese pagodas, Arab palaces, Italian houses, English cottages, Moresque fountains and architecture."[22] These facades did not necessarily reproduce a contemporary foreign city's architecture accurately—indeed, in the case of the street in Cairo, the architecture was a melange of elements from different epochs. Henri Loyrette argues that the motivations for reproduction were diverse. He lists several variations in the reproduction of a national architecture, from reduction and diminishment to juxtaposition, pastiche, and specimen: "pure and simple reproduction of an existing architecture . . . reduction . . . model . . . specimen . . . pastiche . . . miniaturization or summary . . . juxtaposition of two different elements . . . and, diminishment" (Loyrette 224–25). And these could be combined. Of the Cairo Street at Chicago's Columbian Exposition (Fig. 10), a contemporary commented that "[f]rom the window of the ticket seller to the front door of the Temple of Luxor was a varied succession, *a laughable jumble of the sublime and the ridiculous*":

Fig. 10. "A Group of Natives." From *Midway Types.*

> Looking down Cairo Street from the West end, one saw a bewildering complication of objects in the fantastically decorated and shaped buildings, and in the motley dressed throngs of its inhabitants and visitors. In the distance the eye catches the shadows of the Egyptian Cafe where were sold lager beer and peanuts, and where a lonesome Egyptian girl wandered about selling flowers. The minaret of the mosque of Abou Bake Mazhar, from whose heights the muezzin called the faithful to prayer, rises to the right like a dainty carving on the sky. *The street, which was a combination of the peculiarities of various streets of old Cairo, and not a reproduction of any one in particular,* was honeycombed on its sides with over fifty shops, none of them over six feet square, in which were displayed the work of quaint artisans of Egypt. (*Midway Types,* "Cairo Street Looking East," my emphasis)[23]

Some architects, such as Frantz Jourdain, felt that, for the vertiginous spectator of the great disparities among these different architectural styles, the accomplishment of the Haussmannism evident at the expositions was to *harmonize* and *unify* the violence of such juxtapositions of strange sights: "the *tour de force* of the Universal Exposition is, precisely, that there disparities are harmonized, and a unity is made through violent contrasts."[24] The unity achieved here could substitute, on a metonymic level, for the lack of unity among nations—indeed for the great animosity between Europe and, for example, peoples of the Near East and Africa—in Europe in the nineteenth century. The vertigo and sublimity of the facades resulted in a unification of the various "countries" presented to the eye: one could take them all in on a stroll through the pavilion and, after the initial vertigo wore off, create an aesthetic, if not a global or political, harmony among nations.

Diversity is part of the odd, Huysmanesque jumble that is the fair. Exhibits of colonial peoples and of all that is, like many objects of the fair, freakishly exotic become fragments of a larger amusement or educational tour, of commercial and scientific perspectives.[25] As in the *Visions Lointaines* of Paris, the display of colonial peoples in other parts of Europe and in America created typological classifications of subject races on a "village" scale. The village, like the tasks, dances, and ceremonies enacted in its artificial context, was a miniature of a larger cultural whole—a fragment and ultimately a "ruin" of a cultural group. An example of such exhibits is found in the Trocadero of the 1878 Paris exposition. At the Trocadero, among many attractions, one could view Algerians (in their "Arab tent") or the interior of a Japanese farm. One could stop to smoke a hookah in the "Turkish Bazaar" in Philadelphia in 1876 or savor an Egyptian bonbon. One could see, smoke, taste, and smell the Orient, Africa, or Italy as one wandered along. Similarly, on the Trocadero in 1900 one could walk through the *Pavillons des colonies françaises:* Martinique, Tunisia, Senegal, Dahomey, the Ivory Coast, and so on.[26] At Chicago's Columbian Exposition in 1893, one had the advantage of "A Peep at Algiers" or a "Johore Bungalow." In *Midway Types,* the caption for a photograph of an Algerian village says that in the distraction of the Exposition's "hurly-burly" it was difficult at first to reflect on the bizarre fashion in which so many different nations were brought together on the Midway:

> In the hurly-burly of the Exposition one did not seem to accentuate the peculiarities marking the coming together of the representatives of more nations than, according to history, ever before met at one time and place. Since the Fair has ended a quiet review of its story fills the tale with exclamation points. Almost forgotten lands tendered a type or two of existence. Obsolete people came out of their mist and insignificant powers ranged up alongside the big ones. The memories of them all make a motley heritage. As strange a tribute as any was from Algiers and Tunis, whose shopkeepers and play people filled the building portrayed in the picture. Here they sold wares and trinkets; here their actors and dancers presented phases of human existence startlingly at variance with our own modes and manners. Their book of Chicago life was but a pamphlet, yet that pamphlet repaid the study given it. Doubtless the Exposition was indebted to France, the possessor of the two countries named, for the loan of its people. (*Midway Types,* "A Peep at Algiers")

The "obsolete people" of the misty "almost forgotten lands"—possessed and on loan by France—are part of the tale of the fair. They are "strange tributes" of "play people"; Algiers and

Tunis have "tendered a type or two of existence" for the fair. The "motley heritage" of memory is little improvement over the "hurly-burly" breathlessness of taking in the fair, but it has the advantage of hindsight: it recognizes the peculiarity of what it has witnessed, and it clearly remembers the people exhibited as not only a part of the "past" and "forgetting" but as objects that can be circulated by European colonizing powers. The gaze of the caption writer is in this way inadvertently keen: it sees that the fair is a bizarre fantasy of exotica made possible by loans of European nations. It also sees that the Algerian Theatre pictured is one of many of the fair's "sublime musayums" of "almost forgotten" yet dearly possessed obsolete fragments of exotica. As was true for the vanished Javanese village, "everywhere there is going on the process of oblivion" (*Midway Types,* "Skeletons").

The dialectic between the sublimely monumental or gigantic and the disarticulated fragment or ruin of the exotic is integral to the politics of world fairs and their display of power in the nineteenth and early twentieth centuries. From the ornamental orientalism of the Porte Monumentale to the exotic titillation of Little Egypt, the exotic was part of the "curiosity" and the fantasy of the fair. The attitude of the *flâneur* was entirely appropriate to a cultural form that promoted the visual aesthetics of a series of curiosity cabinets strung along vast panoramas of monumental architecture. The fairs were made both for gaping astonishment, excitement, and passive consumption of fragmented objects and experiences, *and* the creative imagining of exotic communities.

In the latter half of the nineteenth century, exhibitions and department stores made ready use of exotica to sell their merchandise. In this context it is not the *understanding* of objects from foreign places that is emphasized but their indiscriminate *consumption*—they are there to satisfy a desire for unfamiliar things, for incorporation or excitement and not understanding of other cultural realities. Rosalind Williams suggests that exotica and mass consumption attain a somewhat symbiotic relationship to the extent that department store displays utilized fascination with the exotic to provoke consumption. Consumption and its needs dictate that there must be ever-new products—therefore, the "exotic" can be seen as a metaphor for the perpetually *nouvelle,* embodying the inherent drama of all products that promise to satisfy desires which are in principle unsatisfiable.

Williams uses "exotic" in a broad sense to mean anything highly ornate or decorative. She claims that the exotic is an "illusion of art," a "fake" made available for mass consumption, rather like a kitsch equivalent of the foreign, a substitute or quick fix for the incredible, shocking, and new:

> As a quality of aesthetic judgment, taste does not apply to transient decor whose purpose is "to attract and to hold" the spectators' attention. Why the reliance on fake mahogany, fake bronze, fake marble? Because the purpose of the materials is not to express their own character but to convey a sense of the lavish and foreign. Why the hodgepodge of visual themes? Because the purpose is not to express internal consistency but to bring together anything that expresses distance from the ordinary. Exotic decor is therefore impervious to objections of taste. It is not ladylike but highly seductive. In this aesthetic demi-monde, exotic decor exists as an intermediate form of life between art and commerce. It resembles art, it has recognizable themes and stylistic traits, its commercial purpose is wrapped in elaborate visual trappings; yet it does not participate in traditional artistic goals of creating beauty, harmony, and spiritual significance. This hybrid form is an illusion of art, a "so-called artistic element" posing as the genuine article. (71)

"In environments of mass consumption," Williams says, "the logic of art gives way to the logic of fantasy" (72). The interesting part of Williams's argument is that the department stores and exhibitions, like other forms of exotic display, bring together the pieces necessary for fantasy and forego artistic considerations in favor of entrancing engagement with the exotic as a consumable product.

A particularly intriguing fantasy produced at the 1900 Paris Exposition was the illusion of travel to distant places. A technological miracle, the "distant Visions" or "Visions Lointaines" provided the spectator with simulated world tours. Discussing a review article by Michel Corday (Louis-Leonard Pollet, 1869–1937), Williams mentions his classification of the "tours" into twenty-one categories: "'ensembles in relief,' panoramas in which the spectator moves, those in which the panorama itself moves, those in which both move, and moving photographs" (73; see also Altick 1985). Two of the illusions of voyage Williams describes, via Corday, used various mechanical and painted devices to give the "tourist" the impression of "seeing" different countries in succession as part of a "chaotic-exotic style":

> [T]he tourist walked along the length of an enormous circular canvas representing "without solution of continuity, Spain, Athens, Constantinople, Suez, India, China, and Japan," as natives danced or charmed serpents or served tea before the painted picture of their homeland. The visitor was supposed to have the illusion of touring the world as he strolled by, although Corday hardly found it convincing to have "the Acropolis next-door neighbor to the Golden Horn and the Suez canal almost bathing the Hindu forests"—the chaotic-exotic style, the universe in a garden, only on canvas! On a somewhat more ingenious level, the Trans-Siberian Panorama placed the spectator in a real railroad car that moved eighty meters from the Russian to the Chinese exhibit while a canvas was unrolled outside the window giving the impression of a journey across Siberia. Three separate machines operated at three different speeds, and their relative motion gave a faithful impression of gazing out a train window. A slight rocking motion was originally planned for the car, but the sponsoring railway company vetoed the idea because it advertised that its trains did not rock. (73–74)[27]

Something similar to the delirious excitement of these hysterical tours was dreamt by the narrator of Flaubert's *Novembre.* In this early work, a young man dreams of traveling to foreign lands, among them China, India, and the Sudan, in the hope of curing a fatal case of ennui. Having devoted several paragraphs to his fantasied pictures of these places he says:

> Whirl me away, you storms of the New World. . . ! Let the torrents of Norway cover me with their spume! Let the snows of Siberia, piling down, wipe out my path! Oh, to travel! to travel! to travel and never stop; to see everything surge up

and pass away in this enormous dancing whirlwind until your skin bursts and your blood spurts! (108–9)

This comes from an author who once expressed the idea, to Louise Colet, that he was "no more French than Chinese" (Flaubert, *Correspondence* 1: 314).[28] Momentary reflection on this statement brings to mind photographs of Pierre Loti or Toulouse Lautrec dressed out in fabulous assortments of Asiatic garb (Figs. 11 and 12) or the dreamlike image of the composer Saint-Saëns sailing off in a Nile boat with the Orientalist painter Georges Clairin. Saint-Saëns is dressed in a Japanese robe and barbouches; in his hand he holds a fan (see Thornton 163). Such images and sentiments provoke the idea that the yearning for exotica, for a hysterical procession of new worlds, was not only quite deeply felt but also part of an anxious cosmopolitanism, if not an occasional spasm of Europhobia. Something in these images urges us to consider the ironic possibility that the stereotypes of fairs were themselves also mirrors for the fair-going *flâneur,* not simply observed but enthusiastically imagined, savored, embraced, ridiculed, or cast off.

The fairs were, quite obviously, not the only forms of sublime exposition of the exotic. Fantastic creations of exotic lands were familiar in other popular European media as well. I will name only a few here to make the point that the geographical distance between Europe and the Orient and Africa was not only shrinking but those areas were also readily available for dreaming in popular culture and material objects. A seemingly "natural" avenue of exploiting exotic themes presents itself in the operatic stage. Many operas, from Puccini to Bizet to Massenet, carried Orientalist themes and used the Orient as a stage for sublime passions. When considering the heavy influence of Orientalism and exoticism on opera, one thinks immediately of Puccini's *Turandot* (China) and *Madame Butterfly* (Japan); Verdi's *Aida* (Egypt); Bizet's *The Pearl Fishers* (Ceylon); and Saint-Saëns's *Samson and Delilah* (Egypt). Perhaps less readily recalled are Meyerbeer's *L'Africaine,* Gounod's *La Reine de Saba,* Bizet's *Djamileh* and *La Guzla de l'emir,* Massenet's *La Roi de Lahore,* or Delibes's *Lakme* (see Jullian 27–28). Through the use of props and costumes—and stereotypical characters—an exotic visual aesthetic was created in opera as

Fig. 11. Pierre Loti. From *Exotische Welten.*

well. Librettos for operas like *Abduction from the Seraglio* reinforce cultural stereotypes of a violent Orient of marauding Turks, while *Aida,* with its vast pageantry and parade, reinforces the singularly monumental character of the Orient.

Fig. 12. Toulouse Lautrec. From *Exotische Welten*.

Other modes of display were able to "contain" the excessiveness of the Oriental and exotic, to channel its excess into particular objects which serve as miniaturized fetishes of exotic places. Examples of this desire to miniaturize—in order to make accessible, possessable—include picture postcards, cigarette cards, posters, and such seemingly innocuous things as tea and biscuit tins, all produced toward the end of the century. Thus, at the time, such mundane items as biscuit tins bore illustrations of fanciful themes from other countries (including ornamentation which mimicked styles of architecture or painting popular in those countries) and labeled "Japan," "Mexico," and so forth, as if to designate the successful incorporation of entire countries into a neatly packaged tin (see Franklin; Doggett). For an illustration of the fantastic dreams set adrift by such mundane items as tea tins we may again turn to Flaubert, who attributes great influence to these objects of daily life and exclaims, "Oh! que les boîtes à thé m'ont fait faire de voyages!":

> In a cedar-wood canoe, a long canoe with paddles, so slim that they seem feathers, beneath a sail of plaited bamboos, to the sound of tom-toms and tambourines, I will go to that yellow land they call China. You can hold the women's feet in one hand, they have little heads, narrow eyebrows which curve up at the corners; they live in arbours of green reeds and eat velvet-skinned fruits from painted porcelain. The mandarin, pointed moustache falling to his chest, head shaven, pigtail dropping low on his back, walks, round fan between his fingers, in the gallery where tripods smoke, passes slowly over rice-mats; he has a little pipe in his pointed cap and black writings are imprinted in his red silk robes. Ah, the voyages on which tea-boxes have sent me! (*November* 108)[29]

Observing the contexts in which exotic peoples and objects are displayed, one sees not only how they lent themselves to stereotypical perceptions of "yellow lands" or eaters of "velvet-skinned fruits," but also in this jumble of traits can be seen their genealogy from such seemingly innocuous phenomena as the curiosity cabinets of the sixteenth and seventeenth centuries. Filled with rare and exotic objects gathered from voyages, these cabinets served as early museums of cultural treasures. Generally a jumble of items, species, materials, these objects, when put together in this fashion, did not so much represent the shells, fish skeletons, spears, and so on, that they were but the "exotic" or strange in itself—what Francis Bacon called "the shuffle of things" (Turner 220).[30] Sometimes the cabinets themselves were encrusted with the found objects of foreign lands, and entire rooms were packed with their randomly displayed exotic items. From these objects one looks through and past the fairs to what James Clifford calls "a truly global space of cultural connections and dissolutions" (4) and the jumble of "Western" and "Exotic" in twentieth-century travel and experience. We have a vision of our modern curiosity cabinet in Pico Iyer's *Video Night in Kathmandu:*

> Abroad, we are not ourselves; and as the normal and the novel are transposed, the very things that we might shun at home are touched with the glamour of the exotic. I had never seen, or wished to see, a Burt Reynolds movie until I found myself stuck in a miserable guesthouse in Bandar Sari Begawan; I had never been to a Dunkin' Donuts parlor until I decided to treat myself to my first ever Yorkie bar in Surabaya. . . . (10)

When abroad, we become wondrously exotic curiosities to ourselves. Illusions of voyage, exotic objects displayed at exhibitions, world fairs, in curiosity cabinets, department stores, or operatic sets encouraged the dreaming or hallucination of the exotic other and exotic place—much as they would be dreamt up in the operatic sets of *Turandot, Madame Butterfly,* and *Abduction from the Seraglio,* for example. It is no accident that nineteenth-century writers such as Nerval, Gautier, or Baudelaire would speak of the East as something seen through a veil of hashish—an image hallucinated in opiated dreams. The involvement of anthropologists, to a greater or lesser degree, lent a "scientific" air to fair exhibits of exotic places, people, and things, and increased the chance that they would be ethnologically informative (see Rydell). While the ideology of photographic or anthropological "realism" might dispel the blue haze of pure dreams of the exotic, the fantastic quality of exotic objects persists in the spectacles discussed here.

Somewhere between the hysterically sublime "world tours"

of the Champs de Mars or the Chicago Midway and the glass envelopes and tea tins of exotic souvenirs, a cosmopolitan sensibility emerges in the nineteenth century. Within this sensibility lives the "jumble of foreignness" of these great spectacles, the confused stereotypes of race and gender that produced and were reproduced by the aesthetic of the "sublime musayum." In the creative process of this aesthetic, we see not only the vicious work of stereotypes of savages and Cleopatras but also the hysterical self-fashioning of Europeans and Americans in the mirrors of the Rest. As Saint-Saëns sails down the Nile, as Cairo Street Dudes and Irish beauties stroll the Midway, Flaubert dreams of being "no more French than Chinese."

Notes

1. In an appendix to the *Reminiscences of the Colonial and Indian Exhibition* held in London in 1886, this "jumble" is apparent in the list of "natives" who were exhibited. Burton Benedict summarizes this list: "There were forty-five Indians, one Burmese, ten Senegalese, ten Red Indians from British Guiana, five Cypriots, five Cape Malays and nine Kaffirs from South Africa, four Malays, and eight Hong Kong Chinese" (46). Although the "jumble of foreignness" refers primarily to the display of "non-Americans" at an American fair, there is often reference in contemporary documents to the many different "nationalities" (naturalized United States citizens) who helped to build the fair (see Chicago Record 13–14), and America is seen as a "medley" of such nationalities (75).

2. Indeed, Mr. Molony's Muse is stunned by the *number* of things contained in the "Palace made o'windows": "My Muse's words / Is like the bird's / That roosts beneath the panes there; / Her wings she spoils / 'Gainst them bright toiles, / And cracks her silly brains there" (188–89).

3. The dialectic between exotic sublimity and racial and gender-based stereotypes is a product of the conjunction of the Idealist and Romantic aesthetic of sublimity with growing Orientalist and Exoticist discourses in the early nineteenth century. This dialectic can be demonstrated in various literary and artistic contexts throughout the nineteenth century, as well as in subversions of exotic sublimity in modernism and postmodernism. The parody of sublimity in Thackeray's verse suggests awareness of the relationship between sublimity and stereotype in the developing aesthetic of exoticism.

4. Timothy Mitchell interprets the representations of Egypt at the exhibitions as part of a process of "framing" the other, of making an orderly "picture" out of the chaos the European spectator originally perceives in it. In his analysis, Mitchell uses Heidegger's concept of the "world picture" to emphasize the placing of the Egyptian in a contained space apart from the European spectator, and the conception of that space as one upon which European technologies and discourses of power could be instrumental:

> These symbolic representations of the world's cultural and colonial order [museums, theaters, gardens, zoos, exhibitions], continually encountered and described by visitors to Europe, were the mark of a great historical confidence. . . . Exhibitions, museums and other spectacles were not just reflections of this [new political] certainty, however, but *the means of its production,* by their technique of rendering history, progress, culture and empire in "objective" form. They were occasions of making sure of such objective truths, in a world where truth had become a question of what Heidegger calls, "the certainty of representation." (7)

While I agree that the concept of the "world-as-picture" is convincing in Mitchell's analysis, I would question the broader applicability of Heidegger's critique of anthropology and "worldviews" to studies of cultural difference; it may be that Heidegger's analysis replicates the distancing and insularity he criticizes.

5. See Robert Rydell, who argues that the overriding feature of ethnological exhibits of exotic peoples was the emphasis on establishing visual and spatial hierarchies among the races, promoting the argument for an evolutionary progression from the darkest and most barbarous races to the enlightened white races of Europe and America. He believes that this ideology dominates the fair, and while he believes that the midways were important, he does not spend much time with the competing aesthetic of the popular midway amusements. "Were the world's fair midways just for fun?" he asks. "Hardly. . . . World's fair midways constituted 'living proof' for their imperial calculations by exposition sponsors" (236). While this may be true, a look at the maps in Figures 1 and 2 is enough to convince us that this hierarchy was *not* adhered to on the Midway Plaisance. Indeed, on the Midway, the progression is from the Bedouin Encampment to the Hungarian, the Lapland, and Dahomey exhibits and then to Old Vienna. Although inhabitants of the Bedouin village were perceived as racially inferior to the Viennese, the ladder to Austria did not detour from the Bedouins through the Laps and the Dahomeys. Other scholars of fairs have repeated Rydell's emphasis on hierarchies; see, for example, Zeynip Çelik, 5.

6. "Entering the avenue a little to the east of the Woman's Building, [the fair-goers] would pass between the walls of medieval villages, between mosques and pagodas, Turkish and Chinese. . . . They would be met on their way by German and Hungarian bands, by the discord of Chinese cymbals and Dahomeyan tom-toms; they would encounter jugglers and magicians, camel drivers and donkey boys, dancing-girls from Cairo and Algiers, from Samoa and Brazil, and men and women of all nationalities, some lounging in oriental indifference, some shrieking in unison or striving to outshriek each other, in the hope of transferring his superfluous change from the pocket of the unwary pilgrim" (Bancroft 353).

7. Thomas Richards contrasts the orderly (and seemingly endless) display of English commodities with the cacophony of the foreign exhibits at the Crystal Palace. "Next to the virtual encyclopedia of manufactured objects crammed into the English half," Richards says, "the foreign half looked like a disheveled cabinet of curiosities. . . . [E]ven the *Official Catalogue* of the Exhibition had to admit that the foreign half of the building was at best a mutilated copy of the English half" (25).

8. Çelik argues that the mixing of colonies in French exhibits served to em-

phasize the power of the colonizer by virtue of its ability to contain such a variety of different cultures:

> The architecture of the Algerian and Tunisian colonies of France projected an image of Islam correlating with that of the noncolonial presentations. Yet the indigenous character of the pavilions played a different role in the colonial context, aggrandizing the image of France by making it more varied and complex. The greater the spectrum of differences in colonized cultures, the stronger was the impression of the colonizer's power and the vastness of his domain. One French observer asked: "Are we not a grand Muslim nation, given our vast African colonies?" In effect, Islamic countries were only a small part of the much larger French empire. (134)

9. This was the *Midway Types* caption for "A Dancer of the Persian Palace." This volume is not paginated; references will be to the captions of the photographs. The term *olla-podrida* here means *heterogeneous.* The definitions given by the *Oxford English Dictionary* suggest the connection of this term to *taste* since *olla podrida* basically means a "rotten pot." (1) "A dish of Spanish origin composed of pieces of many kinds of meat, vegetables, etc. stewed or boiled together" and (2) "A hotchpotch, medley; a mixture of languages." This phrase seems even more fitting given a similar description of the display of racial types offered by the 10 Sept. 1893 *Chicago Tribune:* "Sort of Universal Stew/A Pot Pie of the Earth" (cited in Rydell 68).

10. See Appelbaum (97–98) and Çelik. Çelik claims that the belly dance was a central attraction, *especially at Parisian fairs,* for it fit well with *the indigenous entertainment industry* in Paris, "specifically . . . the popular dances performed in the cabarets, cafe-concerts, *jardins d'hiver,* and the *bals publics.*" Çelik lists the derogatory names of the dancers, which emphasize the degradation of exotic women that was reinforced by these "casual" amusements:

> The cult of the star, which originated in these establishments, extended to the fathmas, Feridjees, Aichas, and Zohras who took their place among the exotic female dancers of the time: La Goulue (the Glutton), Nini Pattes en l'air (Nini Paws-in-the-Air), Môme Fromage (Mistress of Kid Cheese), Grille d'Égout (Sewer Grate), and many others. The Islamic theaters of the expositions complemented the city's own cabarets. In these theaters, amid architecturally "authentic" settings, belly dancers presented the element of Muslim life most intriguing to Europeans, one that for at least seventy-five years had been the focus of Orientalist painters and writers. (27–28)

Çelik discusses in many places the horrified reaction of Islamic visitors to the fairs *and* Paris, specifically with regard to the degradation of women and Islamic religion, the latter in the use of facades of Mosques for such cabarets.

11. Although the comparison between "Oriental women" and the Sphinx had become stereotypical in nineteenth-century Orientalist art and literature, an immediate source of association between Egyptian women and the Sphinx was provided in a sculpture called *The Secret* by Theodore Baur, an artist from New York. The sculpture was exhibited at the Columbian Exposition east of the Arts Palace on the Exposition Grounds. A photograph of this odd monument appears in the Werner Company's *The Columbian Gallery.* The photograph is titled "An American Myth"; it is, apparently, a woman's face and breasts on the body of a lioness. "The incompleted group," the caption reads, "is named 'The Secret,'

of which a meaning may be gathered from the Cupid whispering into the ear of a curious sphinx, apparently half woman and half lioness in form. The pleased and yet sinister radiance on this creature's face, though it be wellnigh as brutish as her feline body, is considered by many to be a masterpiece of sculptural expression. From the very dawn of art the sphinx has been a vehicle for the sculptor's weird imaginings."

12. "Tea Garden People" commends Commodore Perry for introducing the world to the sedate Japanese, and claims "no race prejudice" against the Japanese, amidst statements of racial stereotyping:

> Commodore Perry made a mighty transformation when he unlocked the doors of Japan with his cannons for keys, and introduced to the public the people of one of the most intelligent and ingenious nations in the world. To-day the Japanese have representatives in all great cities and not a race-prejudice exists against them. . . . Two marked peculiarities about the Japanese are their sedate but not excessive politeness, and their fluent use of the English language. These traits may be easily recalled by those who were fortunate enough to be brought into business relations with these interesting people.

The temporal dimensions of the captions revolve around the time of the fair and its dismantling. That no race prejudice exists "to-day" does not, of course, preclude such prejudice from surfacing after the fair.

13. At the 1939 Pacific Exposition in San Francisco, Cleopatra and the Amazon merge in the "Palace of Monsters": "The Monster Show provided an extracurricular activity during its first season that had the operators worried. It was in the matter of Cleopatra, the South American boa constrictor, and her 'bundle from heaven' . . ." (James and Weller 210).

14. A contemporary visitor to the Congress of Beauties displays his obvious favoritism for the American woman:

> The beauty of the girls varies, ranging from the attractive presence of the maid of Tyrol and the girl of Poland to the soapy discoloration of the black-and-tan lady who represents Cuba in a gorgeous costume of yellow silk and black lace. Nationality and costume are said to go together here; but the Yankee appearance of the houri from Arabia Felix, and the guttural low Dutch of the Oriental garbed odalisques, are things that breed skepticism. The melancholy and lonely looking little Chinawoman is unhappy enough to be genuine; but the Irish colleen in spectacles is a fraud. The peasant girl of southern France has a flavor of comic opera about her, for her garments are too clean and the girl too pretty to be the genuine article. The American girls in the exhibition are boldly genuine, and their good looks and big eyes have in them memories of that district that New York calls the Tenderloin. But the costumes are handsome, picturesque and geographically correct. (*The Columbian Gallery* 21)

15. This remark on the "wrinkled and rugged" aspects of the Oriental beauty displays a more general concern with the "decay of women" that may be attributed to their domestic use in patriarchal society. In their discussion of Simone de Beauvoir's cave parable, Sandra M. Gilbert and Susan Gubar observed that "[d]estroyed by traditional female activities—cooking, nursing, needling, knotting—which ought to have given them life as they themselves give life to men, the women of this underground harem are obviously buried in (and by) patri-

archal definitions of their sexuality" (94). The concern with the overworked Oriental woman may be symptomatic of issues of gender at home, particularly with the relationship between women's roles at home and in the workplace.

16. The "hysterical sublime" is a term Fredric Jameson uses to refer to the fluid motion of commodities and images in postmodern experience. The hysterical sublime also indicates the experience of the postmodern subject who travels, according to Jameson, in a fluid, unmapped world (83). I think, however, that this term can be applied as well to experiences of spectacles I am describing here.

17. In fact, the "process of oblivion" was not so much at the fair as in the home countries of those displayed. For example, the Isma'il Pasha, then Governor of Egypt, visited Napoleon III during the Universal Exhibition in Paris in 1867. His purpose was not simply to serve as a representative type of his country at the exhibition, but also to obtain a loan of 296 million francs from France. These funds were to be used to replace old, irregular streets of Cairo and Istanbul with "straight, regular streets and gridpatterns," and to provide modern street lighting, following European models (see Çelik 6). Mitchell also discusses the refashioning of Egyptian cities along similar Haussmannian lines (see 34–62).

18. The "anthropology" of Benedict's *The Anthropology of World's Fairs* is interesting because it is constituted by his (uncritical) comparative references to "other cultures"—the Kwakiutl or the Maori, for instance—who "also" enact the "total prestation" or ritual of competition at the basis of world's fairs. "[A]pplying the potlatch model" helps make the argument that fairs "serve to rearrange status hierarchies and to validate the rise of the middle class." Not wishing to agree or disagree with Benedict's analysis of the relationship between the middle class and the fairs constituted in the total prestation, I would simply like to point out that comparisons like this one, or those which compare Iowa's "River of Corn" and Santa Clara's knight and horse of prunes to "competitive display by rival Maori kin groups," are not straightforwardly analytical. Rather, the non-European other is used here to validate or universalize a process Benedict has difficulty criticizing. The fact that the Kwakiutl and the Maori participate in "total prestations" makes phenomena such as the fair, and the jumble of foreignness promoted by them, oddly acceptable to Benedict. Thus the irony of Benedict's argument: on the one hand, he asserts the primacy of the monumental in European and American fairs; on the other, the monumentality of the fairs is inadvertently made an original product of exotic cultures—they are the "primitive" referents for this modern manifestation of competitive consumption. The by-product of Benedict's essay is that those who are non-European (those who are exotic) are twice consumed: first as spectacles of the fair and second in Benedict's comparisons, which refuse the *critical* analysis merited by such displays of European hegemony.

19. The fragmentary and disarticulated character of the exotic object or other in the fair context achieves a status similar to that Barbara Kirshenblatt-Gimblett attributes to the "ethnographic object":

> The artfulness of the ethnographic object is an art of excision, of detachment, an art of the excerpt. Where does the object begin and where does it end? This I see as an essentially surgical issue. . . . Perhaps we should speak not of the ethnographic object but of the ethnographic fragment. Like the ruin, the ethnographic fragment is informed by a poetics of detachment. Detachment refers not only to

> the physical act of producing fragments, but also to the detached attitude that makes that fragmentation and its appreciation possible. Lovers of ruins in seventeenth- and eighteenth-century England understood the distinctive pleasure afforded by architectural fragments, once enough time had passed for a detached attitude to form. . . . Nor were ruins left to accidental formation. Aesthetic principles guided the selective demolition of ruins and, where a ruin was lacking, the building of artificial ones. (388)

20. Foreign nations participating in the exhibit were Egypt, Portugal, Holland, Rumania, Hungary, Switzerland, England, South Africa, Belgium, Persia, West Indies, India, Netherlands, East Indies, Brazil, Mexico, Argentina, New Zealand, Ecuador, Peru, Chile, French Indo-China, Costa Rica, El Salvador, Australia, France, Italy, Panama, the Philippines, Johore, Norway, Colombia, and Japan (James and Weller 100, 116). Ironically, the motif of peace and unity in the Pacific was disrupted by the war conditions of many of the countries, making it impossible for them to continue participation during 1940.

21. "The grand facade of the Universal Exposition at Anvers is achieved like a fantasy. It does not have any determinate style, it gives rather the idea of one of those prodigious Indian monuments in which fantasy dominates. With its gigantic proportions and its central portico, which rises to 66 meters, this construction, which honors the architect Bordiau, looks like a palace from 'A Thousand and One Nights.'" (*Le livre des expositions universelles 1851–1989* 80).

22. *L'Exposition de 1867 illustrée, publication internationale autorisée par la Commission Imperiale* (cited in Loyrette 221). It is interesting that the facades of strange cities—non-European cities or cities outside England, France, and Germany most often—are complemented by facades of architecture from prior periods, such as the Renaissance. This suggests that, on a visual plane as presented at the expositions, geographically distant cities are equivalent to historically distant times, promoting what Johannes Fabian calls a "denial of coevalness" (Fabian 31).

23. The commentator of *Midway Types* adds the terms "lump" and "bunch" to the "jumble" of foreignness observed by Julian Ralph. The caption for a "A Group of Natives" (Fig. 10) declares, "[H]ere we have them in a lump—Cairo Street types caught by a sun-flash—magnate and subordinates, camel driver, donkeys, donkey drivers and the elusive urchins. . . . No magician in Arabic legend produced a vision so wonderful for its seeming improbability as was done by the hand of the realist who put the people of this group on the sandy beach of Lake Michigan." In "A Street Entertainment" the commentator tells us, "The foreigners are bunched." I find these comments odd, for we may be sure that thousands of people were crowded on the Midway each day. That foreigners are described as a "lump" or "bunched" indicates, I think, not so much a spatial configuration of bodies but the homogeneity of the "foreign" for the commentator. In "A Street Entertainment," the foreigners who are close to one another are standing to the left, as if for a portrait, while others move about the street; the photograph is not well composed or does not seem to have been staged as much as the others; in "A Group of Natives," the subjects are literally standing side by side, single file.

24. Here Loyrette cites *Revue de l'Exposition Universelle de 1889,* 224.

25. Perhaps the most relevant scientific enterprises in the display of exotic people in the nineteenth century were evolution and archaeology. A picture

advertising the contributions of the latter to The Ethnographic Exposition of Scientific Missions at the Industrial Palace in Paris in 1878 depicts objects (Egyptian and Mexican monuments, pottery, huts, tombs, mummies, a piece of a Northwest coast totem pole) spread around its surface. This display is meant, of course, to indicate the *variety* of objects on view at the Exposition. An alternative significance of the picture is the decontextualization of the objects which suggests, through the fragmentary and eclectic collection of exotic *things,* that these objects need no context or are more interesting *as* fragments.

26. Paul Morand wrote, regarding the 1900 Exposition, "The French remain ignorant of geography, geography comes to them." (Qtd. in Marie-Noelle Pradel-de Grandry 289.)

27. Burton Benedict says of the Panoramas of the 1900 Exposition: "Panoramas made some pretense at being educational, but unlike the dioramas in the exhibit halls of the main fair, they tended toward the sensational, the mythological and the fantastic. In a sense they were caricatures of the serious exhibits. They exploited the sensational as though it were an educational or scientific display" (56).

28. 26 August 1846: "I am no more modern than ancient, no more French than Chinese, and the idea of the fatherland, that is to say the obligation to live in one corner of the earth marked in red or blue on the map and to detest the other corners in green or black, has always appeared to be narrow, born of a fierce stupidity. I am the brother in God of all that lives, of the giraffe and of the crocodile as of man, and the fellow-citizen of all those who inhabit this grand furnished hotel of the universe."

29. Coincidentally, the famous Orientalist painter, Jean-Leon Gerome (a student of Gleyre, who advised Flaubert on his African scenes), upon returning from a voyage on the Nile in 1857, arranged a series of ateliers for artists, which was commonly known as "la Boîte à Thé." This was because of two Chinese paintings on the wall, which recalled the decor of such boxes. See Ackerman, 48.

30. He cites Bacon's *Gesta Grayorum.*

Works Cited

Ackerman, Gerald M. *La Vie et l'oeuvre de Jean-Leon Gerome, Les Orientalistes,* Vol. 4. Paris: ACR Edition Internationale, 1986. 4 vols.

Alloula, Malek. *The Colonial Harem.* Trans. Myrna Godzich and Wlad Godzich. Minneapolis: U of Minnesota P, 1986.

Altick, Richard. *The Shows of London.* Cambridge and London: Harvard-Belknap, 1985.

American Engraving Company. *Midway Types: A Book of Illustrated Lessons About the People of the Midway Plaisance World's Fair 1893.* Chicago, 1894.

Appelbaum, Stanley. *The Chicago World's Fair of 1893: A Photographic Record.* New York: Dover, 1980.

Bancroft, H. H. *Book of the Fair,* Chicago: Bancroft, 1894.

Benedict, Burton. *The Anthropology of World's Fairs: San Francisco's Panama Pacific International Exposition of 1915.* London and Berkeley: Scolar, 1983.

Benjamin, Walter. *Charles Baudelaire: A Lyric Poet in the Era of High Capitalism.* 1969. Trans. Harry Zohn. New York and London: Verso, 1989.

Brechin, Gray. "Sailing to Byzantium: The Architecture of the Fair." Benedict 94–113.

Çelik, Zeynip. *Displaying the Orient: Architecture of Islam at Nineteenth-Century World's Fairs.* Berkeley and Los Angeles: U of California P, 1992.

Chicago Record Co. *History of the World's Fair.* Chicago, 1894.

Clifford, James. *The Predicament of Culture: Twentieth-Century Ethnography, Literature and Art.* Cambridge: Harvard UP, 1988.

The Columbian Gallery: A Portfolio of Photographs from the World's Fair: Including the Chief Places, Interiors, Statuary, Architectural and Scenic Groups, Characters, Tropical Exhibits, and Marvels of the Midway Plaisance. Chicago: Werner, 1894.

Doggett, Frank. *Cigarette Cards and Novelties.* London: Michael Joseph, 1981.

The Economizer: How and Where to Find the Gems of the World's Columbian Exposition Chicago: Rand, 1893.

Fabian, Johannes. *Time and the Other: How Anthropology Makes Its Object.* New York: Columbia UP, 1983.

Flaubert, Gustave. *Correspondence.* Ed. Jean Bruneau. Vol 1. Paris: Gallimard, 1973. 3 vols.

———. *November.* Trans. Frank Jellinek. New York: Roman, 1932.

———. *Novembre, Fragments de style quelconque.* Paris: Editions Clancier-Guenaud, 1988.

Franklin, M. J. *British Biscuit Tins, 1868–1939.* London: New Cavendish, 1979.

Gilbert, Sandra M., and Susan Gubar. *The Madwoman in the Attic: The Woman Writer and the Nineteenth-Century Literary Imagination.* New Haven and London: Yale UP, 1979.

Gilman, Sander. *Difference and Pathology: Stereotypes of Sexuality, Race and Madness.* Ithaca and London: Cornell UP, 1985.

Greenhalgh, Paul. *Ephemeral Vistas: The Expositions Universelles, Great Exhibitions, and World's Fairs, 1851–1939.* Manchester: Manchester UP, 1988.

Hinsley, Curtis M. "The World as Marketplace: Commodification of the Exotic in the World's Columbian Exposition, Chicago, 1893." Karp and Lavine 344–65.

Impey, Oliver, and Arthur Macgregor, eds. *The Origins of Museums: The Cabinet of Curiosities in Sixteenth- and Seventeenth-Century Europe.* Oxford: Clarendon, 1985.

Iyer, Pico. *Video Night in Kathmandu: and Other Reports from the Not-so-Far East.* New York: Vintage, 1988.

James, Jack, and Earle Weller. *Treasure Island: "The Magic City" 1939–40.* San Francisco: Pisani, 1941.

Jameson, Fredric. "Postmodernism, or the Cultural Logic of Late Capitalism." *New Left Review* 146 (1984): 53–92.

Jullian, Philippe. *The Orientalists: European Painters of Eastern Scenes.* Trans. Helga and Dinah Harrison. Oxford: Phaidon, 1977.

Karp, Ivan, and Steven Lavine, eds. *Exhibiting Cultures: the Poetics and Politics of Museum Display.* Washington, DC, and London: Smithsonian Inst. P, 1991.

Kinglake, Alexander. *Eothen, Or, Traces of Travel Brought Home from the East.* Oxford and New York: Oxford UP, 1982.

Kirschenblatt-Gimblett, Barbara. "Objects of Ethnography." Karp and Levine 386–443.

Le livre des expositions universelles 1851–1989. Paris: Union Centrale des Arts Decoratifs, 1983.

Loyrette, Henri. "Du pavillon isolé a la ville dans la ville (1851–1900)." *Le livre des expositions universelles 1851–1989* 219–32.

Mitchell, Timothy. *Colonizing Egypt.* Cambridge: Cambridge UP, 1988.

Orvell, Miles. *The Real Thing: Imitation and Authenticity in American Culture, 1880–1940.* Chapel Hill and London: U of North Carolina P, 1989.

Pollig, Hermann, et al. *Exotische Welten, Europaïsche Phantasien.* Stuttgart: Edition Cantz, 1987.

Pradel-de Grandry, Marie-Noelle. "XIX siecle, la decouverte des civilisations dans le temps et dans l'espace." *Le livre des expositions universelles 1851–1989* 289–96.

Ralph, Julian. *Harper's Chicago and the World's Fair: The Chapters on the Exhibition Being Collated from Official and Approved Sources by the Department of Publicity and Promotion of the World's Columbian Exhibition.* New York: Harper and Brothers, 1893.

Richards, Thomas. *The Commodity Culture of Victorian England: Advertising and Spectacle, 1851–1914.* Stanford: Stanford UP, 1990.

Rydell, Robert W. *All the World's a Fair: Visions of Empire at American International Expositions, 1876–1916.* Chicago: U of Chicago P, 1984.

Thackeray, William Makepeace. "Mr. Molony's Account of the Crystal Palace." *Punch,* 3 August 1850; in *The Works of Thackeray, Ballads and Verses and Miscellaneous Contributions to 'Punch'.* London: Macmillan, 1911. 188–192.

———. *The Paris Sketch Book of Mr. M. A. Titmarsh, and Eastern Sketches: A Journey from Cornhill to Cairo, The Irish Book, and Character Sketches.* New York: John W. Lovell Company, n.d.

Thornton, Lynne. *The Orientalists: Painter-Travellers, 1828–1908.* Paris: ACR Edition International, 1983.

Turner, Gerard. "The Cabinet of Experimental Philosophy." Impey and Macgregor 214–22.

Williams, Rosalind H. *Dream Worlds: Mass Consumption in Late Nineteenth-Century France.* Berkeley: U of California P, 1982.

BOOKS RECEIVED

Adorno, Theodor W. *Notes to Literature.* Vol. 2. Ed. Rolf Tiedemann. Trans. Shierry Weber Nicholsen. New York: Columbia UP, 1992.

Ahmad, Aijaz. *In Theory: Classes, Nations, Literatures.* London: Verso, 1992.

Ahmed, Akbar S. *Postmodernism and Islam: Predicament and Promise.* New York: Routledge, 1992.

Allen, Elizabeth Cheresh. *Beyond Realism: Turgenev's Poetics of Secular Salvation.* Stanford: Stanford UP, 1992.

Altman, Rick, ed. *Sound Theory, Sound Practice.* New York: Routledge, 1992.

Armstrong, Isobel, ed. *New Feminist Discourses: Critical Essays on Theories and Texts.* New York: Routledge, 1992.

Bahti, Timothy. *Allegories of History: Literary Historiography After Hegel.* Baltimore: Johns Hopkins UP, 1992.

Bataille, George. *Theory of Religion.* Trans. Robert Hurley. 1989. New York: Zone Books-MIT Press, 1992.

Bergson, Katherine, and Philip V. Bohlman, eds. *Disciplining Music: Musicology and its Canons.* Chicago: U of Chicago P, 1992.

Black, Edwin. *Rhetorical Questions: Studies of Public Discourse.* Chicago: U of Chicago P, 1992.

Blau, Herbert. *To All Appearances: Ideology and Performance.* New York: Routledge, 1992.

Bourdieu, Pierre, and Loïc J. D. Waquant. *An Invitation to Reflexive Sociology.* Chicago: U of Chicago P, 1992.

Bové, Paul A. *Mastering Discourses: The Politics of Intellectual Culture.* Durham: Duke UP, 1992.

Butler, Judith, and Joan W. Scott, eds. *Feminists Theorize the Political.* New York: Routledge, 1992.

Chaloupka, William. *Knowing Nukes: The Politics and Culture of the Atom.* Minneapolis: U of Minnesota P, 1992.

Charvat, William. *The Profession of Authorship in America, 1800–1870.* New York: Columbia UP, 1992.

Costa Lima, Luiz. *The Dark Side of Reason: Fictionality and Power.* Trans. Paulo Henriques Britto. Stanford: Stanford UP, 1992.

Court, Franklin E. *Institutionalizing English Literature: The Culture and Politics of Literary Study, 1750–1900*. Stanford: Stanford UP, 1992.

de Jongh, Nicholas. *Not in Front of the Audience: Homosexuality on Stage.* New York: Routledge, 1992.

Easthope, Anthony. *Literary into Cultural Studies.* New York: Routledge, 1991.

Finnegan, Ruth. *Oral Poetry: Its Nature, Significance and Social Context.* 1977. Bloomington: Midland-Indiana UP, 1992.

Fraser, Nancy, and Sandra Lee Bartky, eds. *Revaluing French Feminism: Critical Essays on Difference, Agency, and Culture.* Bloomington: Midland-Indiana UP, 1992.

Fout, John C., ed. *Forbidden History: The State, Society, and the Regulation of Sexuality in Modern Europe.* Chicago: U of Chicago P, 1992.

Gearhart, Suzanne. *The Interrupted Dialectic: Philosophy, Psychoanalysis, and Their Tragic Other.* Baltimore: Johns Hopkins UP, 1992.

Gibson, Ross. *South of the West: Postcolonialism and the Narrative Construction of Australia.* Bloomington: Indiana UP, 1992.

Gonzalez, Eduardo. *The Monstered Self: Narratives of Death and Performance in Latin American Fiction.* Durham: Duke UP, 1992.

Grossberg, Lawrence. *We Gotta Get Out of This Place: Popular Conservatism and Postmodern Culture.* New York: Routledge, 1992.

Gumbrecht, Hans Ulrich. *Making Sense in Life and Literature.* Trans. Glen Burns. Minneapolis: U of Minnesota P, 1992.

Gunew, Sneja, ed. *Feminist Knowledge: Critique and Construct.* New York: Routledge, 1990.

Hannawalt, Barbara, ed. *Chaucer's England: Literature in Historical Context.* Minneapolis: U of Minnesota P, 1992.

Hardt, Hanno. *Critical Communication Studies: Communication, History and Theory in America.* New York: Routledge, 1992.

Harpham, Geoffrey Galt. *Getting It Right: Language, Literature, and Ethics.* Chicago: U of Chicago P, 1992.

Harth, Erica. *Cartesian Women: Versions and Subversions of Rational Discourse in the Old Regime.* Ithaca: Cornell UP, 1992.

Hartley, John. *Tele-Ology: Studies in Television.* New York: Routledge, 1992.

Helgerson, Richard. *Forms of Nationhood: The Elizabethan Writing of England.* Chicago: U of Chicago P, 1992.

Helly, Dorothy O., and Susan M. Reverby, eds. *Gendered Domains: Rethinking Public and Private in Women's History.* Ithaca: Cornell UP, 1992.

Holub, Renate. *Antonio Gramsci: Beyond Marxism and Postmodernism.* New York: Routledge, 1992.

Holub, Robert C. *Border Crossing: Reception Theory, Poststructuralism, Deconstruction.* Madison: U of Wisconsin P, 1992.

Jameson, Fredric. *Postmodernism, or, the Cultural Logic of Late Capitalism.* Durham: Duke UP, 1991.

JanMohamed, Abdul R., and David Lloyd. *The Nature and Context of Minority Discourse.* Oxford: Oxford UP, 1990.

Julien, Eileen. *African Novels and the Question of Orality.* Bloomington: Indiana UP, 1992.

Kott, Jan. *The Gender of Rosalind: Interpretations: Shakespeare, Büchner, Gautier.* Evanston: Northwestern UP, 1992.

———. *The Memory of the Body: Essays on Theater and Death.* Evanston: Northwestern UP, 1992.

Kransniewicz, Louise. *Nuclear Summer: The Clash of Communities at the Seneca Women's Peace Encampment.* Ithaca: Cornell UP, 1992.

Kruger, Loren. *The National Stage: Theatre and Cultural Legitimation in England, France, and America.* Chicago: U of Chicago P, 1992.

Livingston, Paisley. *Models of Desire: René Girard and the Psychology of Mimesis.* Baltimore: Johns Hopkins UP, 1992.

Longxi, Zhang. *The Tao and the Logos: Literary Hermeneutics, East and West.* Durham: Duke UP, 1992.

Mellencamp, Patricia. *High Anxiety: Catastrophe, Scandal, Age, and Comedy.* Bloomington: Midland-Indiana UP, 1992.

Pavis, Patrice. *Theatre at the Crossroads of Culture.* New York: Routledge, 1992.

Perkins, David. *Is Literary History Possible?* Baltimore: Johns Hopkins UP, 1992.

Pieterse, Jan Nederveen. *White on Black: Images of Africa and Blacks in Western Popular Culture.* New Haven: Yale UP, 1992.

Seideman, Steven. *Embattled Eros: Sexual Politics and Ethics in Contemporary America.* New York: Routledge, 1992.

Shiach, Morag. *Hélène Cixous: A Politics of Writing.* New York: Routledge, 1991.

Shires, Linda M., ed. *Rewriting the Victorians: Theory, History, and the Politics of Gender.* New York: Routledge, 1992.

Siebers, Tobin. *Morals and Stories.* New York: Columbia UP, 1992.

Silverman, Kaja. *Male Subjectivity at the Margins.* New York: Routledge, 1992.

Smith, Joseph H., and Humphrey Morris, eds. *Telling Facts: History and Narration in Psychoanalysis.* Baltimore: Johns Hopkins UP, 1992.

Spadaccini, Nicholas, and Jenaro Talens, eds. *The Politics of Editing.* Minneapolis: U of Minnesota P, 1992.

Spigel, Lynn. *Make Room for TV: Television and the Family Ideal in Postwar America.* Chicago: U of Chicago P, 1992.

Spigel, Lynn, and Denise Mann, eds. *Private Screenings: Television and the Female Consumer.* Minneapolis: Camera Obscura-U of Minnesota P, 1992.

Stam, Robert. *Reflexivity in Film and Literature: From Don Quixote to Jean-Luc Godard.* New York: Columbia UP, 1992.

Stein, Edward, ed. *Forms of Desire: Sexual Orientation and the Social Constructionist Controversy.* New York: Routledge, 1992.

Stoller, Paul. *The Cinematic Griot: The Ethnography of Jean Rouch.* Chicago: U of Chicago P, 1992.

Sugano, Marian Zwerling. *The Poetics of the Occasion: Mallarmé and the Poetry of Circumstance.* Stanford: Stanford UP, 1992.

Traub, Valerie. *Desire and Anxiety: Circulations of Sexuality in Shakespearean Drama.* New York: Routledge, 1992.

van Erven, Eugène. *The Playful Revolution: Theatre and Liberation in Asia.* Bloomington: Midland-Indiana UP, 1992.

Vattimo, Gianni. *The Transparent Society.* Trans. David Webb. Baltimore: Johns Hopkins UP, 1992.

Walkowitz, Judith R. *City of Dreadful Delight: Narratives of Sexual Danger in Late-Victorian London.* Chicago: U of Chicago P, 1992.

Western, John. *A Passage to England: Barbadian Londoners Speak of Home.* Minneapolis: U of Minnesota P, 1992.

Wilde, Oscar. *The Importance of Being Earnest and Related Writings.* Ed. Joseph Bristow. New York: Routledge, 1992.

Wood, David. *On Paul Ricoeur: Narrative and Interpretation.* New York: Routledge, 1991.

Zavala, Iris M. *Colonialism and Culture: Hispanic Modernisms and the Social Imaginary.* Bloomington: Indiana UP, 1992.

Zeitlian, Hraztan, ed. *Semiotext(e)/Architecture.* New York: Semiotext(e), 1992.

CONTRIBUTORS

Meg Armstrong is currently completing her doctoral dissertation, "Sublimity and Embodiment: Dialectical Images of Exoticist Discourse," at the University of Chicago. Her dissertation is a cultural study of the relationship between the aesthetics of sublimity and the production and subversion of stereotypes of race and gender in 19th- and 20th-century European and American exoticism.

Margaret Cohen is assistant professor of comparative literature at New York University. She is the author of the forthcoming *Profane Illumination: Walter Benjamin and the Paris of Surrealist Revolution* and journal articles about issues of gender and genre. She is currently working on a book investigating why women authors did not participate in the consolidation of realism in nineteenth-century France.

Teresa L. Ebert teaches postmodern critical theory and feminism at the State University of New York at Albany. Her writings have appeared in, among other places, *Rethinking Marxism, Cultural Critique, The Women's Review of Books, College English, American Journal of Semiotics, Poetics Today,* and *The Future of Feminist Theory*. She has completed two books, *Patriarchal Narratives* and *Ludic Feminism and After,* as well as having co-edited a book on ideology.

Jennifer Hayward teaches English at the College of Wooster and is working on a study of the cultural contexts of serial production from Dickens to soap opera.

Mahmut Mutman has recently completed his PhD in sociology at the University of California at Santa Cruz. He currently teaches media and culture in the sociology and anthropology department at Tufts University.

Judith Newton is in women's studies at the University of California, Davis. She is the author of *Women, Power, and Subversion: Social Strategies in British Fiction 1778–1860* and of the forthcoming *Starting Over: Feminism and the Politics of Cultural Criticism.* She is collaborating with Judith Stacey on an ethnographic study of academic male cultural critics.

Klaus R. Scherpe is a professor of literature at the Free University of Berlin. He is the author of numerous books on German and European literature and on aesthetic theory, especially genre theory, from the eighteenth through the twentieth centuries.

Judith Stacey teaches in the sociology department and the women's studies program at the University of California, Davis. She is the author of *Brave New Families: Stories of Domestic Upheaval in Late Twentieth Century America* and of *Patriarchy and Socialist Revolution in China.* Currently she is collaborating with Judith Newton on an ethnographic study of academic male cultural critics.

THE NIETZSCHE LEGACY IN GERMANY, 1890-1990
By STEVEN E. ASCHHEIM
"One of the most important works of German and European intellectual history published in years. . . . It will be welcomed by intellectual historians as a long overdue history of the multivalent reception and reworking of Nietzsche."
—Jeffrey Herf, author of *Reactionary Modernism*
Weimar & Now: German Cultural Criticism, £27.50 cloth, illustrated

NEW WORLD ENCOUNTERS
Edited by STEPHEN GREENBLATT
"Many of these essays form the cutting edge of scholarship on the expansion of Europe and its cultural consequences. . . . This work is so solid, so elegantly presented, and at the same time so innovative that the book should attract considerable attention."—Anthony Grafton, author of *Defenders of the Text*
A Representations Book, £32.50 cloth, £10.95 paper, illustrated

UNIVERSITY OF CALIFORNIA PRESS
BERKELEY LOS ANGELES NEW YORK LONDON

UNIVERSITY OF CALIFORNIA PRESS 100 SINCE 1893

S0-ARH-142

The Good-Day Bunnies

MOVING DAY

By Harriet Margolin and Carol Nicklaus

A GOLDEN BOOK • NEW YORK.
Western Publishing Company, Inc., Racine, Wisconsin 53404

Copyright © 1987 by Harriet Margolin. Illustrations copyright © 1987 by Carol Nicklaus. All rights reserved. Printed in the U.S.A. by Western Publishing Company, Inc. No part of this book may be reproduced or copied in any form without written permission from the publisher. GOLDEN®, GOLDEN & DESIGN®, and A GOLDEN BOOK® are trademarks of Western Publishing Company, Inc. Library of Congress Catalog Card Number: 86-82374 ISBN 0-307-11645-X/ ISBN 0-307-61645-2 (lib. bdg.) A B C D E F G H I J

Western Publishing offers a wide range of fine juvenile and adult activities, games, and puzzles. For more information write Golden Press, 120 Brighton Road, Dept. M, Clifton, NJ 07012.

Most mornings, the Good-Day Bunnies awoke and greeted the new day. "Good day! Good day! Good day!" each of them said to the others.

But this morning was different. Papa woke everyone early and said, "It's moving day! Hurry up and let's get packing!"

Mama was already dressed. Becky and Bumper, the twins, put on their clothes as fast as they could.

Grandma gave breakfast to them and to the baby, Bonnie. Then she hurried all the children out of the house. "Why don't you all wait on the front steps for the moving van," she said.

Everyone sat down. Becky said, "I'm not scared to move—I'm not!"

Bumper answered, "I'm not scared either, but I bet Bonnie is. She's so little."

"I have an idea," Becky said. "Let's try to make Bonnie laugh."

And they began to clap and sing, "Pat-a-cake, pat-a-cake, baker's man..."

Just then the moving van pulled up in front of the house. The movers jumped out of their truck and lowered a ramp to the sidewalk. BANG!

The movers asked Becky to move Bonnie out of the way. Then they propped open the front door with an umbrella stand and began to work.

Out of the house came a sofa, a table, a chair, a lamp; a picture, a pillow, a mattress, a rolled-up rug.

When Bonnie saw her crib being carried out, she began to cry. Bonnie kept crying, even when Papa hugged her and told her she would see her crib again soon at the new house.

Everything was out of the house and on the truck. Papa said, "It's time to say good-bye to our old house." Everyone waved.

Papa pulled the GOOD-DAY sign out of the ground, and the family headed for the car.

Papa followed the moving van. While the twins played geography, Bonnie took a short nap.

It wasn't long before Papa said, "Here's our new house. Hope it's ready for all of us!"

While the movers unloaded, Becky and Bumper played in the yard. There was a tree to sit in, with a branch to swing from. There were some bricks for building and there was dirt for digging.

There was even a board that was just right for balancing.

"Look what I can do," shouted Bumper as he stood on one foot.

"And look what I can do," yelled Becky.

When Becky and Bumper ran around to the front of the house, everything had been unloaded. One of the movers closed the doors of the truck and pulled the latch. Then he wiped his forehead and said to Papa, "Have a good day!"

Bonnie, who was sitting on top of a carton, knew it was just the right time to wave "bye-bye."

Mama called from the house, "I think you all had better come inside. There's a lot of work to be done!"

Becky raced Bumper to their room. Everything was piled in the middle of the floor.

Becky unpacked the books. When she started to put them on the shelves, Bumper said, "You're doing it wrong."

And when Bumper put some toys on a shelf, Becky said, "Not that way, dummy!"

Becky and Bumper argued about the right way to unpack. Becky shouted, "I think we should make a line down the middle of this room. You can fix your half, and I'll fix mine."

Just then Grandma walked by. "Calm down!" she said to the two of them. "I'll help you, then you can both help me unpack in Bonnie's room."

Bonnie's room was different from the one she was used to. She tugged at Grandma's sweater and wanted to be picked up.

"Look, Bonnie, here's your crib," Grandma said.

Bumper started unpacking. He found a truck, a rubber ball, a bunch of blocks, some storybooks, and a drum. Bumper banged on the drum and sang a funny song—"RUMBA...RUMBA...TUM-TUM-TUM!" Bonnie hardly smiled.

Then Becky found Bonnie's bear at the bottom of the box. "Bear," Bonnie shouted. "Mine!"

When Becky gave the bear to Bonnie, Bonnie grinned from ear to ear.

When Papa needed a rest from unpacking, he took a walk outside. As he walked he said, "I need to fix the shutters...cement these steps...and fix the swing!"

When Papa got to the front yard, he set up the Good-Day sign. He said to himself, "Now this place is beginning to feel like home."

They all walked down the street. They passed an empty lot, then four houses. At the fifth house, laughs and giggles were coming from the backyard.

"I hope those are some children we can play with," Becky said.

But when the children peeked out from behind some bushes, Becky and Bumper thought they looked mean. Becky and Bumper wondered if they'd be nice playmates.

When Grandma, Becky, Bumper, and Bonnie returned, a picnic supper was ready.

Becky and Bumper sat on some cartons. Bonnie shared her supper with her bear.

"An inside picnic is fun," said Bumper. "I like these paper plates and drinking from straws."

After supper, Grandma took Bonnie upstairs for a bath. The warm water made Bonnie sleepy. She didn't fuss about putting on her pajamas and getting right into her crib.

Becky and Bumper played a few games, then climbed into their beds with books.

When Mama and Papa came to say good night, Mama said, "You'll hear new sounds tonight. We'll all have to get used to the nighttime noises in this house.

"Good night, Becky and Bumper. Good night, Bonnie. Good night, new house! Tomorrow should be a good day."